THE GLOBAL CONSTRUCTION OF GENDER

THE GLOBAL CONSTRUCTION OF GENDER

Home-Based Work in the Political Economy

of the 20th Century

Elisabeth Prügl

COLUMBIA UNIVERSITY PRESS   NEW YORK

▄▟▙

COLUMBIA UNIVERSITY PRESS
Publishers Since 1893
New York   Chichester, West Sussex
Copyright © 1999 Columbia University Press
All rights reserved
Library of Congress Cataloging-in-Publication Data
Prügl, Elisabeth.
   The global construction of gender : home-based work in the
political economy of the 20th century / Elizabeth Prügl.
      p.   cm.
   Includes bibliographical references.
   ISBN 0–231-11560-1 (cloth). —ISBN 0-231-11561-X (pbk.)
   1. Home labor.   2. Sex role in the work environment.   3. Women—
Employment.   4. Foreign trade and employment.   5. International
trade.   I. Title.
HD2333.P78   1999
331.4′25—dc21   99–24851
                                                            CIP

To Peter and Helen

Contents

Acknowledgments

Over the years that it took to research and write this book I incurred debts to many people who generously gave their time and suggestions and to institutions that provided resources. I started my first forays into the politics of home-based work while a student at The American University and completed a dissertation on the topic. Since working at Florida International University I added historical materials to my original narrative and conceptually reoriented it to more strongly foreground my constructivist approach. I am grateful to all who facilitated this work.

At American University, Irene Tinker first pointed out that home-based work was a matter of international debate and an issue that needed serious scholarly attention. She followed the gestation of this project from the very beginning and accompanied it with her advice and encouragement. I am grateful for everything she has taught me and her continued friendship. Nicholas G. Onuf's writings on constructivism and our spirited discussions on our commutes to work in Miami have profoundly influenced the argument of the book. Nick not only supervised my dissertation, but also read along as I revised the manuscript, and thought along as I was trying to figure out some of the intricacies of constructivist International Relations. He influenced me in more ways than I can acknowledge. I count myself fortunate to call him a teacher, colleague, friend, and mentor. Renée Marlin-Bennett and Bob Gregg served as second and third readers on my dissertation committee, both offering valuable suggestions. I owe them a big thanks.

In conducting my research I have benefitted greatly from the work of homeworker advocates who generously shared their knowledge about contemporary politics of homework. I owe them for letting me listen in on their deliberations and for taking me in as an ally in their cause. Jane Tate of HomeNet International gave me access to her notes summarizing meetings of homeworker advocates and her journals of visits to homeworker organizations in Asia. She kept me up to date on international organizing and lobbying activities concerning the homework convention and homeworker organizing in Europe. It is to no small degree her deep commitment that has kept alive the international network of homeworker advocates, thus providing a critical source of information. Renana Jhabvala and Ela Bhatt of the Self-Employed Women's Association (SEWA) in India took time out of their busy schedules to explain to me the approach of SEWA to the issue of home-based workers. Their vision of a better world for women workers and their tireless lobbying efforts were crucial in passing the homework convention. I owe them not only insights on SEWA and home-based workers but also a particular view of the world, what feminists call a standpoint.

At the ILO, Gisela Schneider de Villegas facilitated my access to materials on homework in the Conditions of Work and Welfare Department, and made it possible for me to attend ILO meetings on homework. Thank you for making me feel welcome in the department and for easing my work there. Mr. Zoganas hosted me at the ILO Archives, dug up valuable sources, and patiently explained to me matters of history. Lucita Lazo of the ILO Office in Thailand was a source of information on ILO projects in Southeast Asia, and she freely shared conference and research reports. Staff at the ILO Office in Washington, D.C., fielded many of my calls for information and endured me sometimes for days at a time in their library and at their copymachine. I owe them all for their support and hospitality.

A number of my colleagues and students provided valuable feedback on the manuscript. Patricia Price closely read all of it, giving helpful suggestions on interpretation, and alerting me to the work of geographers of scale. Marc Linder also read the revised manuscript, clarified matters concerning labor law and encouraged me to push further on the matter of employment status. Eileen Boris read parts of the book in earlier iterations and identified relevant historical materials. J. Ann Tickner offered feedback on an early version of the theoretical chapter and challenged me to dive more deeply into feminist materials. Rob Walker read chapter 2 and pointed me toward investigating the role of social movements. Kristina Jacobson did a fabulous job compiling the bibliography and checking for consistency in notes. In less tangible terms, many of my students have engaged me in discussions that have helped me clarify my thinking on gender, social construction, power, and global politics. I would like to thank in particular the members of the Miami International Relations Group who have been a continuous source of intellectual engagement.

I received material support from several institutions. The American University granted me graduate and postdoctoral fellowships that financed my dissertation research and allowed me the first steps toward revising the dissertation. The American Association of University Women provided funding that supported me while I was writing the dissertation. Finally, the Department of International Relations at FIU offered an environment conducive to good work, including institutional support and a great group of colleagues. I am grateful to all of them.

This book is a product of home-based work, written exclusively in my home office. Here writing encountered both the comforts and the demands of home. I am grateful to my family for helping me keep home and work apart, at least at times. Rosalie provided the best child care in the world; Peter often did more than his share of housework and cooking; Helen made sure to engage me in her play for relaxation and often just simply left me alone. Thanks for humoring me while obsessing about my research. I dedicate the book to Peter and Helen, the two people in my life who make it all worthwhile.

1 Feminism, Constructivism, and the Global Politics of Home-Based Work

"Victory for Homeworkers" screamed the front page of the July 1996 newsletter of the International Network for Homebased Workers.[1] The International Labor Conference, the policymaking assembly of the International Labor Organization (ILO), had passed a multilateral convention (treaty) on homework, setting international standards for people working at home for pay. This was a major step in a global debate that stirred passions in countries around the world since the beginning of the twentieth century. It formalized rules in the interstate arena about a group of mostly female workers widely recognized as underpaid and exploited. Ubiquitous in urban and rural areas around the world, home-based workers sew garments, embroider, make lace, roll cigarettes, weave carpets, peel shrimp, prepare food, polish plastic, process insurance claims, edit manuscripts, and assemble artificial flowers, umbrellas, and jewelry. Some subcontract with factories, large firms, intermediaries, or merchants; others are quasi-independent and sell their goods and services to traders, merchants, or companies. Some work alone; others are embedded within family enterprises.

According to economic theory—both Marxist and liberal—home-based work was destined to disappear as production moved into factories. However, large numbers of predominantly female homeworkers appeared in Europe with the industrial revolution; Karl Marx described them as tied to the factory system through "invisible threads."[2] By the early twentieth century, the vast majority of industrial homeworkers in Europe, North America, and Australia were women, often wives of working-class husbands, and in the U.S. often immigrants. Desperate for any type of income they typically worked under extremely exploitative conditions for puny wages. During the world wars some governments drew on homeworkers to sew uniforms and pack car- tridges, often under a tightly regulated system, while others discouraged the practice in favor of drawing women workers into factories. Under the postwar factory-based production system, industrial homework in Europe, North America, and Australia apparently went into decline although homework persisted widely in such important productive sectors as the garment indus- try. Furthermore, industrial homework became an important ingredient in the labor-intensive industrialization strategy of Japan and took on consider- able importance in newly industrializing countries such as Taiwan and Hongkong. In the 1960s, home-based work also emerged in the literature as widespread in less modernized economies of Africa, Asia, and Latin Amer- ica. Home-based workers in these economies were crafts producers and workers in what became known as the "informal sector."[3] In many countries they constituted the majority of the nonagricultural labor force. The crisis of capitalist accumulation, which appeared in the 1970s, and the new strat- egy of firms to counter the effects of the crisis by becoming more flexible, reversed the decline of homework in industrialized countries. New service sector home-based workers joined industrial homeworkers and informal sec- tor workers as the ideal work force under a global economic regime of flex- ible accumulation. Considered outdated and bound to disappear a hundred years ago, home-based workers in the 1990s seemed to set the standard for the flexible work force of the future.

From a state-centric perspective, the ILO Home Work Convention con- stituted an insignificant technocratic intervention on the part of a func- tionally oriented intergovernmental organization, and is barely worth a foot- note. From the feminist constructivist perspective I adopt in this book, the convention was a climax in movement activism, in a global debate in the course of the twentieth century over the relationship between home and work and the implied relationships of gender. Encoded in everyday prac- tices, such as commuting from home to work; in the regulatory practices of states, such as denying home-based workers labor rights; and in practices of international relations that isolate "the domestic" from "the international," the separation became the fulcrum of the twentieth-century global gender order.[4]

V. Spike Peterson has argued that the domestic and the household as a unit of production did not exist before the state but emerged only in the process of state formation. From the Athenian city state, built on a public realm of politics as distinguished from the private realm of necessity, to the early modern state, legitimized on the public-private distinction of liberal philosophers, to the industrial capitalist state that conceptually and physically separated a devalued realm of reproduction from the sphere of production, centralized states drew legitimacy from the distinction of opposing realms.[5] This distinction effected powerful consequences, participating in the dualistic construction of masculinity and femininity, marginalizing the feminized in political processes, and positioning women as disadvantaged in the distribution of goods and values.

Although public-private distinctions constructed women as outside of politics, gender relations were never purely domestic. They were not contained in households or, from the perspective of International Relations (IR), in states. The identity of the security state, and thus of the interstate system, fundamentally built on an opposition between masculinized protectors and feminized protectees. Similarly, the development and spread of capitalism entailed a separation of home and work and the "housewifization" of women.[6] In this way, gender relations have always interwoven relations between states—the rules that guided conduct between capitalist and security states. Indeed, the construction of the work-home dichotomy took on distinctive forms under various hegemonies within the Westphalian system. It was the Dutch who in the seventeenth century invented the home as an architectural space, separating the downstairs as a place of public interchange from the private upstairs. It was the Victorian British whose industrial capitalism enhanced the move of work out of the home and who fiercely gendered the middle-class home to make it a sphere of femininity and comfort that could support the gestation of a superior race intent on creating an empire. It was the Americans who in the twentieth century rationalized the home as a space for consuming women and children that supported a form of hegemony based on a Fordist regime of accumulation.[7] Finally, the increased obfuscation of home-work boundaries at the turn of the twenty-first century parallels the emergence of new economic and political world orders.

The purpose of this book is twofold. First, I wish to affirm a contention that feminists in International Relations have made for some time: that gender politics pervades world politics. They have shown this to be the case in the practices of militaries and diplomats and in the way in which IR scholarship obscures the role of women in interstate practices and the international economy. The book focuses on an additional area of International Relations: international organizations and global governance as the regulatory complements of the global economy. It is part of a burgeoning post-Cold War literature on gender politics in this arena.[8] Second, I wish to show that gender is a global construct, one that results from practices that connect arguments at all levels of politics and society, including the international. A significant strand of feminism today argues that gender is a social construct. In other words, notions of female and male, feminine and masculine, are not naturally given but emerge from particular sociohistorical practices. I seek to add to a growing literature that approaches international politics as one set of practices engaged in gender construction by extending the argument to the regulatory edifice of the global economy. I do so from a self-consciously feminist constructivist perspective that integrates theoretical approaches from the constructivist and gender literatures in International Relations.

Constructivism

The argument that gender is a social construct belongs in the metatheoretical realm of constructivism. The fact that constructivism is becoming popular in IR augurs well for an integration of gender analysis in the field. Constructivism achieves an ontological shift from a focus on given agents and solidified structures in neorealism and neoliberalism to the processes that constitute the world. In this way, constructivism puts in the center of analysis issues that are critically important to feminist theorizing: the construction of identities, power, and processes of change.[9]

As its popularity has increased in IR, diverse understandings of what exactly constructivism is have proliferated. Contention exists around its core assumptions, its philosophical foundations, as well as its proper methods. Some subsume constructivism under writings probing ideational causation,[10] some take norms and social context as its crucial explanatory variables,[11] some consider institutionalization and intersubjectivity its key concerns,[12] while others find its central preoccupation to be language.[13] Some constructivists draw their insights from philosophical realism, some from the sociological classics (Durkheim and Weber via Anthony Giddens), some from Wittgenstein and speech act theory, some from the writings of French poststructuralists.[14] Some insist that a constructivist method is by definition interpretive, hermeneutic, or genealogical whereas others see no contradiction between an intersubjective ontology and a positivist methodology.[15]

Despite this diversity, there is one core feature that distinguishes self-identified constructivists from other IR scholars:[16] They argue that international life is social, and they insist that the focus of inquiry in world politics should be "social facts" such as norms, rules, institutions, and language. The levels of analysis problem has importantly served to organize constructivist thinking. Rather than subscribing to the incompatibility of explanations from different levels of analysis, constructivists have argued that agency and structure are co-constituted.[17] Structures reproduce through the practices of knowledgeable agents while at the same time enabling these practices.[18] Depending on their particular orientation, constructivists take norms, rules, institutions, or language as the media of this reproduction. These social forms are intimately implicated in world politics not only because of their regulative, but also because of their constitutive effects: they guide conduct while at the same time creating objects and agents.

The constructivist orientation toward the social puts the focus on phenomena of world politics that neorealism and neoliberalism obscure or cannot account for. First, constructivism has put into the center of attention the constitution of agents, their identities and interests. No longer are states considered as given or politically preexisting, but national interests and state identities now appear in need of explanation.[19] Second, because the social is by definition unstable, constructivists account for change. This has made the approach attractive to those who seek to understand the transition from the medieval to the Westphalian system, the disintegration of the post-World War II system, or the transformation of world politics through the strengthening of "global civil society."[20]

Gender

The constructivist focus on identities as well as its understanding of reality as fluid and changing make it a promising approach for gender analysis. Indeed, the notion of social construction is at the core of contemporary feminist writings, and there is broad agreement that gender itself is a social construct.[21] Feminists in International Relations have focused on the way in which gender is being constructed in the field and on the way in which gender has produced particular understandings of central IR concepts such as state and sovereignty. For example, they have explored the gendered process of state-making, the gender politics in revolutions, and the masculinist identities of developmental states.[22] They have described state sovereignty as a gendered concept, the way in which sex, gender, and sexuality affect it, and the way in which female bodies have shaped it.[23]

My concern here is not with the gendered construction of International Relations, but with the construction of gender itself—with notions of masculinity and femininity in the international political economy. There is a growing body of IR literature on the way in which states and the scholarly study of international relations construct masculinity and femininity. J. Ann Tickner has introduced Robert W. Connell's notion of "hegemonic masculinity," to suggest that the celebration of male power in the field of International Relations produces a stereotypical image of masculinity that contributes to legitimizing a patriarchal political and social order.[24] Others have adopted the concept to describe the construction of masculinities through wars and through the military.[25] Jean Elshtain has argued that wars evoke specific gender identities constructed and passed down in myths and memories.[26] Cynthia Enloe has interpreted women's encounters with various global actors—politicians, tourists, colonial travelers, militaries, diplomats, multinational corporations—as manipulations and contestations of masculinity and femininity.[27] Sandra Whitworth and Deborah Stienstra have shown how material conditions, institutions, ideas, and discourses interact in social movements and international organizations to produce different policies toward women and different understandings of gender.[28] In the area of International Political Economy, feminists have explored the way in which development practices and global restructuring have employed and reproduced gender constructions.[29]

While these writers use the language of social construction, few have self-consciously positioned themselves in the context of constructivist IR literature. Yet, many of their assumptions are compatible with constructivism. First, like constructivists, many feminists are concerned with "the social" as opposed to material capabilities, static structures, unquestioned positivities, or pregiven identities. They make the social come alive in discourses, stories, and practices. Second, like constructivists, many feminists employ a theoretical orientation that implies impermanence, historicity, and malleability. Stories can be rewritten, discourses can be deconstructed, practices change, stereotypes alter, ideologies can be revealed, institutions and ideas change.

Feminist inquiry is far too diverse to subsume it under a constructivist research program. Yet, I find that a cross-fertilization of feminist and constructivist ideas can be mutually beneficial and seek to develop here the outlines of a "feminist constructivism" that adds to the diversity of feminist research in IR. A feminist constructivism would have to put feminist politics in the center of inquiry. That is, it would have to provide the tools to investigate social practices that realize relationships of power resulting in the subordination of women and provide knowledge for a struggle against such relationships of power. Two feminist debates seem of particular significance in orienting this type of constructivism. First is the feminist debate on epistemology focusing on the social positioning of knowers and their relationship to the known, and on ways to justify critical knowledge. Second is the debate on the relationship between sex and gender, or more broadly between the social and the material, a debate that is crucial to a constructivist understanding of power.

Constructivism and Feminism

In an influential essay published in 1986, Kratochwil and Ruggie recognized that the preoccupation with intersubjective phenomena (they focused on the study of international regimes) had profound epistemological implications. Positivist methods could not account for the force of norms.[30] But those who reject positivism invariably risk the charge of relativism: if knowledge is constructed and contingent, how could any type of knowledge be considered more accurate or better? Rejecting positivism, so the charge goes, invites "explanatory anarchy." This has led many self-identified constructivists to cling to positivist methods, treating culture or norms as causal variables that can be held constant, but inviting considerable problems of analysis.[31]

The notion of relativism itself issues from its opposition to objectivism; and the dualism between the two is caught up in the Cartesian quest for foundations. Objectivism finds a foundation in reason. The critique of reason has occupied philosophers at least since Hegel but has gained new vibrancy in recent years as theorists of post-Modernity increasingly conveyed "that there may be nothing—not God, reason, philosophy, science, or poetry—that answers to and satisfies our longing for ultimate constraints, for a stable and reliable rock upon which we can secure our thought and action."[32] Philosophers have thus pushed beyond the opposition of objectivism and relativism to develop notions of reason that are socially embedded. Both constructivists and feminists have participated in developing new forms of inquiry that account for the constructedness of knowledge.

Ruggie introduces "narrative explanation" as an alternative to positivism that is based not on deduction but abduction: "The aim is to produce results that are verisimilar and believable to others looking over the same events."[33] That is, the standard for justification is the judgment of others. From a feminist standpoint the question is who these others are. Ruggie's narrative explanations presumably receive validation from colleagues in the academy, who judge the explanation as "verisimilar and believable." But Ruggie, together with most other self-identified constructivists, chooses to ignore that the community of scholars is rather exclusive, not only in the sense of excluding people who lack power, but even more so in excluding ways of knowing that make sense from the perspective of those excluded.

For feminists this is the crucial issue: it matters who is the knower. If knowledge is social construction, the enterprise of knowing creates power and the social positioning of the knower makes a difference. Yet, this raises new questions of justification. Few feminists are prepared to follow relativist notions of knowledge production, insisting that their critique has grounds. Feminist debates about the grounding of emancipatory knowledge have centered importantly around the notion of a "feminist standpoint," introduced in 1983 by Nancy Hartsock. Hartsock argued that material circumstances set limits to what can be known, that the perspective of ruling groups is partial and perverse but structures the material relations in which all are forced to participate, that consequently oppressed groups must struggle for their own vision to expose existing relations as inhuman. She called her version of this vision the "feminist standpoint," and saw in it a vehicle for women's liberation.[34] The notion has since received considerable scrutiny. Many have denounced the presumably essentialist implications of a feminist standpoint that apparently was based on common biology, the same psychosocial situation, or a shared experience of motherhood and domestic work. Yet, Hartsock has denied the charge of essentialism, pointing to her Marxist view that knowledge is historically specific and accomplished through practice. From a constructivist perspective such practice emerges not from frozen material circumstances but from rules that create power differentials and circumscribe agency, including the production of knowledge.

The debate over essentialism, over the question whether there is a common something that makes women what they are, has occupied feminists since the 1980s. The debate received ammunition in controversies over theories seeking to explain the roots of women's oppression. Critiques from the perspective of women of color, "Third World women," and lesbians showed that such theories often projected the experience of privileged, white, Western, and heterosexual women onto all women, subsuming heterogeneity under a common narrative of oppression, and obscuring differences arising from identifications based on race, ethnicity, class, sexual orientation, or national location.[35] Poststructuralist feminists supported these arguments. Critical of the exclusionary implications of modernist logocentrism, its concern with origins and foundations, and its silencing of "Others" through the naturalization of identities, they rejected an understanding of women as a universal category with a common essence and insisted that women needed to be analyzed as outcomes of discursive practices. Humanist feminists replied that this understanding did away with emancipatory agents. As subjects disappeared, so did notions of intentionality, accountability, self-reflexivity, and autonomy, ideas they claimed were central to feminist critique and practice.[36] Feminists were groping for a middle ground in this debate. Marysia Zalewski's effort to destabilize the oppositional construction of women and gender, essentialism and constructivism, is indicative. Concerned that the substitution of "gender" for "woman" had the effect of shutting up women before they were ever heard, she questioned whether talk about "woman" by definition assumed a feminine essence. Instead, it was necessary to maintain "woman" as an unstable category.[37]

For the purposes of a feminist epistemology, the debate about essentialism has created a broad understanding that there is no unitary feminist standpoint but that there are many standpoints of groups involved in different relationships of power. Hartsock has acknowledged that her original conceptualization of the feminist standpoint did not allow theoretical space for differences arising from race or sexual orientation and has argued the need for pluralizing the notion of a standpoint.[38] Similarly, Donna Haraway has called on feminists to develop "situated knowledges," advocating "a doctrine of embodied objectivity that accommodates paradoxical and critical feminist science projects."[39] In International Relations, Christine Sylvester has made the case for a "postmodern feminism" in which "people called women" find temporary homesteads that allow them agency and engage in a method of "empathetic cooperation."[40] The construct "woman" may be one such homestead that provides a basis of solidarity for differently positioned people called women.

Feminist epistemologies have been at the forefront of a paradigm shift in the second half of the twentieth century, of which constructivism is a part. This paradigm shift entails, in Susan Hekman's words, "a movement from an absolutist, subject-centered conception of truth to a conception of truth as situated, perspectival, and discursive."[41] Feminism enriches constructivism with an epistemology that provides justifications based in politically constituted groups of knowers. It gives purposes to the search for truth. The point of such an epistemology is, to quote Haraway's echo of Marx, "to make a difference in the world, to cast our lot for some ways of life and not others."[42]

Feminist constructivism also differs from other versions of constructivism in its concern for the way in which social practice carries codes of power. Constructivists rarely investigate power as a phenomenon of construction; many implicitly subscribe to an understanding of power as located in individuals or states, disregarding the intersubjectivity of power, the interweaving of rules with rule.[43] In contrast, for many feminists power is intersubjectively constituted together with the categories gender, race, class, ethnicity, etc. As Joan Scott has argued, gender is "a primary way of signifying relationships of power."[44] Jean Cohen and Andrew Arato agree that "power operates through gender codes, reducing the free selectivity of some and expanding that of others."[45] Notions of masculinity and femininity and the matrix of compulsory heterosexuality realize power by constructing gender. The Foucaultian understanding of power as "capillary," i.e. as operating in all aspects of social practice, is suggestive in this context and has influenced many feminists. The Foucaultian understanding is compatible with constructivism.

Constructivists agree that military and economic power is not purely material, that it has social content. Norms influence what weapons governments choose to acquire and use, in which situations they will employ military power, how they will define their security position in the world, and what doctrine their militaries will follow.[46] And global economies have been constructed differentially depending on how "social purpose" interacts with state capabilities.[47] Yet, these constructivists retain an understanding of power as something that states "have," reserving a presocial world of capabilities. In addition, many make a distinction between the material and the ideal, separating a world of construction from a world outside construction.[48] Feminist views on this issue profoundly impact the meaning of social construction.

In the 1960s, feminists introduced a distinction between sex and gender to attack notions that described women's secondary status as natural. In this strategy, sex described the material, i.e. biological and pre-given, aspect of what it meant to be a woman or man, whereas gender designated socially constructed inequalities. Writings on sexed bodies have since destabilized the distinctions between sex and gender, biology and society, nature and culture, yielding important understandings on the production of the material. Linda Nicholson has described how the rise of materialist metaphysics paralleled "a significant shift in the eighteenth century from a 'one-sex' view of the body to a 'two-sex' view." While earlier the female body was seen as "a lesser version of the male," now the female body was considered altogether different and physical characteristics became the explanations for these differences.[49] Her analysis shows that physical differences between women and men were the result of historical constructions, and that the separation of a material realm from a social realm is untenable.

Donna Haraway has further contributed to destabilizing the distinction between the social and the material. Her investigations of the political dimensions of science have shown that "technoscience" engages in a social construction of biology and nature through the genetic mixing of species (including humans and animals) and the mutual penetration of technology and life.[50] Similarly, Judith Butler has rejected the treatment of the body as a "site or surface" where social construction takes place, and suggested that matter itself is "a process of materialization that stabilizes over time to produce the effect of boundary, fixity, and surface."[51] She conceptualizes materiality as the most productive effect of power. Butler's concern is with sex, but her theorizing opens up important, yet uncharted venues for understandings of the material, or capabilities, in International Relations.

There have been steps in this direction. I read Carol Cohn's exploration of the language of nuclear experts as an example of a feminist study that shows how the power of nuclear weapons is realized socially. In recalling her experience in the world of defense intellectuals, she recounts with terror how in learning their language, the use of nuclear weapons became a possibility. The idea that nuclear weapons are useful appears perverse and irrational to outsiders, but learning the language makes it possible to " 'think about the unthinkable,' to work in institutions that foster the proliferation of nuclear weapons, to plan mass incinerations of millions of human beings for a living."[52] J. K. Gibson-Graham offers a similar attack on the fixity of the material in her effort to destabilize capitalism through counter-representations. She shows that the power of capitalism issues from its representations and seeks to undermine this power by opening up discourses that construct capitalism as "hegemonic" to allow space for non-

capitalist practices.[53] Such feminist explorations undermine suggestions of
the existence of a separate material world of power capabilities in which
power resides with individual agents. They open up the "material" world
for creative research from a constructivist perspective while significantly
broadening the notion of social construction itself.

In sum, the feminist constructivism I propose here is distinct in that it
adopts an emancipatory epistemology and in that it casts doubt on understandings of power as presocial. I would argue that a constructivism that
wants to meet these requirements has to put language in the center.

A Linguistic Constructivism for Feminist Purposes

In International Relations, the turn to language has often been associated
with poststructuralist writings, especially of Michel Foucault, and indeed
these writings have strongly influenced feminists. At the same time, as shown
earlier, some feminists have been critical of the move toward poststructur-
alism because it entails the loss of the notion of agency. Some feminists
sympathetic to linguistic analysis have found inspiration in the writings of
Jürgen Habermas and his notion of communicative action.[54] Like poststruc-
turalism, the theory of communicative action puts language in the center of
an understanding of the social. But unlike poststructuralists, Habermas focuses on communication between reflexive agents. He conceives of identities not as produced in narratives, stories, and discourses, but as outcomes
of the development of a capacity to reflect on validity claims. Together,
Foucault and Habermas provide conceptual tools for a feminist constructivism that postulates socially constituted agents embedded and implicated in
networks of power. I use Nicholas Onuf's elaboration of Habermasian and
Foucaultian insights for International Relations as a starting point for a constructivism adapted to feminist purposes.[55]

Habermas proposes the notion of communicative agency against notions
of instrumental agency (the rational choice perspective), normative agency
(the perspective of role theory), and dramaturgic agency (the perspective of
ethnomethodology). Communicative agency arises from the interactions of
subjects capable of speech who through their communication get to understand each other by negotiating common definitions of the world. Communicative agency avoids the presumption in instrumental agency of a
choosing subject with given preference orderings, the presumption in role

theory of pregiven roles that individuals simply fill, and the presumption in ethnomethodology that individuals operate on a stage. Instead, agency and society are realized through communication, through the affirmation or challenge of validity claims. All communicative statements entail validity claims, i.e. a speaker claims that a statement is factually correct, normatively right, and nondeceptive. If the hearer accepts these claims, understanding is accomplished and speech acquires a binding force. Communicative agents renew their interpersonal relationship, affirm their agreement about objective facts of the world and about subjective experiences.[56] In other words, they reproduce the world by communicating. Onuf argues that rules provide the "missing link" between social structures and the temporary agreements that emerge in communicative exchanges. The normative force resulting from a speech act agreement becomes a convention when others join in the agreement and when propositions with complementary content are repeated. Conventions have a tendency to substitute for agreements; they become instituted into rules. Institutions are patterns of rules and related practices.[57]

Onuf argues that rules engender rule because all rules distribute privilege. In other words, rule-guided practice always entails a reproduction of power. At this point his constructivism departs from Habermas, and links up with Foucaultian power analysis and with the arguments of feminists who have long proposed that power pervades all aspects of life, ranging from the household to the international, from the very intimate to the very public. Because gender is a code for power, social agents by definition participate in negotiations of both gender and power. In this Foucaultian and feminist understanding, power is not possessed by individuals or located in a central source, whether a king, ruling classes, or elites. Power is not exercised over others but has an unmediated presence in society where it operates to constitute subjects.[58] Linking Foucaultian notions of power to the operation of rules in social communication preserves reflexive agency while taking advantage of the insights of poststructuralist power analysis.

From the feminist constructivist perspective I propose, it is then possible to conceptualize gender as an institution that codifies power, a constellation of rules and related practices that distributes privilege in a patterned way and is reproduced in communication. This institution of gender cuts across other institutions, such as the state, the household, and the economy, and interacts with the configurations of rule they effect. The purpose of gender analysis is to specify the rules of gender in particular contexts and describe interlinking patterns.

Gender as a Global Construct

To argue that gender is a social construct implicated with power is hardly news. To argue that gender is a global construct, on the other hand, requires specification. Who is doing the constructing in a supposedly anarchical world of states? What are the loci of such construction? Is there a community of constructors and who makes up this world? Answers to these questions require an elaboration of the global as a social space.

From a state-centric perspective, scholars often employ the term "global" to describe activities, structures, and processes that reach beyond the inter-state arena: interdependencies, the interconnectedness of domestic and international politics, and the proliferation of non-state actors in such politics.[59] Thus identified, the global is a negative category—it describes all that is not captured in state and interstate politics and is of interest primarily because of its effects on traditional forms of governance centered in the state.

Social theorists, often from outside the field of International Relations, approach the global differently. For them the global designates a social space in which distance and time have become largely irrelevant. Telecommunications and transportation technologies have enormously increased density of contacts and enabled instantaneous connections. The proliferation of transnational corporations, nongovernmental organizations and regulatory agencies; ecological changes resulting from human intervention; around-the-clock financial markets and global assembly lines; the development of shared cultures; and various networks of resistance all form aspects of globalization. Thus, the global does not simply indicate that which is not contained in the state, but designates the world as a single place of "supraterritorial . . . social relations."[60] It is the political space of a network of agents (including agents of states) enabled by new communications and transportation technologies and responding to transnational practices that endanger the natural environment, people's economic well-being, and physical security.

While the global has become a buzzword only in the 1990s, it is possible to discern a trend toward globalization at least since the end of the nineteenth century. As Scholte points out, after the telegraph appeared in 1840, the telephone, international short-wave radio programs, and international airline service enabled progressively more global communication, while the global influenza epidemic of 1918–1919 and multilateral discussions of transboundary pollution in the 1930s attested to the impacts of global forces even before the second world war.[61] At the end of the twentieth century global flows of capital, goods, communications, and people have accelerated significantly and contributed to an expansion of global space.[62]

The global is thus not a geographical term that designates a territory. Rather, a specific set of influential agents, through practices that reach beyond state boundaries, define the global as a social space. The fact that there are local differences in the way gender is constructed, and that global process may have touched some regions of the world less than others, does not invalidate the argument that these construction processes exist and create their own realities.

I take social movements as the perhaps most significant political agents in global space, interpolating agents that self-consciously construct. Following Habermas, Cohen and Arato interpret new social movements as an aspect of the process of rationalization that has characterized modernity. Social movements have become uniquely "self-reflective" about their relationships to the world and in this way embody the very essence of emancipatory communicative action.[63] As reflexive and communicative agents they participate in the continuous (re)construction of global rules. The identities of movements need not be fixed. As shown earlier, feminist theorists have argued that agency is possible even if identities are shifting. Walker agrees: social movements are social (i.e. they construct), but they also move (i.e. they change identities).[64] They do not have definite boundaries but continuously reinvent themselves through political practice.

Drawing on language-based constructivism, I find it useful to think of social movements as institutions supporting sustained argumentations geared toward changing rules. Argumentations capture the self-reflective character of social movements and evoke the linguistic basis of movement politics while signaling the instability of movement identities. To distinguish social movements from spontaneous rebellions or acts of resistance, their argumentations need to be sustained over a certain time period. Furthermore, I find it useful to think of the argumentations of movements not so much as geared toward influencing "elites, opponents and authorities," but toward changing rules that define elites and the appropriate scope of their conduct. In changing such rules the arguments of movements redistribute resources that constitute the foundations of power.[65]

Movement politics can then be understood as social construction in a global space. This implies, contra Habermas, Cohen, and Arato, that communications do not have to yield emancipatory outcomes; indeed if rule-guided communication always implies rule, then relationships of power always taint the constructions inherent in communications.[66] Furthermore, my understanding of social movements encompasses not only the "critical" social movements that dominate the literature, but also those that seek to limit, exclude, and disempower. In this book I treat neoclassical economic liberalism as a social movement that has helped bring about recent changes in capitalist modes of regulation.[67] There is no convincing reason why different forms of capitalism should not be treated as effects of social movements. Indeed, a broad range of Marxist literature has long emphasized the historical contingency of capitalism.

The character of social movements has changed with globalization. The literature often distinguishes "old social movements," such as the labor movement and the socialist movement, that typically operate like interest groups, often organized hierarchically and intending to influence or even take over the state, from new social movements, such as the environmental and the women's movements, that target cultural and normative change. The politics of new social movements are not limited to strategic exchanges with their adversaries, and seek as well to mold the power relationships realized in identities.[68] However, the movements literature may have overdrawn the distinction.[69] Indeed, Cohen and Arato have argued that a proper understanding of social movements encompasses both the influence-oriented politics of the old movements paradigm and the identity-oriented politics of the new movements paradigm.

But there may be another change that the sociological movement literature has overlooked: the impacts of globalization on the way movements operate. In the West, scholars have described the first sustained social agitations, replacing spontaneous and unorganized local rebellions, in connection with the rise of nationalism, democracies, and nation-states.[70] In the global age, resistance and politics has again taken on a new form, providing influence to skilled individuals, not necessarily agents of organizations or states. Their politics, mediated in social movements, effect a reconfiguration of political space. In Walker's words, the practices of these movements "do not always conform to the codes of inner and outer, to the account of spatiotemporal relations that informs the normative horizons of modern politics."[71] The changed character of movement politics emerges in the history of women's movements in the twentieth century. The themes of internationalism and transnational solidarity appeared in nationally and class-based movements before the first World War. The targets of activism were mostly states and, in the 1920s, international organizations. At the end of the century multiple issue-oriented movements pursue common strategies in a shared global space in which the presumption of commonality is fiercely contested, and debates often revolve around the "translations" of ideas from and into various local contexts.[72]

Gender and Global Politics

Because the global is a social space without territory, there is no obvious location from which to study it. A sizable body of feminist research takes local communities as the preferred sites of inquiry, exploring the way in which global economic forces have differentially impacted women and reproduced inequalities.[73] Others have focused on "women on the move" to explore international domestic service, mail-order brides, and sex tourism as elements of globalization.[74] A third group of studies has explored the politics of the internationalist women's movement and its engagement with multilateral institutions, many centering on the United Nations conferences of the 1990s.[75]

The development of multilateral institutions in the twentieth century offered a novel site of international politics that increasingly has provided a locus of communication between states and social movements. In a sense, interstate politics and global politics meet in multilateral institutions and the literature reflects this straddling of boundaries. Feminist studies describe how nongovernmental organizations have agitated in multilateral fora to help create norms on violence against women, challenged gendered definitions of human rights, put women's empowerment in the center of population policies, and committed states to enhancing the status of women.[76] Others have focused on the clash between economic ideologies and feminist visions in multilateral discourses. They have described the disempowering effects on women of the "neoliberal frame" and of economistic language that has come to dominate multilateral negotiations, whether at the Beijing Women's

Conference or at the negotiations of the North American Free Trade Agreement, and they have explored gendered, sexed, and racialized metaphors in regional economic "regimes."[77]

Writings about gender politics in the area of labor, the main focus of this study, typically take the interstate arena as their point of departure—i.e., the ILO and its formal policies. At the same time, these studies invariably highlight the influences and interventions of internationalist women's movements that operate in global space. For example, while the purpose of Carol Riegelman Lubin and Anne Winslow's study of the ILO is to survey conventions, recommendations, declarations, and programs on women; the presence of women in policymaking processes; and the status of women in the ILO bureaucracy, they also describe how the activities of individual women and feminist lobbies have impacted ILO practices.[78] Similarly, Ann Therese Lotherington and Ann Britt Flemmen have internationalist feminists as their audience when they explore the way in which "mainstreaming" gender into the ILO's policies touches core values of the organization and when they document successful subversive strategies.[79] Neither study focuses on internationalist feminist politics in a global space explicitly, but both take such politics as a crucial parameter.

Global politics move into the center of inquiry when the topic becomes rule change. Lubin and Winslow describe a change in the ILO from a focus on protection in its early years to a contemporary focus on equality.[80] Sandra Whitworth agrees that, while efforts to pursue equality and protection have always coexisted in the ILO, the mix of policies has shifted as policies stressing equality have virtually replaced protective measures. Whitworth explicitly links these changes to larger processes. She treats ILO outputs not as end products advancing the status of women (as Lubin and Winslow do), but as elements of a historical structure that (re)produces gender relations. Her focus is not women but gender. ILO policies are elements of a complex process that constructs notions of the feminine and the masculine while organizing the international. Using Robert Cox's analytical framework, Whitworth explores the interplay of material circumstances, ideas, and institutions. At the material level the decrepit conditions in factories at the turn of the century, the rise of fascism in the 1920s and 1930s, women's growing labor force participation since World War II, and increased employment opportunities in the expanding service sector all influenced ideas about gender and the international organization of such ideas in protective conventions and conventions promoting equality for women.[81]

This book builds on Whitworth. Like her, I am concerned with the construction of gender and take the ILO as my analytic point of departure. Like her, I see the ILO embedded in global processes. But there are also differences. Because Whitworth bases her constructivist argument on Coxian critical theory, she considers global processes to be "material"—related to the historically specific organization of production. Constructions of gender parallel material developments. In contrast, my language-based version of constructivism leads me to consider global processes as discursive practices in a social space that encompasses material developments. Furthermore, I argue that gender construction is global, rather than international, which I take to be Whitworth's argument. Instead of seeking to "uncover the social construction of gender within ILO policies,"[82] I want to describe construction processes in a global space that entail conversations between a diverse set of agents including those speaking for states, international organizations, nongovernmental organizations, private companies, and unions.

A Word on Method

Home-based work provides an ideal terrain for an exploration, such as this one, designed to shed light on gender, constructions of femininity and masculinity, in the global arena. Since the industrial revolution the home has in various ways been defined as a feminine space devoid of work. Home-based work violates rules prescribing the separation of home and work and notions of femininity and masculinity that map onto this separation. It thus functions as a methodological wedge that breaks up ideas about proper womanhood and manhood. Debates in international fora about home-based work have entailed debates about gender rules and therefore provide an ideal point of entry to probing gender in global space.

Like the social movements that are the focus of my investigation, the home-based workers, who are the target of movement arguments, are not easily delimited as a group, and indeed the boundaries of the group move in the course of the history that I sketch. Global debates before World War II largely concerned female European, North American, and Australian industrial homeworkers tied to factory production. After the War, this group moved into the background as home-based craft producers in Latin America, Asia, and Africa took center stage. Contemporary home-based workers comprise both of these groups as well as consultants, freelancers, and home-based workers in the service sector. Indeed, the contemporary understanding of home-based work directed my selection of historical topics. I owe the insight that dependent homework and self-employment are not fundamentally different to the leaders of the Self-Employed Women's Association (SEWA) of India whom I had the opportunity to meet in the course of my research. Their understanding made it possible to conceive of diverse forms of home-based work as part of one large communication concerning gender and workplaces that has spanned the twentieth century.

In writing this book, I found an epistemological standpoint within the interpretations of the "global homeworker movement," a movement that seeks emancipatory space in the context of global restructuring. It is a small movement that straddles the labor, microenterprise, and women's movements. Seeking to improve the economic status of home-based workers, to gain them legitimacy and legal recognition, it has spawned a diverse set of organizations, from global networks to local advocacy groups and banks that offer credit. It is also a movement rife with controversy, between those who see home-based workers as self-employed and those who see them as dependent workers, between those who see home-based work as an alternative to capitalism and those who insist that, in a capitalist economy, all workers are dependent and exploited, between those who think that home-based workers should be unionized and those who think they need primarily access to capital.[83]

My particular vantage point has been a small group of activists from India and Europe, who organized in the early 1990s in order to lobby for an ILO convention on homework. I attended a meeting in the Netherlands in May 1990 under the auspices of a Dutch NGO (IRENE—International Restructuring Education Network Europe), which brought together advocates from various countries and laid the grounds to formalize an international network, HomeNet International. I maintained contact with the network, renewing relationships at various ILO-sponsored meetings that led to the passing of the convention, and helped facilitate a meeting in the U.S. in the context of the 1991 Forum of the Association for Women in Development. HomeNet members have provided me with valuable information about the situation of home-based workers in different countries and the difficulties of organizing. HomeNet also provided me a way to see the world. I am not sure that HomeNet activists would have written this book the way I did but I hope that they will agree with much of what I have to say.

My other major source of information was the International Labor Organization. As an organization that systematically collects information from a diverse set of agents engaged in labor politics and that facilitates communication between them, it served as a convenient site for my broader investigations. In the summer of 1991, I spent a month at the ILO, browsing the vast information that the Office had gathered on home-based work and attending a Meeting of Experts on the Social Protection of Homeworkers. I returned in the summer of 1995 to work my way through relevant materials in the ILO Archives and to attend the International Labor Conference which in that year had put homework on its agenda for a first round of discussion.

All these activities thrust me in the middle of a vast conversation on home-based work that employed and problematized rules about gender. My purpose was to identify these rules. I gained leverage in this effort from historical comparisons. I also employed, as a methodological tool, Onuf's classification of rules into instruction-rules, directive-rules, and commitment-rules.[84] This distinction allowed for insight into the changing politics of social movements in the context of globalization, their identity-and interest-oriented politics, their efforts to change definitions and gain rights. Derived from speech act theory, the three categories of rules provide the ontological grounds for Onuf's language-based constructivism. Without delving into the philosophical arguments from which the distinction arises, I briefly describe them.

Instruction-rules define, state identities and beliefs about the way things are. They make claims about facts, elicit agreement about these facts on the part of others, and thereby bring about conformity. Foucaultian analyses exploring the production of subjects are concerned with instruction-rules. So are feminist analyses focusing on the creation of sexed bodies and gendered agents. A large part of this study is taken up with identifying instruction-rules.

Directive-rules imply commands, requests, demands, permissions and warnings. They elicit compliance, conformity, obeisance, submission. Directive-rules define hierarchical relations such as the one between employers and employees. They often imply negative consequences that would result if one were not to follow directions, e.g. a home-based worker loosing future assignments if she did not carry out the work in precisely the way specified, or a woman adjusting her habits because of a fear of violence. More formally, governments can issue directive-rules that force employers to provide certain benefits or abstain from certain practices under the threat of punishment.

Directive-rules often have preoccupied the work of political scientists and defined their concern with enforcement. However, they play a subordinate role in my analysis of interventions to change the rules of home-based work.

Commitment-rules imply promises and offers that oblige individuals to act accordingly. Commitment-rules fix socially mediated identities into self-understandings, create role-identifications, and build understandings of rights and duties. For example, when feminists argue that women's rights should be considered human rights, they lay claim to commitment-rules. This category of rules focuses attention on the "rational" aspects of modernity, such as rules of law and democracy, which are missing in poststructuralist depictions of society as normalized. Focusing on commitment-rules in the context of this work means showing the potential and limits of talk about workers' and women's rights.

Onuf developed his distinction between these three categories of rules on the basis of theoretical arguments, and it is often difficult to empirically identify which categories particular rules fall into. In part this is because language itself is often ambiguous. Furthermore, any written body of law or convention typically includes all three categories of rules. For example, human rights law not only specifies commitments but also instructs about identities and, more rarely, implies negative consequences. But instruction-rules, directive-rules, and commitment-rules can serve as heuristic tools that yield practical insight into the way change takes place and in that way inform feminist practice.[85]

Overview of the Book

Although the ILO has only now set standards for their employment, home-based workers have been a point of discussion ever since the organization was founded in the early part of this century. Chapter 2 analyzes how the creation of Western welfare states involved constructions of gender. In the first two decades of the twentieth century, the labor movement, the consumer protection movement, and the women's movement all used industrial homework as a cause that legitimized state intervention into the economy. Debates at international homeworker congresses at the eve of World War I built an ideal of women as mothers who did not work, and of home as devoid of work. In parallel, they constructed those who violated these rules as dirty, diseased, and miserable creatures and created homeworkers as nonworkers outside the working class. In the late 1920s, such constructions facilitated agreement among states in ILO discussions about setting minimum wages. At the same time, the feminist movement began to challenge constructions of women as motherly and not real workers, and used the debate about minimum wage fixing to stage demands for equal pay. Their radicalism pitted equal rights feminists against feminists in the labor movement who favored protective legislation and in some cases a ban on homework. Under U.S. influence, the ILO Regional Conference of American States called for a ban on homework but efforts to gain similar directives at the global level were unsuccessful.

The two decades after World War II are the subject of chapter 3. Home-based workers appeared in global politics as indigenous crafts producers in Latin America and in the newly independent states of Asia, and Africa. Unlike the Western industrial homeworkers in the early part of the century, these home-based workers were not constructed as nonworking mothers, but as marginal workers and supplemental income-earners. Nation-building rhetoric ambiguously framed them as representing the essence of the new nations on the one hand, and as a sign of backwardness on the other. Prescriptions for modernization devalued home-based industry, painted feminine activities and the crafts of feminized indigenous peoples as backward, and styled masculine types of activity as worthy of modernization. On the other hand, nationalist rhetoric celebrated indigenous crafts as a source of national identification. In technical assistance literature, the increasingly feminine character of home-produced crafts inspired erotic metaphors that cast the developing nation as the seductress of foreign buyers, exploiting images of femininity for economic purposes.

Chapter 4 focuses on the revived feminist movement and developmentalist themes valorizing the provision of basic needs, appropriate technologies, and small-scale undertakings in the 1970s, introducing into global debates the notion of the "informal sector." The literature subdivided the informal sector into typically feminine marginal survival activities and masculine, vibrant enterprises, reproducing an understanding of the economic marginality of women. In parallel, the Women in Development (WID) movement attacked rules that constructed the home as private and women's work as nonwork. Policy interventions increasingly targeted "microentrepreneurs," many of them women. In the context of the 1980s debt crisis, structural adjustment policies, and accelerating economic restructuring, development agencies supported women and their home-based work because they saw in them a way to raise families out of poverty. Home-based women workers were no longer viewed as dupes or signs of backwardness but emerged as morally superior and economically savvy.

Chapter 5 describes the legislative history that led up to the passing of the ILO Home Work Convention. I explore the influence of the home-worker movement and the role of the International Labor Office in putting home-based work on the ILO agenda. I argue that the convention consti-tuted an attack on the gender rules that underpinned Fordist modes of regu-lation, rules that built extensively on the opposition between home and work. Debates leading to the convention reveal the multiple and often divergent notions of femininity and masculinity that informed various arguments, ranging from an understanding of homeworkers as passive and exploited dupes to a degendered notion of homeworkers as the ideal workers in an economy built on flexible accumulation.

Chapter 6 documents the interlacing of class and gender in Fordist modes of regulation. It explores the ways in which the debate on homework desta-bilized Fordist constructions of social class formulated around the opposition between employers and the self-employed on the one hand and employees on the other. Debates about what it means to be a homeworker reveal the opposition not only as gendered but also as untenable under conditions of flexible production. The chapter shows how the arguments of homeworker advocates intersected with those of the neoclassical liberal movement to challenge Fordist instruction-rules about class and gender. I conclude the study by assessing the extent to which my feminist constructivist approach and my focus on movements succeeded in offering practical and emanci-patory knowledge and raise questions for feminist research that emerge from a treatment of global construction processes from the locale of an interna-tional organization.

2 Motherly Women—Breadwinning Men: Industrial Homework and the Construction of Western Welfare States

The debate about home-based labor in the first part of the twentieth century was embedded in social struggles around the creation of modern welfare states. Poverty and misery had accompanied the reorganization of home-based manufacture into industrial production, fostering political consciousness among the newly emerging working class which increasingly organized and threatened the political order in European countries. Specific responses to "the social question" varied in national contexts, but by the beginning of the century, most Western governments had begun to regulate factory employment and were adopting measures to ease some of the worst impacts of unfettered capitalism by inaugurating the construction of welfare states. The fight for the creation of welfare states absorbed the energies of reformers, academics, bureaucrats, socialists, and feminists in addition to labor organizers. They constructed rules that redefined the identities of workers and citizens; asserted the obligations of states, the bourgeoisie, and employers toward the proletariat and the poor; and condemned those who violated these obligations.

Home-based workers played a significant role in arguments about state intervention in the market. While economic theory had predicted that, in the long run, industrial development would move all production into factories, a new type of home-based worker emerged in the mid-nineteenth century. As Karl Marx observed, the "old-fashioned [domestic] industry has now been converted into an outside department of the factory, the manufactory, or the warehouse."[1] These workers no longer produced the whole piece but were integrated in the industrial division of labor. Marx was quick to add that the brutal exploitation of female and child labor had limits and "so soon as this point is at last reached . . . the hour has struck for the introduction of machinery, and for the thenceforth rapid conversion of the scattered domestic industries and also of manufactures into factory industries."[2] Modern production techniques would overcome an outmoded form of work. Factory legislation would help speed this process. While social insurance schemes and labor laws in nineteenth-century Europe excluded home-based workers,[3] Marx saw "an irresistible tendency towards the general application of those principles."[4]

Ironically, it appeared that labor legislation had precisely the opposite effect; at least in some branches of industry it drove work out of factories and into urban homes. Industrial homework allowed employers to circumvent the new labor laws; it was particularly attractive to women because it enabled them to earn an income while meeting their child care and household duties. In France, the proportion of garment workers at home increased from 51.8 percent in 1896 to 58.6 percent in 1901.[5] In Germany their number almost doubled between 1882 and 1907, and women were responsible for most of the increase.[6] By the turn of the century, armies of women from London and Paris to Berlin and New York sewed clothes and shoes, assembled artificial flowers and feathers, made match boxes, brushes, umbrellas and toys in their homes. Their low wages, and often despicable working conditions inspired arguments around the world for state intervention to improve labor conditions.

Australia, New Zealand, Britain, Germany, Austria, Norway, and several states in the United States all wrote homeworking laws before World War I. Australian legislation, which established tripartite "trades boards," provided an important inspiration for other countries. The boards comprised representatives of employers, unions, and the government, set wages and maximum hours, and required that employers keep lists of the homeworkers they employed. The British law of 1909 imitated the Australian trades boards, applying them to all "sweated industries" and giving them additional authority to mediate disputes. The German law of 1911 established similar boards but only granted them power to set wages in the revised version of 1923.[7] In the U.S., the state of New York banned the (mostly male) home-production of cigars in the late nineteenth century, but courts declared the law unconstitutional on the basis that it infringed upon a citizen's right to contract. In the aftermath of the ruling, states confined measures to regulate homework, such as minimum wage laws, to women only, thus reducing the risk that courts would invalidate such measures.[8] At the international level as well, there were efforts to achieve an agreement on how to deal with homework. All these interventions entailed rule changes that effected a separation of home and work and affirmed the role of male breadwinners.

Rules

The industrial revolution entailed not only a separation of home and work but also a spatial reorganization of gender relations that created the home as a female sphere and the public world of work and politics as a male one. Historians have amply criticized the "myth of separate worlds," documented the multiple ways in which the home remained a work place even after the industrial revolution, and the ways in which family processes have always intertwined with both women's and men's income earning.[9] But debates leading up to the formation of early Western welfare states extensively drew on the myth, and labor laws reproduced the home-work separation. Debates about industrial homework at the beginning of the twentieth century both confirmed and contested instruction-rules that had come to define gender relations in the late nineteenth century. At issue were in particular the following: the spatial relation between home and work; the gendering of the home as feminine and of work as masculine; the identification of womanhood with motherhood and of masculinity with income earning.

The exclusion of work from home played a central role in the formulation of a new gender order that emerged with the industrial revolution. In preindustrial agricultural and artisan households it was understood that wives and children contributed economically; the insecurity of income precluded reliance on one breadwinner. While family members collaborated in economic endeavors, men were constructed as household heads. A crucial source of male honor and power, especially in artisan households, was the "property in skill," which legitimized men's status as heads of households. The industrial revolution fundamentally changed this family structure, creating the role of a single male income earner. As Sonya O. Rose has shown for England, the emergence of the male breadwinner was closely related to the move of work into factories and the loss of male artisan skill that this entailed. Because it required increasingly less skilled labor, factory production devalued men's status. The notion of the male breadwinner re-created men's dominance under different rules. Agitations to remove women and children from industrial production, or at least to sideline them into unskilled "women's work," together with the emergence of male cultures of protest, progressively excluded women from wage earning as well as the public rostrum, creating a new form of industrial patriarchy. The full-time housewife became a symbol of working-class respectability.[10]

Cults of domesticity and true womanhood formed the corollary to the idea of the male breadwinner. In bourgeoise culture, the home became the retreat from harsh factory life, a place of harmony and regeneration. Replacing the lost, pre-industrial community, the new home formed the cornerstone of a healthy social order. Women emerged as the guardians of this order; they held together a world in which men had to act self-interestedly to succeed as free agents in a liberal economy. As Ellen Carol DuBois has put it, "women's essential selflessness was a necessary corollary to men's individualism, the means of reconciling the pre-eminence of the self-determining man with the requirements of social order."[11]

One of the main arguments that legitimized women's confinement to the home revolved around their child-bearing capacity. Motherhood became an all-encompassing definer of womanhood. All women, regardless of whether they had or wanted children, were potential mothers, and this condition came to guide policies and debates. Motherhood required that women stayed home to ensure the well-being of their offspring, for which they were assigned sole responsibility. Motherhood and womanhood became virtually exchangeable at the turn of the century, inspiring not only state regulation but also the argumentations of social movements.

Given the centrality of the home-work separation to the new gender order, it is not surprising that industrial homework became a fiercely contested practice. In the first part of the twentieth century, arguments around industrial homework demanded state intervention, i.e. directive-rules, to abolish a practice that proved contradictory in its effects on a gender order celebrating female domesticity and motherhood. The ideal of the male breadwinner had rarely been achieved in working-class households that needed women's income for a decent living; for many industrial homework provided a means to maintain respectability while enabling women to earn an income. In this way, industrial homework enabled at least an appearance of nonworking mothers. But, on the other hand, the mixing of home and work threatened the health of the social body as well as industrial patriarchy. The households of industrial homeworkers did not measure up to middle-class standards of orderliness, and industrial homework threatened to undermine the job security of male workers/breadwinners that were the counterpart to the domestic housewife. Demands for change must be read as efforts to rationalize a gender order built on the home-work separation and the house-wife-breadwinner opposition.

Much of the debate around homework in the first part of the century concerned changes in directive- and commitment-rules. Activists sought to create labor legislation and international labor conventions demanding that employers and governments make provisions for the welfare of work-ers and in this way committing themselves to the notion of workers' rights. Labor laws to ameliorate exploitation, protective legislation for women, and social security provisions all entailed the creation of both commit-ment- and directive-rules. But debates also affected and effected instruction-rules about gender identities. Indeed, arguments about homework were most effective and most contentious when they concerned instruction-rules about gender. Welfare and labor legislation gained legitimacy through notions of workers identified as male breadwinners and women workers identified as dependent and not-real workers. Gender rules legitimized protective legis-lation for women and helped introduce the principle of state intervention in the economy. And contentions which attacked definitions of femininity as motherliness not only opposed conservatives and progressives but also ripped apart the feminist movement.

Movements

The labor movement and the women's movement crucially shaped de-bates about homework in the first half of the twentieth century. Both con-stituted global movements that consisted of conversations across national boundaries, of social networks organized supernationally. Both also reflected the power politics of the era in that their reach rarely extended outside Europe and North America or took seriously input from other areas. Thus, the debate at the time transcended state boundaries, but it was also geograph-ically confined and fairly euro-centric.[12]

Before World War I, the Socialist International constituted the most vocal and influential organization of the labor movement at the global level. While the First International disintegrated over ideological squabbles between the followers of Marx and Bakunin, the Second International, established in Paris in 1889, found cohesion under the banner of a social democratic orientation which combined demands for immediate practical reforms with a long-term vision of revolution. In their pragmatic approach, socialists and labor leaders sacrificed the rights of women workers, including home-based workers. Many demanded restrictions on women's work in the nineteenth century and, while the International passed a resolution in support of women's suffrage in 1900, it also advocated protective legislation in the sphere of work. The rhetoric of the labor movement participated in a construction of women as motherly and of home-based workers as outside the working class.

In the mid-nineteenth century, there apparently was a broad understanding, at least in Britain and Germany, that home-based workers belonged in trade unions, and they had a presence there. They voiced their positions even when these contradicted the interests of factory workers, such as opposing the extension of the British Factories and Workshop Act to homework. According to Sheila Rowbotham, the understanding that homeworkers belonged in unions changed as organized labor turned to the state for protection from the effects of the capitalist mode of production and increasingly defined homeworkers as outside the labor movement. From the labor perspective, homework undermined factory legislation and thereby the foundations of the male breadwinner role that was a crucial element of the industrial-era patriarchy. By the beginning of the twentieth century, socialist parties all over Europe passed resolutions condemning homework and agitated for its abolition.[13]

The Second Socialist International dissolved with the First World War when some of its most important members rallied around the national cause rather than choosing pacifist internationalism. The Russian revolution and the Soviets' attempts to impose their interpretations of history and policy on socialist allies world-wide split the socialist/labor movement in the postwar era. The International Federation of Trade Unions (IFTU), an alliance of trade union centers from mostly European countries, founded in 1901 with headquarters in Berlin, emerged as the leading noncommunist voice of labor after the war. It participated in the negotiations of the Versailles Treaty to establish the International Labor Organization and came to represent labor within the ILO, collaborating closely with the revived Second International.

The IFTU's positions on women's work carried significant weight at the ILO whose first conference in 1919 passed a convention to prohibit night work for women, a major IFTU demand. The IFTU considered the possibility of an international campaign for the regulation of homework at its 1907 conference. Overall however, the IFTU largely ignored the interests of working women. Union women formed their own organizations to focus attention on issues such as organizing women and minimum wages. They also carried the banner in the fight against homework. The International Federation of Working Women, created by the British and the American Women's Trade Union Leagues in 1919 and including union women from all over Europe, discussed homework at its 1923 convention, and discussions at the International Congress of Women Workers in 1927 stressed the need for eradicating the practice.[14]

Before World War I, labor women found a home within the first wave of the feminist movement. Voting rights were the main rallying cry of this movement, but it concerned itself as well with issues of war and peace and with women's economic status. After women won the vote in most European countries and the U.S. at the end of World War I, concerns for equal treatment in the economic sphere moved to the foreground. But the issue of special legislation for women created a vast split within the global women's movement. Was it necessary to legislate prohibitions of night work and dangerous work for women, but not for men? Was it desirable to have minimum wages for women but not for men? Was maternity protection a benefit for women or did it hinder women's employment? While equal rights feminists castigated the discriminatory effects of such legislation, union women defended protective legislation as necessary in a situation where women's conditions of employment objectively differed from those of men. The homework question got entangled in this debate as those favoring protective legislation also favored a ban on homework. In the late 1920s, differences about special legislation led to a split of the International Alliance of Women (IAW) dominated by U.S. women that favored protective legislation. Excluded from the IAW, equal rights feminists took their fight to the international level in separate organizations. They established the Open Door International for the Economic Emancipation of the Woman Worker in 1929, Equal Rights International in 1930 and the World Women's Party in 1938. The purpose of the later two was to promote an Equal Rights Treaty at the League of Nations. The purpose of Open Door International was to monitor developments at the ILO, to fight for the repeal of protective legislation, and to prevent further ILO conventions on protective legislation.[15]

The goal of both defenders and enemies of protective legislation was the same: to gain women equal status in the economic sphere. Both rejected a gender order that stipulated a male breadwinner supported by a non-earning housewife and mother. But they differed in their understanding of women's identities. They subscribed to different instruction-rules about the connection of womanhood and motherhood, a difference that may have resulted from their class positions. Those who, in the name of working-class women, favored protective legislation, tended to view women as actual or potential mothers, and they considered motherhood a disadvantage in the labor market (as it most likely was for those who could not afford to hire maids). In contrast, equal rights feminists, many of them middle-class professionals, tended to define women as individuals in the liberal sense, i.e. as free agents, and thereby challenged instruction-rules that associated womanhood with weakness and dependence.

The debate about protective legislation at the international level was so fierce largely because of the influence of U.S. feminists who fought each other about the issue of an equal rights amendment to the U.S. Constitution. Leaders of different factions in the U.S. carried their arguments and personal animosities to the international level. But many global feminists actually found a middle-ground on the issue of protective legislation, rejecting most restrictive laws but supporting maternity protection. Indeed, for many (including many in the U.S.) the language of maternalism became a basis to argue for equal laws that would allow women to exert their "special" influence in the world. In this revaluation, the maternal experience was not a source of weakness but of superiority; the identification of womanhood and motherhood preserved while demands for equal rights legitimized.[16]

The labor movement and the women's movement created a global space for conversations about gender rules. After the end of the first World War, the new multilateral institutions of the League of Nations importantly focused these conversations. The Swiss and Belgian governments had long sought to establish an international organization in charge of labor regulation, but had found little support from other governments. In 1900, they created the International Association for Labor Legislation (IALL), made up of social reformers, academics, doctors, lawyers, social workers, and some government officials. Organized into local affiliates and headquartered in Basle, Switzerland, the IALL was to publicize findings about labor conditions and in this way "have a moral and educational effect" on governments.[17]

Homework was a major concern of the IALL because it was seen to undermine factory legislation. Starting in 1904, the Association called on its affiliates to initiate studies on homework resulting in extensive research on the practice all over Europe. Researchers explored the connection between homework and international competition, outlined the effects of new labor legislation on the expansion of homework, detailed the social situation and wages of homeworkers, and reported on the successes and failures of labor legislations.[18] At the IALL's 1906 conference, government representatives from fifteen countries, agreed to a convention prohibiting night work for women and committed themselves to extend this prohibition to women homeworkers.[19] In 1907, a Swiss Homeworker Congress resolved that the IALL initiate proceedings for governments to arrive at international agreements in those areas of homework where international competition pushed wages to unacceptable levels.[20]

In connection with the 1910 world exhibit in Brussels, Belgian advocates organized the first International Homework Congress, bringing together 250 participants from nine nations who compared the situation of homeworkers and legislation in these countries. The Congress resolved to create an International Homework Office with the mandate to organize a follow-up congress in 1912. Negotiations with the IALL led to an agreement that its Belgian affiliate assume leadership of the International Homework Office, and the office was established with its headquarters in Brussels.[21] The IALL and the International Homework Office became focal points for the global debate on homework before World War I. Their activities were closely intertwined with those of various Consumers' Leagues on both sides of the Atlantic. The two international congresses of Consumers' Leagues in 1908 and 1913 brought together many of the same people as the homework congresses organized by the International Homework Office, and regulating homework emerged as a crucial strategy of Consumers' Leagues.

After the war, the Versailles Peace Treaty established the International Labor Organization, the international agency in charge of labor legislation that the Swiss and Belgians had envisaged. When the Allied powers created the ILO, they did so because of commitments they had made to labor unions during the war in order to ensure their collaboration in the war effort. The Bolshevik revolution and the fear that it might spread to other countries bolstered these commitments. Labor unions and socialists agreed that social welfare could be advanced through international action, and their leaders actively participated in the negotiations at Versailles. The organization constituted the regulatory counterpart of welfare states at the international level. It was to work toward the regulation of working hours and wages, establishing social security protection, and ensuring the free operation of trade unions.[22]

The ILO took on many of the issues the IALL had been debating, including restrictions of women's work. Organized in a tripartite structure, it allowed a voice and a vote to employer organizations and unions in addition to governments. Feminists lobbied the ILO from the outside. Industrial homework appeared on its agenda in connection with debates about minimum wage setting in the late 1920s, and again in the 1940s, when U.S. women in the Roosevelt administration sought international action on homework. Thus, the ILO together with the congresses of the International Homework Office and the Consumers' Leagues provided a place for global arguments about homework including the contestation of gender rules.

Argument: Homework Means Dirt, Disease, and Disorder

In the decade before World War I a series of "homework exhibits" in Berlin, London, Frankfurt, Zurich, Amsterdam, and Brussels attracted global attention. Organized by unions, consumers' leagues, academics, and even one by a sympathetic newspaper, they portrayed the diversity of homework, the way homework was organized, and—most importantly—attested to the meager wages of homeworkers. The exhibits were highly effective and became part of the "repertoire of contention" of social movements concerned with industrial homework. The empress of Germany visited the 1904 exhibit in Berlin and reportedly was moved to tears. The 1906 exhibit in London created an "explosion of pity," and led to the creation of the Anti-Sweating League. The purpose of the exhibits was to show that homework was an "evil," to raise indignation about the situation of homeworkers and to create a sense that something needed to be done.[23]

Homework exhibits evoked intense emotion and repulsion, in part because they documented the disorder that resulted from violations of gender rules that were meant to make more secure a world rent by industrial strife and social change. These rules stipulated that home and work did not belong together; rather their spatial and temporal union represented social disorganization. The language of public health, which resonated widely at the time, often provided metaphors to express this disorganization, and debates at international congresses effectively articulated the fear of disorder that the mixing of home and work seemed to cause. At the International Congress of Home Work in 1912, advocates described homeworkers' households as disorganized, their children as roaming the streets exposed to vice and maladies. Homework was said to threaten the health of the family and of consumers who were "exposed to collecting deadly germs in the products" of homeworkers. Homeworking families emerged as breeding grounds of alcoholism, tuberculosis, and sexually transmitted disease. Consumers' Leagues demanded a ban on the home-based processing of foods and called for the disinfection of clothing assembled in homework. Homeworkers even were held responsible for the spread of prostitution: "Through competition [homeworkers] will arrest the lot of women workers capable of earning their living and they will enter into misery and prostitution."[24] Because they polluted the feminine home with paid work, homeworkers were held accountable for the pollution of proper womanhood.

The global debate echoed some national themes but was silent on others. Most importantly, at the international level voices that defended homework as a desirable practice were virtually absent. In contrast, in France and Germany, social reformers, while accepting the need for regulating homework, also insisted that it was a valuable option for women and that regulation should not endanger the practice.[25] In the words of Käthe Gaebel, general secretary of the Gewerkverein der Heimarbeiterinnen, a Berlin-based organization of homeworkers under the leadership of Christian women, homework's "internal legitimacy" derived from the fact that it "preserved women for the family."[26]

The connection of homework to the preservation of family life apparently did not play a role in the British and American contexts.[27] But other arguments, including the creation of homeworkers as miserable creatures and the use of medical metaphors were pervasive in Europe and North America and easily agreed upon at the international levels. For example, activists in the United Kingdom associated "sweating" with dirt and disease and abundantly employed medical metaphors. When sponsoring legislators introduced the Trade Boards Act of 1909 in the House of Commons, they argued that the "application of this measure [i.e. the Act] is very limited. It is intended to be applied exclusively to exceptionally unhealthy patches of the body politic where the development has been arrested in spite of the growth of the rest of the organism. It is to the morbid and diseased places—to the diphtheritic spots that we should apply the antitoxin of Trade Boards."[28] In the U.K. concerns with the purity of homes and of women ranged, in Vivien Hart's words, "from the literal ('domestic uncleanliness, as it is sometimes called—where the beds are not properly made, and that sort of thing') to darker hints ('the worker, in the case of women, finds money in a way that is far more common than many people think')."[29]

Like the British, many French saw homework both as a medical and an economic pathology. A Parisian doctor described it as "a painful sore on the social body," and "a criminal waste of human life and effort." Hygienists argued that "crowded, damp, and unventilated homes, overwork, and exhaustion" made homeworkers vulnerable to disease. Furthermore, homeworkers spread germs through the clothes and toys they produced. According to Judith Coffin, the French literature became strangely macabre and repulsive: "The women cough while bent over their sewing machines, 'and each cough spews forth drops filled with virulent tubercular bacteria.' " In the U.S., the Consumers' League similarly played on the effectiveness of health metaphors, circulating "graphic stories of food and clothing custommade in the presence of deadly disease—like the consumptive crone licking boxes for wedding cakes." And in Germany, an advocate in the academy described homework as "a creeping, gnawing disease of the body politic."[30]

Talk about a healthy body politic easily merged into talk about a healthy race and nation. Nationalists argued that women, as mothers, were the backbones of nations, civilizing agents and the preservers of the race, and considered homework under this aspect. The cause of the nation demanded the protection of women from the travails of industrial labor, whether this cause involved higher birth rates (as in France) or romantic notions about the strengthening of the "Volkskraft," i.e. the vigor of the people, (as in Germany). Homework could facilitate motherhood, but only if it was not exploitative. For example, a 1918 medical treatise about preserving the strength of the German people demanded minimum wage laws for homeworkers not in order to eradicate homework but to enhance its potential role in preserving family life: "Adequate remuneration allows female homeworkers not only a more humane existence, but in many cases is the necessary prerequisite for marriage at the most appropriate age and for the raising of numerous healthy children. . . . The homeworker as well must be allowed to exercise above all her natural profession—to be a wife and mother."[31] National Socialist labor legislation adopted this argument to strengthen Germany's homeworking law in 1933, regulating wages and working conditions and, for the first time in German history, ensuring the implementation of these rules, through tripartite councils tied to the authoritarian control structure of the Nazi Party.

Not surprisingly, nationalist themes rarely appeared in global fora that generally gathered progressive forces with an internationalist outlook, and nationalists and internationalists arrived at different policy prescriptions regarding homework. But nationalist and internationalist arguments agreed that there was a need to preserve women's motherliness. Indeed, Leila Rupp has observed that the emphasis on women's motherliness was much more pronounced in internationalist feminist circles than at the national level. Emphasizing women's distinct qualities provided the grounds for a collective identity that cut across the bonds of nationalism.[32] The maternalist worldview of internationalist feminists joined that of international labor activists who wanted to preserve the role of the male breadwinner and that of nationalists. In their joined social horizon, mixing home and work amounted to a mixing of womanhood and manhood, the building blocks of a society constructed as orderly.

Manufacturing at home, which had been the norm a hundred years earlier was now considered a sore on the body politic, dangerous to families and consumers. While factory work apparently contributed to the wealth of nations and the well-being of families, homework seemed to have quite the opposite effect: poverty, disease, and immorality. The talk of disorder, malady, and impropriety prepared the grounds for technocratic state intervention, for the rationalization of work and gender relations. Clinical metaphors combined with an appeal to gender rules justified international and state action in a historical context where the legitimacy of state intervention in the economy was fiercely contested.

Argument: Industrial Homeworkers Are Not Real Workers

The separation of home and work affirmed men as breadwinners and constructed an image of workers as independent and unattached to homes. The masculine worker was a free agent, free to sell his labor power, free to enter contracts, and capable of representing himself in political society. His corollary was the politically and economically dependent housewife/mother. Although feminists and labor women made inroads into politics, men often spoke for women in the labor movement, and upper- and middle-class women, with their own tenuous right to self-representation, spoke for working-class women. Paternalism and maternalism in the labor and the women's movements combined to construct industrial homeworkers as ignorant dupes and hapless victims who needed reformers to look after their real interests.

At the International Congress of Home Work in 1912, advocates portrayed homeworkers as "miserable creatures" incapable of securing a job which paid a living wage and who even "begged" for jobs that paid puny amounts. Homeworkers did not have the equipment to do real jobs; they were not real workers. Accordingly, they could not speak for themselves in the political arena. They did not have "the necessary mental and economic independence to appoint on their own useful and appropriate representatives." Homeworkers' resistance to legislation only showed their political immaturity. As reformers saw it, homeworkers themselves were the biggest obstacle to legislation, and legislation would be a delicate matter because "the people who stand to gain the most by any legislation on the subject are more inclined than any others to commit breaches of the law." Homeworkers were not yet "sufficiently enlightened" about their own interests.[33]

Again there were national differences. According to Sheila Rowbotham, homeworkers in Britain were active in unions and resisted exploitation in the nineteenth century. Only when demands for state intervention came to dominate debates about homework did they get painted as outside the working class. By 1907, Gertrude Tuckwell of the British Women's Trade Union League told the Select Committee on Homework that it was "absolutely impossible" to organize homeworkers. The Trade Boards Act of 1909 covered homeworkers and encouraged attempts of the National Federation of Women Workers to organize homeworkers, although with little lasting success.[34]

In Germany, socialists and feminists eyed each other with hostility in the early part of the twentieth century, and the organization of women homeworkers became the preserve of more conservative Christian reformers. Accordingly, the idea that homeworkers did not belong in the working class, were incapable of developing class consciousness, becoming real proletarians, and joining the struggle for the emancipation, was more deeply ingrained here. In the opinion of Robert Wilbrandt, an academic writing on the homework problem in Germany, homeworker organizations were not real workers' organizations. They answered to a need for community and companionship but could not become agents of change. Members of the Gewerkverein der Heimarbeiterinnen met with "the aid of the pastor's wife and the "extraordinary members" [i.e. the bourgeois leadership]," but they would never "be capable of proletarian class struggle, of a victorious unfolding of power." When they left their meetings, they were ready "to let themselves be exploited further."[35] Apparently in France similar associations prevailed. In the words of Aline Valette, a French factory inspector, member of the workers' party, and delegate of the seamstress union: "Their isolation leads [needleworkers] to believe that they are utterly and forever helpless, and they recoil before any initiative that needs to be taken."[36]

Given these instruction-rules about homeworkers, it is not surprising that socialists, labor unions, and progressives favored the eradication of homework. Because homeworkers were not real workers, they, unlike their male factory counterparts, did not have a right to work. Indeed, homeworkers undermined the struggles and achievements of the working class; they were enemies of the working class rather than fellow workers. While socialists and unionists supported demands that homework be regulated, they saw regulation as a first step toward eliminating the practice. They reasoned that strict regulation would make homework unattractive to employers and the practice would die out as a consequence. As one speaker observed at the 1912 International Congress of Home Work, "if these industries die because they are forced to pay their employees appropriate salaries, it provides the proof that they were not worthy of continued existence." The labor movement had defined homework as an artificial system of labor that had no place in the industrial world.[37]

The goal of keeping home and work apart underlay socialist and labor arguments in favor of banning homework. Such arguments entailed contentions to preserve a patriarchal order that privileged men as workers and breadwinners. A wish list that socialists presented at the Berlin Homework exhibit of 1906 explicitly specified the need to separate living and working areas in homeworking households—in addition to standard demands for wage-setting boards and the extension of social insurance and labor laws to homeworkers. A rule to this effect would have ended homework simply because few homeworking households had homes large enough to comply. But the demand also illustrates the underlying anxiety about the mixing of work and home, the degree to which it cemented a gender order that mapped breadwinning and mothering onto these spatial distinctions. Homeworking women not only threatened the working class by subverting factory legislation and collective bargaining agreements, but they also emasculated the men in their own families by threatening their status as breadwinners.

This is how a homework activist from Belgium saw the issue at the International Congress of Home Work:

> In a family where the husband earns two francs and the wife one franc, there will be three francs to live off and the husband will worry no longer about gaining a higher salary. By suppressing the miserable salary of one franc that the woman earns, you will see the husband demand a supplement of his own salary. Thus, in order to ameliorate the salary of men, we need to abolish the small earnings of wives.[38]

The logic implied in this argument—that the family would be better off financially if the woman's income-earning opportunities would be curtailed—made sense on the basis of instruction-rules that framed men as natural providers. The anxiety over losing breadwinner status (and the prestige associated with such status) led to a plea to abolish homework. If men had high-paying jobs, women would no longer need to earn income and the gender order that separated the masculine and feminine realms would be restored.

Gender Rules and Interstate Politics: The Case of Minimum-Wage Fixing

Global debates before World War I had employed instruction-rules that defined home and work in opposition, constructed the identities of masculine breadwinners/workers and feminine, nonworking mothers/homemakers. These themes took on different shades in different local contexts and in various ways shaped welfare states. Because they crossed state boundaries, they appeared as well in interstate negotiations and facilitated understanding in multilateral fora. Debates about industrial homework and the gendered understandings of the practice provided the grounds for an agreement on the ILO Minimum-Wage Fixing Machinery Convention of 1928.

The principle of a minimum wage was strongly contested in virtually all European states and the U.S. before World War I. But global movements gradually converged on the agreement that minimum wages were the best way to improve the conditions of homeworkers and to control the negative effects of the practice. The promising experiences with trades boards in Australia and Britain inspired activists all over Europe to demand similar mechanisms for their own countries. The 1912 International Congress of Home Work called for the establishment of "wages boards" and for setting minimum wages. The 1913 International Conference of Consumers' Leagues likewise demanded minimum wages in "home industries." Delegates argued that low salaries were at the root of the homework problem. Low pay forced homeworkers to put in long hours, to neglect their children and even enlist their children to work. Homeworkers themselves were incapable of raising salaries through their own action because they were isolated, weak, and timid. Legislation therefore was the only solution.[39]

But the question of minimum wage legislation was intimately linked to gender identities as some sought to reserve minimum wages to women only. Instruction-rules that defined women workers as not real workers guided such a strategy. Reformers drew on and reproduced such rules often for pragmatic reasons. Limiting demands for a minimum wage to women was more likely to be successful and, many hoped, would establish a precedent that ultimately allowed the extension of the minimum wage to all workers. As a French law professor argued at the International Congress of Home Work:

> Every time the question [whether to extend minimum wages to all workers or to women only] is raised before the French Association for Labor Legislation we are told: You will have already great difficulties succeeding if you limit yourself to the protection of women and regarding women your action is singularly facilitated by emotion, the storm of opinion roused by revelations about the situation of many homeworkers. Do not risk being condemned to certain failure by demanding immediately a general rule applicable to men and women alike.[40]

Apparently broad public opinion understood that homeworkers, and possibly women in general, were outside the working class, they were workers with different rights.

Even before World War I feminists had been fighting the pragmatic argument to limit minimum wage demands to women only and the issue became fiercely contested, even within the feminist movement, in the interwar period. Some feminists, fearing that limiting minimum wage legislation to women would endanger their jobs, challenged the notion of special legislation. At the International Congress of Home Work a French feminist newspaper editor warned: "Employers would simply direct themselves to-wards men, because one cannot forget that in a number of homeworking industries, notably in certain categories of linen goods, men can without difficulty and almost without any apprenticeship replace women workers."[41] While the 1912 Congress defeated an amendment to apply minimum wages to women only and provided a victory to those resisting special legislation, this did not represent dominant opinion at the time.

By the interwar period minimum wage fixing had become acceptable for women and homeworkers, reproducing an understanding that they were not like other workers. French and German legislation limited the minimum wage to homeworkers. The French law of 1915 (although hardly enforced) was even more restrictive, reserving minimum wage provisions for female homeworkers only. In the U.S., minimum-wage laws typically applied to women only. The German argument was that the state should intervene only in those areas where collective bargaining failed. French legislators considered minimum wages an extension of charity to a population defined as minors. And U.S. laws sought to avoid interference with men's right to contract. In Britain, by contrast, a strong coalition of "anti-sweating" activists and progressive politicians had insisted on minimum wages for all "sweated industries." While the category of "sweated labor" potentially included both women and men in low-pay industries, in practice women made up two-thirds of those who benefitted from the minimum wage.[42]

In the late 1920s, controversies about homework and the minimum wage found a forum at the ILO where they got entangled in power politics and reproduced, in the interstate arena, instruction-rules about gender that global debates had generalized. The 1927 and 1928 sessions of the International Labor Conference debated a British proposal to consider establishing an international labor standard on minimum wage fixing machineries. British and German representatives took the debate over such machineries as an occasion to engage in a struggle over prestige. The British had been instrumental in setting up the ILO and held considerable influence at the International Labor Office. Indeed, officers at the British Ministry of Labour and at the International Labor Office knew each other well and carried on an extensive correspondence in advance of the 1927 and 1928 conferences, coordinating draft proposals and strategy.[43] The British envisaged general-izing to the international level their Trades Board Act of 1909 which applied to all "sweated trades." Trades boards had been established with the support of all major parties, which had come to accept the principle of limited state intervention in setting wages.[44] In contrast, Germany had newly joined the League of Nations in 1926 and, as the defeated nation of the First World War, was trying to reestablish its prestige at the international level. The German government and German employers wanted to limit any state intervention in wage setting to an absolute minimum. In their view, the state should intervene only in those areas where collective bargaining was not possible. The Germans sought to extend their Homework Law of 1923 and argued that a wage fixing machinery should be set up for the "homeworking trades" only. Different legal practices provided the grounds for government posturing, but shared constructions of gender facilitated agreement.

During debates in the Committee on Minimum Wages, the British held that homework was not fundamentally different from other types of work, representing simply one form of "sweated labor." In contrast, the German government representative insisted that "no real common basis exists for the two systems [i.e. the homeworking trades and the non-homeworking trades]."[45] In arguing his position, he appealed to the feminine character of the proposed targets of intervention. To ensure that the convention encompass both "sweated trades" and homeworking, the International Labor Office had suggested that the range of application be defined as areas where wages were exceptionally low and organizations "defective." The German government delegate used this formulation to construct homeworking as "naturally defective." He quibbled, "the organisation should not merely be defective in fact, but . . . it should be necessarily defective *in the very nature* of the trade."[46] He thought that this criterion would limit the proposed convention to homeworkers, i.e., mostly women workers, for whom it was apparently "natural" not to have unions or other forms of interest representation. The instruction-rule that defined homebound women as mothers and homeworkers as nonworkers helped him argue the German national agenda.

While the British did not go along with the German argument to restrict minimum wage fixing to homework, they apparently shared with the Germans and other conference delegates the idea that above all minimum wages should apply to populations that were not fully integrated in the working class and could not therefore be expected to organize for their own interests. Despite differences on the surface, they drew on joint understandings of women appropriately attached to the home, and not quite real workers. In the words of the (female Norwegian) Reporter of the Committee on Minimum Wages, "I think both men and women will have need of that help, but it is also clear that it is the women who will need it the most, and who will therefore benefit the most."[47]

Indeed, the recommendation which accompanied the convention on minimum wage fixing included the admonition that "special regard might usefully be had to trades or parts of trades in which women are ordinarily employed."[48] Concern with safeguarding proper womanhood was the major reason why delegates added this clause. The Belgian government delegate urged to include the sentence in response to a call for ILO action by the League of Nations Committee on the White Slave Traffic. This committee had concluded that "unduly low wages were a contributing cause of prostitution" and that it was necessary to "remove the temptations to which underpaid women workers were exposed."[49] The formulation evoked the theme that women's home-based work implied disorder, impropriety, and a violation of standards of proper womanhood, themes that pervasively had informed debates before the war.

Global constructions of gender and shared understandings of feminine propriety facilitated the final compromise on the convention's target, i.e. "workers employed in certain of the trades or parts of trades (and in particular in home working trades) in which no arrangements exist for the effective regulation of wages by collective agreement or otherwise and wages are exceptionally low."[50] The agreement remained that minimum wages were appropriate for those who could not organize, those who were not historical agents, those not part of the working class. Germany and Britain were the first to ratify the convention in 1929. With 100 ratifications as of December 1994, it remains one of the most widely adopted.[51]

Challenging Global Gender Rules: The Fight for Equal Pay

Ironically, ILO debates employed instruction-rules that defined women as motherly nonworkers at a time when such rules were under fierce attack in global debates. In the 1920s, equal rights feminists were locked in a fight with their more maternalist sisters in the women's movement and were targeting the ILO in an effort to dislodge such rules. While the global debate about women's work had largely been formulated around the problem of the working mother, the equal rights feminists of the interwar period brought to the debate notions of independent womanhood. They argued that marital status and motherhood should be irrelevant to women's treatment in the labor market. They attacked a gender order built on the separation of home and work, the ideology of domesticity, and understandings of women as naturally different because of their child-bearing capacities. Constructions of women as mothers had legitimated inequality, and unequal pay was one of its most painful expressions.

Neither minimum wage laws in European countries nor the ILO convention on minimum wage fixing specified the principles according to which wages should be fixed. They contained no requirement that wages should be the same for women and men. Indeed, national machineries set differential pay rates for women and men in both Britain and Germany, with women's rates being 50 to 65 percent that of men.[52] During the 1920s and 1930s, the ILO as well as members of the International Labor Office opposed laws on equal pay and equal protection. They clashed with feminist organizations championing the equal rights of women, most importantly, the Open Door International, an organization whose leaders considered the ILO "a real danger to women when it proposes and uses its international machinery, internationally financed by the governments of the world, to do propaganda in favour of restrictions placed on women alone."[53]

The driving force behind Open Door International was Elizabeth Abbott, founder of the British Open Door Council. She had support from a series of feminist organizations in Britain and recruited allies—mostly upper-class and middle-class women with means to travel and to dedicate time to politics—in countries all over Europe. The manifesto and charter of Open Door International stated that a woman "should be free to work and protected as a worker on the same terms as a man, and legislation and regulations dealing with conditions and hours, payment, entry and training should be based on the nature of the work and not on the sex of the worker."[54] The Open Door dissociated women's status as workers from their marital status and from motherhood. Its fight was about rights, about creating commitments to women's well-being, that paralleled those of men. In order to achieve these "equal rights," the movement needed to dismantle gender rules that celebrated women's child-bearing capacities, and in the process created the female body as weak and unfit for "real" (i.e., paid) work.

Just as public health metaphors had informed the language of dirt, disease, and disorder in talk about homework, so it bolstered interpretations of women's bodies as physically adapted to motherhood, but not paid work, giving a scientific touch to gender rules that defined women as maternal.

Open Door International began to attack such constructions of women's bodies as unsuited for paid work, and it found plenty of material in ILO publications. The ILO's *Encyclopedia on Occupation and Health* included statements such as, "the injurious effects of labour on the female organism are established by quite a series of statistical data" and "the rhythm of machinery is not adapted to the female organism." Furthermore, women were not "suited to work demanding sustained attention or great sang-froid or great professional skill;" and this was because women, presumably given to sacrifice, tended to "feed themselves less substantially than men." Feminists ridiculed such statements in public gatherings, and raised consternation among those wed to old gender rules. An ILO observer who attended a meeting of the Open Door Council reported about the "insolence" of the language used and recommended that the ILO refuse to receive the resolutions produced at the meeting.[55]

At the International Labor Office, the activities of Open Door International and its British affiliate, the Open Door Council, caused considerable concern and hostility. Because the Open Door's rhetoric violated the maternal definition of womanhood, it invited disbelief and outrage. In the judgment of Marguerite Thibert, a French socialist who headed the ILO's service for women and children, the Open Door movement revealed "excessive individualism" and lacked recognition of "natural facts" when it demanded that women should be free to decide whether they wanted to work before and after childbirth, engage in night work, or dangerous work. Albert Thomas, the ILO's Director General, called the Open Door's initiative against the maternity protection convention an "absurdity" and a "monstrosity." He judged that the organization did not represent "the real working women," that it was not taken seriously in the British labor movement and had little influence. But ILO officers reported that Open Door was securing "very considerable influence" and receiving sympathy from many women's organizations and was "doing the Office a great deal of harm."[56]

For the Open Door movement, the minimum wage fixing convention of 1928 became a lightning rod. Representing a coalition of five British feminist organizations, Abbott sent a letter to Thomas in advance of the 1928 International Labor Conference, urgently requesting "that in any Draft Convention and Recommendation concerning Minimum Wage Fixing Machinery, the Eleventh Conference of the International Labour Organisation shall adhere to the Seventh Principle written into the Treaty of Versailles, Part XIII, Article 427, for the guidance of the International Labour Organisation, namely: 'The principle that men and women should receive equal remuneration for work of equal value.' "[57] Feminist lobbying had secured this language at Versailles, but governments had since paid it little heed. The Open Door's request found its way into the deliberations of the conference in the form of an amendment proposed by the Indian labor representative and supported by a female colleague from Poland. But opponents argued that including the amendment would prevent governments from ratifying the convention and the Committee on Minimum Wages defeated the amendment. The hegemony of the old gender rules did not allow the language of equality. In response Open Door International drafted its own equal pay convention and started a campaign to get an opinion from the International Court of Justice to have the ILO declared incompetent in the matter of minimum wage fixing because it ignored a principle laid down in the Treaty of Versailles.[58] Evidently Open Door found no government to bring the issue before the Court and the campaign fizzled. However, the fact that the ILO adopted an equal pay convention only twenty years later (in 1951) shows the degree to which old gender rules were embattled even at the time, and must be attributed to rule changes demanded by organizations such as the Open Door.

Because participants in the global debate about equal pay subscribed to different understandings of womanhood, feminists demanding equal pay sometimes found support among ideological opponents who would have liked to push women out of the labor market. Different instruction-rules led to very different expectations about the impacts of directive-rules. While feminists believed that equal pay regulations would benefit women because their capabilities equaled those of men, those who thought of women as maternal believed that equal pay regulations meant an end to women's competitiveness in the labor market. Equal pay regulations therefore would preserve male privilege. For example, at the International Labor Conference in 1928, the worker representative from France supported equal pay because paying women lower wages was "a serious menace to the employment of men," and "the enforcement of the equal pay rule was the only means of preventing the ousting of men by women."[59] Similarly, the employer delegate from the Netherlands believed that "wherever there was competition between men and women for the same work for equal pay, men were likely to be preferred, and, in view of the greater family responsibilities they were likely to have, should be preferred."[60] Their arguments paralleled those of a Portuguese employer delegate: "As men worked quicker than women, the

men would be given preference. Besides, women were more liable to illness."[61] Where equal rights feminists expected women to succeed under
conditions of legal equality, those wedded to an understanding of women as
maternal expected them to naturally fall behind. Their understandings of
women's bodies as designed for motherhood and not paid work allowed them
to support equal pay for the benefit of male breadwinners.

The same understanding led some union women at the Conference to
oppose the inclusion of an equal pay stipulation. They believed that it
would hurt women by making them less attractive workers. They shared
with the men concerned about preserving male breadwinners an understanding of women as distinct, or at least were aware that this was the prevalent instruction-rule, and that the rule might work to women's disadvantage. But arguably they became complicit in perpetuating constructions of
women as inferior workers who could not compete with men. The attitudes
of labor women received a boost in the 1930s when women from the Roosevelt administration became active at the ILO. Their push for international action to abolish homework affirmed instruction-rules that defined
home-based women as motherly. But their offensive to accomplish international action on homework was unsuccessful. Instruction-rules of women
as motherly had been undermined to such an extent that special labor laws
for women no longer gained political support.

Projecting the New Deal: The Ambiguous Hegemony of U.S. Women

In 1934, the United States joined the ILO and took on the role of a
hegemonic leader. It sought to project into the international arena a consensus among U.S. elites about the proper organization of welfare states as
reflected in legislation passed under President Roosevelt's New Deal.[62] The
Roosevelt administration gave homework activists in the United States the
opportunity to realize their legislative agendas. Labor women with a long
tradition in the fight against homework held central positions in the administration. Frances Perkins, a former lobbyist for the New York Consumers'
League, became secretary of labor; Clara Beyer, who had been involved
with both the National Consumers' League and the Women's Trade Union
League (WTUL), became assistant secretary for labor standards. Mary An-
derson, a former WTUL leader, initially continued as head of the Women's

Bureau to be succeeded by Frieda Miller, also a former WTUL leader, and the former industrial commissioner of the state of New York who had played a major role in pushing through the New York legislature a State Homework Law that provided the basis for bans in several industries.[63] Miller was the long-time U.S. government delegate to the ILO's Governing Body and after World War II pushed for ILO action on homework.

Their experience with homework laws at the state level had convinced these women that the only way to deal with the practice was to ban it. To justify bans, their rhetoric drew on the repertoire of a gender order that opposed motherly housewives and breadwinning workers. Appeals to saving motherhood joined a concern for the smooth operation of the welfare state. Homework was seen to compete with factory employment and undermine wage and health standards, all crucial elements of stable workplaces for masculine breadwinners. In addition, a Fordist mode of accumulation based on mass production and consumption now required the elimination of homework. Homework contradicted this mode of accumulation because it was said to lower the purchasing power of workers and thereby lower levels of consumption. By 1945, nineteen states in the U.S. banned homework and seven gave administrators the power to prohibit it. At the federal level, the wage and hour administrator issued bans in six industries in 1941 arguing that homework threatened the implementation of the Fair Labor Standards Act of 1938, which regulated wages and working hours. The U.S. Supreme Court sustained these federal bans on homework and they stayed on the books into the 1980s.[64]

The women in the Roosevelt administration took the fight against homework to the international level with little input from the women's movement. The fight for equal rights largely engaged middle-class women who tended to ignore the concerns of working-class women, and while labor women continued to battle equal rights feminists on matters of special legislation, homework was no longer part of their movement politics. At the global level, World War II intervened to mute conversations on women's work. Homework became an administrative and legal matter of governments, international bureaucracies, and courts, the issue fueled by former movement activists turned bureaucrats.

The women in the Roosevelt administration pushed the issue first in the Americas during the 1939 ILO Regional Conference of American States. Mary Winslow, a WTUL member working in the U.S. Department of Labor's Women's Bureau, chaired the committee which discussed a proposed resolution on homework and shepherded it to adoption.[65] The resolution encompassed a dual and somewhat contradictory strategy, calling on the one hand for a ban on homework, but conceding that it may be necessary to regulate homework "as long as [it] continues to exist." Concerns about economic efficiency and the needs of the state dominated the wording of the resolution. It portrayed homework "as being against the interests of workers and of the national economic system" and as "a means of defrauding the interests of the State or of slowing down the development of technical progress in industry."[66] The contradictory nature of the resolution mirrored its gendered subtext and the reality of divergent gender divisions of labor in the Americas. While U.S. legislation was written with women in mind, in many Latin American countries men engaged in homework in substantial numbers. The committee's report cautioned that the total elimination of homework "would involve a transformation of industrial organisation that would affect not merely women and juvenile workers," implying that a ban would be justified for women and children but not for men.[67] Divergent gender constructions of homeworkers in American countries thus inhibited the rigid projection of U.S. policies to the regional level. But, for the first time, the resolution called for a ban on homework at the interstate level, no doubt in large measure due to U.S. influence. Apparently there was a consensus in the Americas that home and work should be separate.

For several reasons, the U.S. government women were less successful in Geneva. First, when the ILO launched its renewed inquiry into homework after the war, homework in European ILO member states, together with other economic activity, was much reduced, making it a low priority for governments. Second, the war had changed political conditions in Western Europe that affected working class politics, including gender identifications associated with such politics. The Cold War and the popularity of socialism had encouraged the inclusion of labor unions into state decisionmaking structures, the institutionalization of labor law that regularized interactions between workers and employers, and the expansion of social security systems. As corporatist forms of interest intermediation proliferated and state intervention for welfare purposes became an accepted principle, homework became less of a threat to the aspirations of a masculinist working class. Finally, equal rights feminists apparently had shaken the association of womanhood with motherhood that had served to curtail women's right to paid work. At the same time, lack of movement activism limited opportunities to hammer out new global understandings of gender. Without activist support, U.S.

women fought a lonely battle within the ILO, reviving old and strongly contested constructions of gender that did little to advance their cause.

In 1946, Frieda Miller presented to the ILO's Governing Body a request on behalf of the U.S. Government to conduct an inquiry into the problems of industrial homework. She employed the language of efficiency in expressing the belief "that it was necessary to see that the high industrial standards of the war years were not undermined" and strongly advocated the abolition of industrial homework, interpreting it as "not an integral part of the national economy."[68] The Governing Body authorized the International Labor Office to study homework over the following three years.[69] A series of articles in the International Labour Review detailed national laws and policies, and showed how little consensus there was on the issue by then. The U.S. position, outlined by Miller, constituted one extreme, employing the old language that defined homeworkers as nonworkers and homework as undermining factory work: "Low wages, long hours, child labour, unhealthy and insanitary working conditions—evils which long have characterised industrial home work in the United States—are part and parcel of the system, . . . and complete abolition alone can actually eliminate them."[70] Miller revived the idea that homework was a source of disorder, threatening now not so much the moral order but the efficient functioning of the welfare state. Furthermore, Miller resurrected old themes that identified homework as a public health hazard: Homework was "a parasitic growth on the industrial system, injurious to the community at large and especially to factory workers, whose standards are undermined by the competition of home workers."[71] These arguments reaffirmed that homeworkers were not working class and that the mingling of home and work invited disorder.

In contrast, articles about Switzerland and France recounted policy approaches that apparently had come to terms with the continued existence of homework and told of collective bargaining agreements that included homeworkers. Here homework no longer was a source of disorder but had been integrated into a new industrial order. Switzerland actually encouraged homework as a way of bringing employment to remote mountain areas. While regulating the working conditions of homeworkers, the government also created a public agency to give out homework, and cantonal authorities sought to persuade private enterprises to send work into homes, provided vocational training to homeworkers, and supplied them with tools.[72] The French also seemed to take an approach more favorable toward homework. According to the woman labor inspector who reported in the International

Labour Review, it was no longer desirable to abolish homework because collective bargaining agreements increasingly included demands for home-workers such as minimum piece rates, equal remuneration for home and factory workers, compensation for overhead expenses, questions of social insurance, holidays with pay and hours of work. New laws extended the terms of collective agreements to whole industries and ensured that all workers and homeworkers were covered. The result was an "assimilation of the con-ditions of home workers to those of factory workers." Homework may have been a source of great suffering but it "also has contributed . . . to the improvement of the lot of many workers" and deserved continued exis-tence.[73] Results of the ILO survey on homework, published in the *Interna-tional Labour Review* in 1948, concluded that regulation focusing on min-imum wages together with "other techniques" apparently could "integrate the home worker into the same system of standards and benefits that applies to regular factory workers."[74]

The same survey showed that homework was no longer a big concern for governments, most of which at the time of the survey were governments of the left. The British reported that "outwork is not an important feature of English industry" and that "for many years past, use of the outwork system has been declining." The governments of Norway and Sweden replied that homework played only a small part in their economies. The French response vividly portrayed the context of war-devastated Europe, citing shortages of raw materials, rationing, a decline in exports, and the effects of monetary devaluation as reasons for the decline in homework. Even the U.S. response prepared by the DOL's wage and hour and public contracts divisions gave little reason to pursue the issue. It stated that "as a result of long run industrial and economic factors and fairly recent State and Federal legislation, home work in the United States of America has been reduced to the point where it is comparatively unimportant, except in a few industries."[75]

Numerical trends apparently facilitated the cavalier attitude of govern-ments regarding homework.[76] But more importantly, there was a new con-sensus, at least in Europe, on what it meant to be a worker, a woman, and a man. The legacy of wartime economic planning combined with electoral victories of the left to broaden the reach of European welfare states, gener-alizing social insurance schemes and often tying labor and employers into corporatist decisionmaking structures. The new rules of industrial relations and welfare entailed new messages about class and gender. On the one hand, they cemented the separation between home and work: For the first time a large number of women could live up to the ideal of the "non-working" mother as increased male income together with family benefits facilitated full-time mothering and reduced the need for homework. The French government, for example, speculated in a communication to the ILO that homework may have become less attractive for women with the introduction of payments for mothers staying home to raise their children.[77] On the other hand, a relatively secure working class no longer saw low-paid female labor as a threat and could adopt the language of equal rights. Women workers no longer were mothers outside the working class but could be integrated into the new corporatist structures and labor laws. With homeworking laws and the inclusion of homework provisions in collective bargaining agreements homework was somewhat controlled and homeworkers could be tolerated. They became part of the female workforce of secondary income-earners.

The situation was different in the U.S. Despite the institutionalization of an old age pension system during the Roosevelt administration, the U.S. never developed social security protection comparable to Europe. It still lacks a state-supported system of health-insurance and leaves it to states to develop policies and administer programs such as unemployment insurance or welfare payments to single mothers. Furthermore, in 1947, a Republican-controlled Congress passed a labor-management relations act (the Taft-Hartley Act) that considerably weakened union power, precluded any efforts to extend collective bargaining agreements to whole industries, and created a division among organized and unorganized workers that formalized access to governmental decisionmaking structures for a comparatively small number of unionized workers. Where unions were weak, homeworkers still appeared as potential foes—a threat to tenuous accomplishments and a source of disorder. Homework bans kept cheap female labor at bay. Yet, in the absence of a strong welfare system, the separation of home and work, feminine and masculine spheres, was never as firmly encoded in the U.S. as in Europe. Not surprisingly, the U.S. led the way in the comeback of home-based work in the 1980s.

From an international perspective, the different paths of European and U.S. welfare states meant a breakdown in shared constructions of gender and class that had enabled agreement between European governments in the 1920s. Europeans had "tamed" homework by reducing women's need to work. The weak U.S. welfare state could not promise the same, and social forces continued to employ constructions of working mothers as a source of inefficiency and disorder that arises from a mingling of feminine and masculine spheres. Although equal rights feminists challenged these constructions in the U.S., the unique form of the American welfare state offered those who defended labor rights strategic reasons to tread cautiously on the terrain of equal rights rhetoric. Divergent understandings of class and gender contributed to the failure of the U.S. offensive to gain an international agreement to ban homework. The new hegemon[78] could not accomplish what global movement politics excelled in—the institutionalization of instruction-rules that facilitated agreement in interstate politics.

From the 1950s to the 1970s the topic of homework lingered and periodically resurfaced in various ILO industrial committees and expert meetings which echoed the concern with the smooth functioning of the Fordist welfare state and economic efficiency. Most notably, the 1964 Tripartite Technical Meeting for the Clothing Industry adopted a resolution calling for a ban on homework, lambasting it as an outmoded activity with low productivity that constituted unfair competition and pushed down wages. The resolution marked the last time the call for banning homework appeared in an ILO document, and a closer look at the dynamics of the meeting reveals that the apparent concordance was built on thin grounds. Government delegates from India and Nigeria (in addition to those from France and Switzerland) forcefully opposed the resolution which was vocally supported by worker-delegates from Australia, France, Italy, and the U.S. The governments insisted that homework was an important source of jobs and that homework regulations were not enforceable in places where many home-based workers were self-employed. Their voices were to take on increasing importance in ILO debates on the issue.

The debate on homework in the first half of the twentieth century illustrates the power of global movements. The labor and the women's movements developed a set of shared instruction-rules in a euro-centric global space that defined industrial homework as a source of disorder and identified industrial homeworkers as dependent mothers outside the working class proper. The gendered separation of home and work became a basic rule enabling labor laws and welfare regulations. Not only did gender constructions based on the separation legitimize state interventions in the economy, but they also became an integral element of Fordist modes of regulation that enabled mass-consumption and mass-production by creating stable jobs and family-wages for many men. Interstate politics confirmed instruction-rules about gender in setting international standards about minimum wage fixing.

But the activism of equal rights feminists fundamentally challenged instruction-rules about women workers as different from male workers together with the special legislation that such rules had enabled. In addition, higher male earnings and generous social benefits allowed many women in Europe to become full-time mothers, removing the threat of home-based income-earning, and facilitating demands for the equal treatment of women workers. In the absence of a consensus on the identities of homeworkers, efforts failed to gain international action on homework and realize U.S. hegemony.

3 Supplemental Earners and National Essence: Home-Based Crafts Producers and Nation-Building in Post-Colonial States

Between 1945 and 1960, a total of forty countries with a population of more than 800 million gained political independence from Western colonial powers.[1] Together with the Cold War, the bipolar system, and the U.S. role as the new hegemon of the West, the newly created states constituted the most salient political fact of post-World War II international politics. The new constellation of international relations profoundly impacted policies and programs of the ILO. Most important for debates on home-based work, the ILO leadership increasingly favored technical assistance and promotional programs as opposed to standard-setting. Such programs allowed the organization to overcome the chasm between the United States and the Soviet Union and at the same time responded to the needs of newly independent countries in Africa, Asia, and the Caribbean.[2]

The United States took a lead in this policy change. By the end of the 1940s, the U.S. had made global economic recovery a crucial element of its foreign policy. In addition to rebuilding war-ravaged Europe, this included President Truman's call to "make the benefits of American scientific advance and industrial progress available for the improvement and growth of underdeveloped areas."[3] When David Morse, the former Acting Secretary of Labor in the Truman administration, became Director-General of the ILO in 1948, he shaped ILO priorities to meet U.S. interests and secured the ILO's participation in international recovery efforts by refocusing the organization's work from standard-setting to technical cooperation.

While much of the organization's activities before World War II had targeted industrial relations, technical cooperation with member states in Latin America, Asia, and Africa meant that it now focused on the overwhelmingly predominant rural sector in these regions. The main thrust of technical assistance programs was to improve labor productivity in agriculture and rural industry. During the 1950s, in an effort to overcome perceived shortages of "skilled labor" and "trained manpower," the ILO poured the bulk of its resources (about 75 percent) into vocational training.[4] Under the heading of assisting rural industry, home-based work remained on the organization's agenda. Together with the new UN Commission on the Status of Women (CSW), it provided a forum for global conversations on crafts production, much of it home-based.

Created in 1946, CSW defined for itself the task of "rais[ing] the status of women . . . to equality with men in all fields of human enterprise." This included ensuring that "women . . . be given equal rights with men with respect to labor, wages, holidays, and other economic and social rights."[5] In the ILO, many saw the extensive way in which CSW defined its competencies as an intrusion in the ILO's field of activity. But initial skirmishes gave way to accommodation as the ILO incorporated the language of equal rights into its conventions, and CSW increasingly urged governments to live up to ILO standards. Indeed, the ILO and CSW began to cooperate on issues affecting women workers, and CSW continuously requested from the ILO reports and special studies.[6]

Equal rights talk did not necessarily contradict instruction-rules about women's identities as motherly. ILO conventions concerning women, including the widely ratified 1951 Equal Remuneration Convention, the 1952 Revised Maternity Protection Convention, the 1958 Discrimination (Employment and Occupation) Convention, and the 1962 Equality of Treatment (Social Security) Convention all maintained the understanding that women held primary responsibility for children and the home. The 1965 ILO Recommendation on the Employment of Women with Family Responsibilities is formulated upon the explicit presumption that women were the primary caretakers of children.[7] But, unlike in the prewar debates on industrial homework, motherhood and work were no longer constructed as contradictory. Women workers were no longer a social problem but emerged as "supplemental income earners."

Gender Rules

Feminists have long postulated a relationship between the development of capitalism and the subordination of women which they have seen as connected to women's confinement to the home. Maria Mies has described a link between the expansion of capitalism and the "housewifization" of women: an ideological construction of women as nonworking housewives. The ideology of the housewife made women readily available for superexploitation and in this way facilitated primitive accumulation. Helen Safa has complemented Mies's argument: capitalism creates male breadwinners. By separating home and work it reproduces patriarchal inequalities at the levels of the state and the workplace. Capitalist penetration into Africa and the Caribbean, together with colonialism, imposed such patterns of male hegemony on indigenous societies and instituted a persistent myth of the male breadwinner.[8]

One does not need to subscribe to the evolutionary and functionalist implications of Mies's and Safa's arguments to find their empirical observations acute. There apparently is a close connection between the introduction of Western modes of production and a particular form of patriarchy legitimized by reference to the housewife-breadwinner dichotomy. Yet, these connections are hardly automatic or purely functional. Capitalist development and expansion, together with the gendered creation of the notions of housewife and breadwinner, were political processes. They entailed diverse local and global arguments, including those in multilateral institutions. While global and local gender rules interacted to create different forms of subordination in specific situations, global rules may help explain the sometimes uncanny similarities in patriarchal rhetoric in different contexts. Debates focusing on development assistance (including those at the ILO) contributed to creating such global rules. As Barbara Rogers has shown, international development practice was implicated in the "domestication" of women around the world. The imposition of individual (mostly male) land ownership and the parallel elimination of women's user rights, the introduction of new technologies that destroyed women's income earning opportunities, together with agricultural extension services that targeted men only, all conspired to relegate women to the home, to the pursuit of housewifely activities.[9]

But exploring the debates on home-based work in multilateral institutions shows that instruction-rules that created the housewife-breadwinner dichotomy changed in the context of different social movements. Where debates around industrial homework before World War II invoked the separation of home and work to question the right of mothers to a job, in postwar debates around crafts production, home and work no longer were incompatible, at least for women and indigenous peoples in newly independent countries. Talk about crafts production redefined the home-work boundary so that housewifely women were allowed to earn income while creating symbols of national tradition.

Three sets of instruction-rules accomplished this redefinition. First were rules that distinguished between artistic crafts and utilitarian crafts. Modernization talk suggested that utilitarian crafts production was economically inefficient. In contrast, artistic crafts did not compete with modern industry and could be promoted to serve the needs of national identification. A second set of rules defined crafts producers and their work as secondary, affirming industrialization and male income-earning as economic priorities. Mies's "housewives" now emerged as supplemental income-earners, modern, artistic women that supported the "myth of the male breadwinner," to use Safa's felicitous phrase. Crafts production became a source of secondary earnings that added on to those of the male breadwinner or, at the national level, to modern factory production. A final set of rules connected women, indigenous peoples, and artistic crafts, so that all three came to symbolize the essence of the new nations. These rules defined women as the mothers of the nation, preserving community in the face of material modernization and guarding national values and cultural tradition. Others defined indigenous peoples as representing life before colonialism, anchoring nationalist claims in an origin and conveying legitimacy to national aspirations. Still others created artistic crafts as symbols of national tradition.

Feminist researchers have commented on the "extraordinary similarities in the ways that very different nationalisms construct 'women', and their construction of the nation as female."[10] Nationalist rhetoric often evokes the nation as a loved female body that symbolizes community, family, and kinship—the harmonious collectivity that the nation supposedly is. In such rhetoric women become markers of difference, the feminine nation defined in relation to a masculine state or a rapist imperial power.[11] Nationalist rhetoric that associated women, crafts, and nation, similarly facilitated an understanding of "Third World" nations as feminine. But where the feminine nation was supposed to evoke the love of citizens at the state level, global talk about marketing crafts created the nation as a seductress of foreign buyers.

Movements

It seems counter-intuitive to treat anticolonial nationalisms as a global movement. Yet, with all their differences, anticolonial movements participated in a global conversation that combined assertions of national distinctiveness with aspirations of modernization. Under the leadership of educated elites, nationalist movements in Africa and Asia employed Western ideas, such as the Wilsonian principle of self-determination and the Leninist critique of imperialism, to effect a "universal revolt against the west."[12] They merged this revolt with a revolt against the past, seeking to create new societies in tune with the demands of a modern world. While bourgeois leaders often appealed to particular pasts and traditions, once nationalist movements broadened their base to include rural populations, universalist calls for social reform and modernization joined the charge for political independence. Modernization did not mean Westernization. Leaders sought to hold on to and reshape traditions and merge them with modern elements to create distinctly un-European identities for the new nation-states; the rhetorics of national distinctiveness and modernization coexisted in global conversations on nation-building.[13]

Home-based work, in the form of crafts production, played an important symbolic role in nation-building efforts. Colonial trade policies had opened markets in Africa and Asia to European manufactured products and compromised the livelihoods of indigenous crafts producers; in this sense home-based producers were some of the most visible victims of colonialism. Anticolonial nationalists came to celebrate crafts producers as the embodiment of indigenous know-how, ingenuity, and culture. The Indian nationalist movement perhaps most extensively and explicitly used crafts as a symbol for a free India. Boycotts of British products and the promotion of indigenous cloth found strong support among the Indian bourgeoisie in the early decades of the twentieth century, and Mohandas Gandhi's patronage of home-spinning and village industries is well documented. Among Indian feminists, supporting women's crafts became a mode of resisting the penetration of colonial manufactures into the domestic economy while gaining women an opportunity for economic independence. Chinese women used similar tactics to protest Japanese imperialism.[14]

Postcolonial nationalist rhetoric increasingly associated handicrafts with women, the guardians of homes, to effect an identification with the nation. Handicrafts attached to women because they socialized children and in that way handed down tradition, the imagined primordial values of the nation. In the words of an ILO adviser, "in many countries women are . . . the custodians of crafts, which are part of the cultural life of the people and have been passed down from mother to daughter."[15] By producing handi- crafts, women tended to tradition and secured the values of community and cooperation, which supposedly characterized traditional societies, for the building of harmonious and healthy nations.

Although crafts were symbols of national tradition and pride, few of the newly formed governments made them the center of their development strategies, emphasizing instead the creation of urban-based, "modern" in- dustries. Among those who planned the modernization of economies and societies, home-based crafts production meant backwardness and tradition. While crafts production could help ease the transition, ultimately modern factory production needed to supersede it.[16] The range of approaches to crafts differed. In most countries, modernization strategies ignored crafts producers, in some cases, such as Nigeria, they inadvertently penalized them; in other cases, governments set up special programs and organizations to preserve or even broaden crafts production. The Gandhian legacy moti- vated the Indian government to establish the Khadi (homespun cloth) and Village Industry Board in an effort to protect rural industries from the com- petitive impacts of modern factory production, increase job opportunities in the crafts sector, promote efficiency, and improve design. Other South Asian and African governments developed similar policies and institutions.[17]

During the 1960s, global development debates created an understanding of crafts promotion as an important component of Third World develop- ment. Aid agencies began to provide training and management assistance to crafts producers, and sought to increase their productivity by introducing "appropriate technologies." The ILO played a crucial role in these efforts, preparing reports for a number of governments and recommending specific policies necessary for the promotion of crafts. Merging modernization talk with nationalist rhetoric, ILO officers argued that handicrafts and cottage industries constituted a critical source of income, aided industrial develop- ment, and helped preserve the cultural heritage of newly independent coun- tries. However, they warned that only those crafts which did not compete with modern industry deserved promotion, in particular artistic crafts. Util- itarian crafts, in contrast, needed to be transformed into modern industry.

Technocratic concerns and talk about nation-building dominated the de- bates about home-based work in the 1960s. After independence, nationalist parties and leaders typically came to rule newly independent countries and nationalist rhetoric routinized to meet the requirements of modernization. Labor unions, engaging only a thin layer of workers in Asia and Africa, had little say, expertise, or even interest in matters of employment in these countries. The internationalist feminist movement, which had been such a vibrant voice in the interwar period, had weakened considerably. Women in Africa and Asia contributed importantly to struggles for national independence, in movements that some have termed "feminist nationalist." Yet, there is little evidence that these women communicated or organized at a global level, and their distinct voices remained inaudible in global conversations.[18] In the Asian countries Jayawardena studied, women's organizations, as far as they existed, either disappeared after independence or "degenerated into social welfare organizations concerned with women's education, handicrafts and home care."[19]

To some extent feminist politics had become institutionalized in the UN and the ILO in institutions such as the CSW and the ILO's Section for Women and Young Workers. Some middle-class women from Africa and Asia gained prominence in these institutions and brought to international development talk the nationalist themes that connected women to crafts production. Their arguments joined those of feminist bureaucrats from Europe and North America to create crafts production as a supplementary and feminine activity that could symbolize tradition without disturbing the larger push toward modernization. Together, they continued to put women's issues on multilateral agendas throughout the 1950s and the 1960s. But their efforts lacked the dynamic dimension of a broad movement, and they tended to embed their demands on behalf of women within the existing terms of discourse.

Argument: Home-Based Work Means Opportunity

In global conversations after World War II, home-based work increasingly meant crafts production. In line with nationalist rhetoric, "preserving genuine traditional values of handicrafts" became a major preoccupation, and various international conferences on "indigenous labor" emphasized the "protection of indigenous homecrafts" as a central concern.[20] UNESCO underscored the cultural wealth embodied in handicrafts, and its education programs "stressed the importance of handicrafts as expressions of traditional cultures and their place in modern life."[21] Debates at the UN Commission on the Status of Women conveyed that handicrafts "made possible the continuance of those traditional and artistic skills which formed part of a national cultural heritage."[22] At the 1957 ILO Asian Regional Conference, the government representative of the USSR suggested that developing handicrafts was important "from the point of view of the spiritual needs and cultural development of the people," and the Indian Workers' member agreed that they were important "for psychological reasons."[23]

Such language sat uneasily with the themes of the prewar debate on industrial homework which still echoed in the multilateral spaces that feminists had carved out after the war. Here feminist bureaucrats needed to come to terms with new nationalist themes that evoked home-based crafts production as an opportunity for women. The debates in the ILO's Section for Women and Young Workers and in the UN Commission on the Status of Women during the 1950s constituted an effort to grapple with crafts production as a new form of home-based work. When Western women and those from newly independent countries came to international fora, they faced the challenge of reconciling their often divergent interpretations of home-based work. In these debates the nationalist and anticolonial celebrations of crafts sometimes clashed with the understandings of some prewar feminists of the dangers of home-based work, and the themes of exploitation and opportunity continuously traded places.

During the 1950s, CSW requested from the ILO a series of reports dealing with economic opportunities for women. The ILO's Section for Women and Young Workers suggested that CSW investigate handicrafts and cottage industries because they were to "economically under-developed countries" what part-time employment was to "economically developed countries."[24] Part-time employment was on the CWS agenda already as the principal form of supplemental income-earning for women in the West. Handicrafts constituted the parallel feminine activity for women in newly independent countries. Home-based work became attached to "underdevelopment" and, despite the large number of male crafts producers, was defined as an activity of particular relevance to women.

To begin with, ILO reports and CSW discussions acknowledged the needs of modernizing countries and asserted that handicrafts and cottage industries played an important role in these countries and were worthy of support. Within CSW positive assessments of handicrafts were more prevalent than in ILO reports. CSW delegates declared that handicrafts provided an opportunity to raise the economic and social status of women.[25] Indeed, some saw considerable potential for women's economic empowerment in handicrafts and called for their modernization in order to benefit women. Handicrafts could emancipate backward women: "Women were not aware of their own opportunities in this field and . . . lack of adequate training and traditional attitudes constituted obstacles to economic emancipation."[26] Governments and international agencies should provide infrastructure, ease access to credit and raw materials, and assist with marketing.[27]

In contrast to this assessment of handicrafts as a source for women's empowerment, the ILO reports also revived the rules of earlier debates about industrial homework. They highlighted the need for "careful planning and organization so as to avoid the possibility of exploitation with regard to wages, working conditions and child labour if [cottage] industries became industrial home work."[28] The report's author apparently doubted whether it was possible at all to prevent such exploitation: "Although . . . handicrafts are different from industrial home work, it is important in our consideration of handicrafts and cottage industries to be aware of the potential dangers of abuses which are inherent in any system where men and women are employed by middlemen to manufacture articles at home."[29] Indeed, the line between industrial homework and handicrafts "is somewhat fluid as the latter may become 'industrial homework' under particular economic conditions."[30] Women apparently were more likely to enter these kinds of dependent relationships and their wages, as a result, were lower.[31]

The scruples shown in the ILO reports reflected the preoccupations of the ILO's Coordinator of the Section for Women and Young Workers, Ana Figueroa. A Chilean diplomat, Figueroa participated in debates in the Americas that had come to reflect the United States' preference for banning homework. In her 1956 report to CSW on handicrafts she included a two and a half page summary of the discussion at the ILO's 1954 Latin American Technical Meeting on the Utilization of Women's Work which reiterated "that while measures should be taken to protect industrial home workers, it should be accepted in principle that industrial home work should be abolished in Latin America as soon as the economic and social circumstances of each country concerned permit."[32] Her report to a meeting of experts and directors of women's labor bureaus, sponsored by the Organization of American States in 1957, emphasized the dependent nature of home-based work and extensively employed the themes of economic efficiency dominant in the American policy debates before the war: The majority of small industries

worked for an agent. Homework was a phase in the process of industrialization: on the one hand it could provide consumer goods and meet demands
that factories could not satisfy; on the other hand, industrial homework could
impede industrialization, providing advantages to employers and thus slowing the introduction of factory production. Homework hampered workers'
organization, both for factory workers and for homeworkers.[33]

But the talk about industrial homework, exploitation, and inefficiency
that had inspired the efforts of women in the Roosevelt administration soon
constituted an anachronism. While modernization rhetoric favored an end
to home-based industry, the significance crafts took on as symbols of the new
nations made talk about abolishing home-based work unrealistic. The debate
in the "feminist spaces" of international organizations in the 1950s constituted a failed attempt to synchronize experiences and understandings about
home-based work between Western feminists and feminist nationalists from
Asia and Africa. It also constituted a failed attempt to keep union women's
critique alive in the emerging talk about modernization. Not until the 1980s
would their interpretations be taken seriously again in development talk, and
not until the 1990s would feminist activists from the South accomplish a
synthesis that married crafts production to industrial homework and that
gained acceptance in global debates.

The Modernization Argument: Home-Based Work
Is Backward

Dualisms patterned on the opposition between the traditional and the
modern pervasively informed modernization debates: closed minds vs. open
minds, static thinking vs. dynamic thinking, an orientation toward the past
vs. an orientation toward the future, concern with the short-term vs. planning, religion vs. science, a particularistic orientation vs. a universalistic
orientation. As Catherine Scott has shown, these oppositions were thoroughly gendered: they connoted value judgments about traits differentially
associated with women and men.[34] Arguably, the home constituted one pole
in various dichotomies that mapped onto these oppositions. In modernization rhetoric home-based work became a marker of backwardness, associated
with inefficient production methods, a particularistic orientation toward the
patriarchal family, and a short time-horizon that contradicted methodical
planning. Modernization rhetoric therefore demanded that home-based

work be overcome, enacting a new quest for a separation of home and work.

In the 1950s, there was a broad perception that handicrafts symbolized backwardness and absence of modernity, to be fostered only as a stage of transition "while the inevitable process of industrialisation is carried out."[35] Accordingly, modernizers criticized the "tendency to over-emphasize the cultural aspects of handicrafts and cottage industries."[36] From a modernization perspective, cottage industries at most were "a means of easing the transition to industrialization."[37] In the words of an employer at an ILO Asian Regional Conference in 1957, "these small-scale industries were needed in the transition stage before the ultimate objective of establishing large-scale industries was reached."[38] Various texts emphasized the need to industrialize handicrafts and turn them into a form of "rational employment."[39]

However, a number of writers, including some at the ILO, shifted rhetoric in the 1960s and began to emphasize the value of small industries for a modern economy. In their minds, these industries had to be developed, and they could be developed out of the crafts industries already in existence. Eugene Staley and Richard Morse's study on "how to guide the transition from traditional to modern small industry" provided the textbook for this approach. It developed the idea that home-based industries were inefficient, constructing a strongly gendered distinction between those industries worthy of promotion and those needing to be replaced.[40] It is worth discussing the study at some length because, judging by the number of citations, it had considerable influence in the development literature and because it reflected the rules of the broader modernization debate.

Staley and Morse developed four categories of small industry, arranged on a scale from traditional to modern: family-use system, artisan system (homework and workshops), putting-out or dispersed factory system (industrial homework and quasi-independent shops), and factory system (small, medium, and large factories). In "less industrialized countries" nonfactory systems predominated (i.e., the first three categories), in "industrialized countries" the factory system. The challenge of development was to transform small industry so that it became a part of the factory system. In parallel, the family-use system largely would become obsolete. Traditional artisans would give way to the modern artisans who did not compete with factory production but supplemented it, producing artistic crafts and servicing factory-made products. Finally, the putting-out system was transitional; it was important as a "bridge from artisan-type to factory-type production" at the "threshold of the industrial revolution," but it would not be necessary for "newly industrializing countries" to go through this stage of development.[41]

With the exception of the factory system, all categories of small industry had a home-based component. This component, which Staley and Morse called "household industry," emerged as something very undesirable, detrimental to economy and society: "Household industry is almost always a barrier to improvements in production technology and managerial practices, is subject to grave abuses, and has psychological and social drawbacks that impinge on, among other things, the status of women and the control of population growth."[42] That is, household industry hurt the modernization of both the economy and the family. It slowed "technical or business innovation" because of "the influence of the elders of the family," and because "expert supervision is less feasible."[43]

Especially interesting in this rhetoric is the concern with the status of women. Like the prewar debates, modernization talk advocated a separation of home and work, but for different reasons. Modernization required emancipated women because "the attitudes and ideas of women have such a determining influence, via child rearing, on the psychological makeup, values, and motivation of the next generation."[44] Home-based work hindered modernization because it kept women home and tied to the traditional family, the repository of backwardness: "The hold of the traditional family on its members is at present too strong, from the point of view of those who would like to see rapid economic growth and national development along modern lines. More activity and contacts outside the home are needed, not less, if the necessary new ideas, valuations, and motivations are to move a society out of centuries-old routines."[45] Where the European home in prewar years was an idyll of harmony and wholesomeness, the place where mothering could take its natural course, African and Asian homes in modernization rhetoric symbolized oppression, backwardness, and doom, a place from which mothers needed to be extricated. The separation of home and work was a solution not because it saved the home, but because it overcame the retarding influence of the home on women, and thereby on society. While modernization talk did not take the next step, which would have been to demand the full integration of women into wage work, the implied logic would have demanded precisely that.

It was not women's rights that motivated modernization rhetoric, but a perceived need for technocratic intervention to enable economic development on the one hand and population planning on the other. In this rhetoric, traditional women were routine childbearers, and household industries maintained them in that position. Insofar as home-based work kept women close to the traditional family and made child-rearing easy, it slowed the demographic transition and retarded modernization:

> Modern health measures have drastically lowered death rates, especially infant death rates, with the result that the traditional family, with its ideas and values geared to the needs of an earlier age, now produces too many children. . . . The answer to population pressure is more individualism, especially emancipation of women, so that parents will want and plan for smaller families. Industrial homework, by tending to keep women in the home and by making children into earners at an early age, tends to encourage large families. As compared with work in factories, offices, or stores, industrial homework no doubt holds women more firmly in subjection to traditional large-family norms, makes it possible to care for more children, and lessens the counter-attraction of ideas and activities outside the routine of childbearing.[46]

Home-based work was problematic because it hindered a modern orientation toward individualism as opposed to the traditional orientation toward the family. Home-based work foiled population planning because it based the organization of production on the family. Moving work out of the home would accelerate the spread of modern ideas, increase the status of women, and in this way facilitate population planning. The need to separate home and work received yet another supporting argument.

Given the premises of modernization talk, it is not surprising that most programs targeting small enterprises benefitted mostly "urban-based modern small businesses" while neglecting and sometimes even penalizing handicrafts and cottage industries which were more likely to be rural and home-based.[47] And programs that did focus on crafts often encouraged producers to move out of homes into "industrial estates" that were supposed to provide improved physical facilities (e.g., water, drainage, electricity) and a better work environment. Centralization would reduce not only the disadvantages resulting from the association with the tradition-bound family, but would facilitate as well the provision of training, technical advice, and marketing assistance.[48] Furthermore, moving work outside the home would allow for the creation of a working environment that met modern standards. As one former ILO official explained, "the working conditions in any of the shacks and shanties used by handicrafts producers and small industrialists are totally antagonistic to the introduction of reasonable working conditions and safety for employees, especially when these are girls and young persons."[49] Program designers gave little thought to the potential disadvantages resulting from centralization, even though at least one study showed that industrial estates actually made it more difficult for some producers to attract labor and to sell their goods.[50] Program designers also did not consider the alternative to moving work outside the home, i.e. improving the physical facilities of homes. The separation of home and work seemed a basic prerequisite for the modernization of both the organization of labor and the family.

Creating Tradition

Nation-building debates needed to accommodate the seemingly contradictory instruction-rules that emerged from the nationalist celebration of indigenous crafts on the one hand, and from the modernizers' labeling of home-based production as backward on the other. One strategy was the creation of the notion of "artistic crafts"—those with little utilitarian value and not in competition with factory-produced commodities. "Artistic ware" was an exception within the category of outmoded crafts and deserved promotion, indeed protection from factory production: "Here, other values, of a cultural nature, are at stake. The production of these wares is part of the national heritage and therefore merits encouragement and, where necessary, protection from undesirable influences in design and from cheaply made imitations."[51] Crafts production emerged as part of a socioeconomic framework that was morally superior to degenerate Western societies and that would prevent the selfishness and the anomic consequences of the Western path of development:

> Rapid industrialisation without any attention to traditional employment sectors would tear society from its moorings, bringing in its train the usual evils of juvenile delinquency, broken homes and a life lived under constant pressure. It may prove fruitful for the Third World countries to remember Mahatma Gandhi's message of self-reliance, of the need to develop village industry, to preserve national cultures, and to avoid consumer-oriented societies.[52]

In nationalist rhetoric, handicrafts and rural industries would root new societies as they embarked upon a perilous path of development.

But the national heritage that this language celebrated was not already there; it had to be developed. The ILO helped create national crafts traditions through its technical assistance efforts and through standard-setting, both of which helped generalize instruction-rules associating crafts with tradition. In the area of standard-setting, talk about developing crafts and tradition centered especially on indigenous peoples. Perhaps because their low standards of living disturbed their symbolic purpose of signifying the historical origins of the nation, development planners saw the task as preserving "the genuine traditional values of handicrafts while at the same time making use of them in improving the living conditions of the communities concerned."[53] "Preserving" crafts and "developing" crafts became two aspects of the same coin: Backward crafts needed to become "traditional" crafts in order to serve as symbols of national attachment. Thus, the 1957 Indigenous and Tribal Populations Convention commits ratifying governments to the seemingly contradictory goals of encouraging handicrafts to help indigenous peoples "adjust themselves to modern methods of production and marketing," but "in a manner which preserves the cultural heritage of these populations and improves their artistic values and particular modes of cultural expression."[54] For the sake of the nation, modernization, and preservation, improving art and saving art seemed perfectly compatible. In the words of ILO experts, "the preservation and, where necessary, the modification—within the framework of regional traditions—of the artistic aspects of these crafts would enable the indigenous peoples to preserve their cultural heritage which enriches the cultural life of the nation as a whole."[55]

In the area of technical assistance, the ILO sent to various countries experts who reported on ways to improve the handicrafts sector. Their reports assessed the quality of existing crafts, capacities for crafts training, marketing efforts and potential. And where necessary the reports recommended the introduction of new crafts. A perhaps extreme example is the island of St. Lucia in the Caribbean where a handicrafts tradition was developed from scratch in the 1960s. An ILO report recommended that "St. Lucia should encourage the production of quality crafts." While "St. Lucia does not possess the hundreds of years of craft heritage which has made possible more rapid economic growth in this field in other developing countries," it was necessary that there be "interesting, locally-made products which the tourist can purchase and can later indentify [sic] with St. Lucia."[56] From an international perspective a nation without a crafts tradition had no identity.

The ILO reports' rhetoric also fostered the identification of crafts and nation, keeping vigilance so that foreign influences did not pollute the purity of primordial cultural productions that nationalist rhetoric imagined. In Libya, for example, weaving carpets provided employment for a large group of women in the 1960s, many living in seclusion. The government justified support for these crafts because they were "part of the artistic and cultural heritage of the country." But, an ILO report found the crafts sullied. The discovery of oil had brought rapid economic growth and wealth to Libya and created a sizable market for indigenous crafts. Designs had changed considerably in order to appeal "to both rural and urban customers as well as to tourists."[57] Furthermore, the carpets and textiles produced in government workshops were "not really part of the indigenous culture," representing instead "a combination of Egyptian, Tunisian and European design influences."[58] Truly national crafts should not adapt to modern demands and needed to be kept safe from foreign influences. By keeping watch over the purity of artistic crafts, ILO and foreign experts helped create distinct symbols of identification that established the boundaries of nations and thereby secured the boundaries of states.

While technical assistance projects defined artistic crafts as especially appropriate for newly independent countries, an ex-post evaluation in the 1970s concluded that such projects had very low benefit-cost ratios.[59] But the cause of the nation, the fostering of tradition, apparently justified the expense. Their separation from utilitarian crafts rescued artistic crafts from the hostile forces of modernization. In creating these crafts, governments and development agencies created a cultural heritage that supported nation-building.

Crafts Indigenized

Once the notion of artistic crafts was established, global talk linked these crafts with populations that deviated from the norm of the mainstream, able-bodied, adult, and masculine wage-earner. This was another step toward reconciling modernization and nationalist rhetoric. The association of handicrafts with women, indigenous tribal peoples, the handicapped, and young people signaled their secondary status in the economy. As such, they no longer constituted an obstacle to development but became the basis for supplemental income-earning. Handicrafts were an important preoccupation of the ILO's Section for Women and Young Workers that treated women and young people as a joint category of special workers for whom handicrafts were especially appropriate.[60] Handicrafts production also emerged as an appropriate form of work for the disabled as various countries taught hand-icrafts in "blind schools" and "deaf schools,"[61] and CSW stressed "the therapeutic value of handicrafts in the alleviation of mental and physical disablement" and "as a means of rehabilitating injured and disabled persons."[62] But handicrafts got their most extensive treatment in their association with indigenous peoples and women. For them, handicrafts were constructed as natural. For them also, it was legitimate to violate the work-home separation that had ruled global debates before the war and that underlay the technocratic visions of a modern society. Nation-building rhetoric justified home-based work for Third World women and for indigenous people, both defined as secondary to the economy.

One of the ILO's first major technical assistance efforts in the 1950s was the Andean Indian Programme which set up centers to provide training in agriculture and handicrafts and sought to develop cooperatives for handi-crafts.[63] The purpose was to modernize indigenous crafts while preserving them for national identification. The presumption was that indigenous peoples had an inborn aptitude for crafts, and experts were directed to utilize "the natural skill in weaving of the Indians."[64] The attitude reappears in the ILO's Indigenous and Tribal Populations Convention when it urges that "the persons concerned . . . receive the training necessary for occupations for which these populations have traditionally shown aptitude."[65] But such technical assistance should not interfere with the "spontaneous creative art of the indigenous craftsman" that was a source of pride in nationalist rhetoric.[66]

Indigenous peoples were constructed not only as naturally skilled crafts producers but also as naturally prone to cooperation because of "existing forms of tribal cooperation," and a "tradition of communal activity."[67] Therefore indigenous peoples were especially suited to the introduction of hand-icraft cooperatives. Here "backwardness" became an asset, a non-Western value to be celebrated: "The communally run village workshop appears to be suited to the culturally less advanced communities where the traditional collectivist relationships and institutions survive, [and] internal cohesion is still great."[68] While cooperatives were thought to overcome exploitative relationships with traders and middlemen and to help strengthen the market position of crafts producers, efforts to form cooperatives for indigenous crafts producers also constructed a utopia that modernization seemed to deny — the dream of an alternative economy based on control by producers, small-scale operations, and nonexploitative relations. Cooperatives realized the image of the harmonious nation, and indeed came to be identified with postcolonial nations *per se*. By the mid-1960s, it was understood that cooperatives "had a long tradition in many developing countries and bore marked affinities to closely-knit tribal and community structures."[69] Indigenous peoples and crafts production, defined as harmonious production, now jointly signified the new non-Western nations. And with crafts attached to populations identified as nonmodern, the rest of the nation could safely proceed on the path of industrialization without threatening national identity.

Crafts Feminized

Realizing instruction-rules that attached crafts production to women constituted yet another strategy to reconcile nationalist and modernization rhetorics. On the one hand, these rules defined crafts as secondary to the modern economy; on the other hand, they preserved them as a source of national identification. Development practices especially linked women with crafts that resembled their unremunerated work in the home. This accomplished the dual goal of keeping women at home and safe from Western influences (and thus available as pure symbols of national identification) while justifying interventions to modernize women and their crafts production techniques (and thus extricating them from the clutches of the traditional family). Furthermore, it affirmed the suitability of home-based production for women and created an identity of women as supplemental income-earners.

Governments and charitable organizations created an association between women and certain types of crafts, by delivering handicrafts training through home economics programs.[70] Indeed, many feminists active in nationalist movements had started their organizing as a way to deliver welfare, including crafts training, to poor women and returned to these activities after independence. In addition to providing education and home care skills they continued to promote crafts.[71] Women's organizations sometimes cooperated with governments in teaching women home economics and crafts skills. For example, an ILO report suggested that the Government of Botswana enlist in its national development efforts nongovernmental "women's clubs" which were already involved in welfare-oriented training activities: "If properly harnessed, [these clubs] could take up the production of handicrafts and home industries to serve the needs of the country."[72] Few of the programs these clubs offered taught women qualifications for skilled employment but instead were intended to improve standards in the home, and there was, at least in the 1950s, some concentration on fabricating luxury items such as gold and silver thread embroidery and other fancy work.[73]

Government vocational training programs equally created women's crafts as an extension of homemaking skills, and they intended to modernize both. In Ethiopia, a school for adult women sought to teach crafts, "to train better mothers and home makers, to prepare better citizens, to develop leaders, and to give vocational training" which included "organised visits to handicraft centers." The curriculum of a home economics school for girls in Gambia covered topics of general education in addition to "typing, cookery, laundry, dressmaking, crochet, arts and crafts." The government's Women Training Institutes in Ghana combined instruction in cooking, dressmaking, and "various crafts," with "better home management, child-care, housewifery, budgeting and self-reliance." Similarly, the Malawi government's Magomero Community Development Training College and various self-help projects trained women in home economics and handicrafts.[74] A comparable tendency to target women for combined training in home-economics and crafts, sometimes in addition to secretarial work, was pervasive in Asia.[75] Clearly, these were not just efforts to keep women in their place, but interventions to modernize the home. Crafts production was incidental to these efforts, but fit neatly into constructions of modern womanhood.

The type of handicraft skills the ILO recommended that governments teach women were strongly sex-typed, reflecting increasingly global notions of what a homemaker should know. Textile and clothing production predominated, in addition to food-processing. For example, ILO expert reports advised the government of Libya to train women in weaving, knitting, sewing and embroidery; the government of Iraq to offer courses in drawing and painting, needlework, dressmaking, embroidery, wool-spinning, food processing and "confectionery," i.e. sewing pre-cut clothing; and the government of Ceylon to teach women textile work, mat weaving and needlework.[76] In Asia governments trained women in spinning and handloom weaving, basketry production, bleaching, dyeing and printing, knitting, cutting, and tailoring, doll making, paper making, soap making, preservation of fruits and vegetables, carpet weaving, embroidery, and needlework.[77] Most of these occupations constituted extensions of production for domestic use and were identified as feminine. An ILO report on Cyprus spelled out that certain crafts naturally attached to women: "In the past weaving was considered a normal attribute of every women [sic] in much the same manner as the art of cooking."[78]

As with indigenous peoples, home-based crafts emerged as an occupation for which women had a natural talent. Delegates to the Latin American Technical Meeting on the Utilization of Women's Work suggested that governments provide women "with methodical training in these industries, for which they were especially suited."[79] In Yemen, an ILO expert recommended that the government teach embroidery skills to women: "The art is simple and could easily be acquired by the nimble fingered womenfolk."[80] In Botswana, women were to learn how to weave although there was no tradition of weaving: "Botswana women, as they are quite hard-working, energetic and keen to learn new things, could easily learn weaving."[81] Women's natural skills and universal aptitudes would facilitate the introduction of various crafts.

The association with women and homemaking created crafts production as a secondary activity that supplemented male breadwinning. Crafts provided women "opportunities to earn *additional* income."[82] In some instances supplemental income meant income that added to value produced in agriculture, in other instances income that added on to a male wage. But the notion of supplementality fudged the different class positions of agricultural and proletarian households and the often very different roles of women in these households. Regardless of the labor they contributed to agriculture, and regardless of their actual earnings from crafts production, women appeared as homemakers and supplemental earners, crafts as secondary and increasingly as feminine.

Crafts production was secondary not only to agriculture or wage work outside the home, but also to women's primary occupation—homemaking. Handicraft work was "spare-time work," that women pursued during "their free hours" and "during their leisure" time.[83] In comparison to the talk about industrial homework before the war, there was surprisingly little reference to motherhood in this rhetoric. Being a woman no longer meant being a (potential) mother; instead women had become housewives tied to the home. And where income-earning and motherhood were contradictory in earlier constructions; income-earning and homemaking seemed compatible. According to an article in the *International Labour Review*

this sort of employment [i.e. handicrafts production] is specially suited to the mode of life of the women: in the country districts in particular they are occupied with work in the house and on the land, so that it is very difficult for them to undertake normal paid work, whereas the spare time left by their traditional pursuits might profitably be employed on handicraft work either at home or in small village centers.[84]

Thus, it was thought that "the promotion and development of subsidiary cottage industries affords a means, particularly for the women, of contributing to family income."[85] Where talk about industrial homework had created home-based workers as exploited mothers, talk about crafts production enabled the creation of women as supplemental income-earners.

The Erotic Economy of Handicrafts

The instruction-rules that created crafts as feminine, when inserted into the international political economy, created economic exchange as erotic. When juxtaposed to the rules of the global economy, the feminine nation came to symbolize the loved country but also the exploited country. Amorous metaphors abounded in the language of crafts promotion to international tourists as handicrafts emerged as the seductresses of foreign buyers and tourists. In their association with the feminine, handicrafts became part of an erotic international economy, effecting supplicant identities vis-à-vis wealthy countries.

Because domestic markets for crafts were limited, ILO expert reports forcefully proposed that governments promote handicrafts primarily by making them attractive for export and to tourist. Evidently their message found fertile ground. In a review of French-speaking African countries' policies toward crafts in the early 1980s, J. Trouvé found export promotion of crafts was a priority: "It is only in the field of artistic crafts, especially those that are export oriented, that any measures have been studied and implemented, or at least planned."[86] Tourists emerged as an important market for crafts, and crafts promotion became closely linked to the promotion of tourism in various African countries. In Malawi, the main agency in charge of developing and marketing "cottage arts and crafts" was Hotels and Tourism Limited, a parastatal body of the Ministry of Trade and Tourism. In Gambia, a new Ministry of Information and Tourism opened in 1974 and took on the task of building "craft centers" located in various hotel complexes, just at a time when "the most significant change that has taken place in the handicrafts and small-scale industries has been the involvement of women in these industries." In Swaziland, "small-scale industry" was the responsibility of the

Ministry of Industry, Mines, and Tourism which set up Swazi Crafts Limited in order to purchase the crafts of rural women.[87]

Crafts should seduce foreigners into buying. They accomplished this through their association with women and through the construction of both women and crafts as one with nature, expressing the very essence of the country. In a report to an international conference called by various development agencies, crafts appeared as the embodiment of the Swazi nation and its nature, including its women, and they were there to enchant tourists: "Since Swaziland is rapidly becoming a tourist centre, many people of different nationalities are discovering that it is a country of scenic wonder and unique character—a paradise where one can appreciate *nature's skills* through local handicrafts."[88] Handicrafts represented natural landscapes that were the pride of the nation, and women who made handicrafts emerged as part of this nature.

Similar constructions appeared in an ILO report on Cyprus. Here a handicrafts tradition was to be developed to create the island nation as a cultured place of beauty in the minds of others. "Within two years after Independence," the government of Cyprus created an organization "to develop folk art and handicrafts of local colour and souvenirs."[89] According to the ILO report, handicrafts should come to embody everything that Cypriots were proud of, from the character of the people living on the island to the beauty of its landscapes: "[Handicrafts] can and should be developed as a major component of the island's attraction for visitors to keep in step with the outstanding kindness of its inhabitants, the scenic beauty of its mountains and seashores and with all its art treasures." This would stimulate tourism and a market for handicrafts by enamoring the (male?) foreign visitor: "An interested and well-informed visitor would discover good reasons for a most interesting trip into the interior of the island, enjoying new landscapes and get in personal contact with the villagers. This would give him some of the most pleasant experiences of his visit and as a reward he would take home a piece of cloth having a very special value for him, and well worth the effort made in finding it."[90] The feminized nation offered feminine charms in the form of an embroidered cloth or a woven shawl over which masculine visitors from the industrial core could swoon as they remembered a lovely island upon their return home.

Formerly a catalyst of anticolonial rhetoric, trade in crafts became a form of neocolonial economic intercourse. Technocratic intervention resolved the contradiction between the demands of modernization and the construction of a national identity by feminizing, and ultimately eroticizing, crafts. Like home-based work in the construction of Western welfare states, crafts production in the new states thus became a fulcrum of national projects that reconstructed sex and gender in intended and unintended ways.

In sum, the rhetoric of nation-building, reconciling the contradictory rules of nationalist and modernization talk, defined global understandings of home-based workers during the 1950s and 1960s. As nationalism got institutionalized in government bureaucracies, conversations about home-based workers increasingly came to reflect the technocratic priorities of nation-builders, including those of experts from international institutions. It is in their language, that crafts got indigenized and feminized to serve as symbols of national attachment while safely relegated to a secondary status behind industry. It is their language that modernized women as supplemental income-earners. And it is their language that prostituted crafts to foreigners. In rationalizing nationalist movements, technocratic talk had veered far away from anticolonial vision.

4 Marginal Survivors or Nurturant Entrepreneurs: Home-Based Workers in the Informal Sector

The modernization perspective that so thoroughly influenced nation-building rhetoric came under attack in the mid-1960s. Writers, many from the countries considered underdeveloped, argued that the economies of the South could not develop within national boundaries, but that their embeddedness in the global economy kept them from prospering. The new "dependency perspective" provided governments from the South a common banner under which to rally. At the United Nations, North and South clashed in negotiations over a "New International Economic Order." While economics and politics in the 1970s stalled these negotiations, they contributed to undermining the unquestioned hegemony of the modernization paradigm. Increasingly development practitioners agreed that the overwhelming emphasis on creating infrastructure and large-scale import-substituting industries had not succeeded in eliminating poverty. The gap between the rich and the poor was increasing and population explosion appeared to absorb any gains that were made. The introduction of large-scale factories and welfare state regulations contributed to the creation of a minority of relatively secure male factory workers; but mass consumption remained elusive.

A new strategy was needed, and the consensus in the 1970s was that development should proceed from the bottom up, that development efforts should seek to guarantee the basic needs of people and enable them to raise themselves out of poverty. The ILO contributed to the new basic needs strategy of the second UN development decade by launching the World Employment Programme (WEP), the aim of which was "to halt and indeed reverse the trend towards every-growing masses of peasants and slum dwellers who have no part in development."[1] The ILO would convince governments and international development agencies to make employment creation a priority in development planning. Creating "full, productive, and freely chosen" employment for vast numbers of unemployed and underemployed people in the "Third World" would help alleviate poverty and foster more equitable development.[2]

The new orientation no longer considered factory employment crucial. WEP studies thrust in the center of development debates the notion of the informal sector, described in the report of an ILO mission to Kenya as the small economic activities of the poor, including "carpenters, masons, tailors, and other tradesmen," in addition to "cooks and taxi-drivers," and the "petty traders, street hawkers [and] shoeshine boys" which were a fixture in cities around the world. The Kenya report, which is credited with bringing the concept of the informal sector into the development mainstream, suggested that these informal workers constituted "a sector of thriving economic activity and a source of Kenya's future wealth."[3]

Academics, development practitioners, funding agencies, and activists enthusiastically embraced the informal sector because it provided an economically rational way to champion the cause of previously neglected slum dwellers. Despite considerable confusion about definitions and the theoretical status of the sector, studies proliferated documenting the diversity of the informal sector and its links to the larger economy.[4] Arguably the vagueness of the concept facilitated its popularity: it became all things to all people, an instrument to push diverse agendas. It provided a way out of the stalemate in the theoretical debate between modernization theorists and dependency theorists and in the policy debate over the New International Economic Order.[5] Supporting small entrepreneurs in the informal sector was attractive to modernizers because it met the requirements of economic liberalism while providing a way to help the poor.[6] At the same time, those critical of the unjust effects of capitalism found in "microenterprises" an alternative way to organize the economy. Environmentalists, advocates of appropriate technology and bottom-up development located in the informal sector indigenous knowledge which could overcome poverty apparently without engendering environmental destruction and the alienating consequences of factory life. The feminist movement saw in the informal sector

proof of women's extensive economic contributions: supporting microentrepreneurs in the informal sector became equivalent to supporting women.

Gender Rules

The debates on the informal sector provided a discursive space where
gender rules came under attack and where international technocrats engaged social movements to grope for new instruction-rules to describe developing economies. These debates created new definitions of womanhood
and manhood. A disproportionate number of women workers had jobs in
the informal sector. In addition, a vast majority of work in the informal sector
took place in peoples' homes, or informal sector workers, such as vendors,
used their homes as a base of operations.[7] Gender and the boundary between
home and work became important sub-themes of the debates, employing
contradictory instruction-rules that defined women workers in the informal
sector as marginal survivors on the one hand, and as motherly and nurturant
entrepreneurs on the other. In the clash between modernizers who saw few
economic prospects in women's home-based work and those who celebrated
their work as the basis of a more humane economy, gender reproduced as
oppositional. But feminist interventions also destabilized the boundary between home and work, providing the grounds for radically new instruction-
rules about gender in the later debates on the ILO Home Work Convention.
    A small number of economists considered the integration of home and
work as a crucial element in the "success" of informal sector activities. They
argued that the "family mode of production" gave informal sector firms a
strategic advantage because they could easily draw on or shed otherwise
nonfungible resources such as work space and labor.[8] But most development
practitioners considered this fungibility an obstacle to turning informal activities into profitable enterprises. In their efforts to rationalize the informal
sector, they drew on instruction-rules of the modernization perspective that
considered the mingling of home and work an obstacle to efficiency. For
example, they emphasized the need for book-keeping training to instill in
microentrepreneurs the idea that they needed to isolate business income
and expenditures from family income and expenditures.[9] While not physically separating home and work, they effected a conceptual separation. Constructions of the relationship between the formal sector and the informal
sector similarly reproduced modernization themes that relied on gender

oppositions and created femininity as subordinate, housewifely, and exploited. This was true as well in the identification of women's work in the informal sector as more dependent and less profitable than that of men.

But feminist "women in development" who participated in these debates challenged the modernization themes in two crucial ways. First, they described women's supposedly subordinate activities as the linchpin of the economy, and as forms of production that ensured family survival in the context of a hostile political economy. In the process they reversed the values that modernization rhetoric had attached to women's home-based work. They destroyed the notion of the male breadwinner and constructed women as the true family providers. And they created home-based work not as a backward activity but as an alternative to exploitative capitalism that built on motherly values. Second, they destabilized the oppositions between work and home, between breadwinning and homemaking, between production and reproduction. They did so by expanding the meaning of home-based work to include the diverse activities of women in homes and on farms—both income-earning and unpaid. In this way, they prepared the grounds for a dismantling of gender rules that built on the opposition between home and work in global conversations.

Movements

The revived feminist movement together with the new microenterprise movement led the attack on the home-work opposition in global conversations. According to Deborah Stienstra, the 1970s and the 1980s were "the most dynamic in the history of international women's movements." New feminist organizations joined established women's organizations from the early part of the century to infuse new "vitality, creativity and links to grass-roots networks of women" into the global women's movement.[10] The United Nations, in sponsoring several international conferences on women and an international women's decade from 1976 to 1985, boosted the global character of the movement. Various international networks emerged in the context of these conferences. Nongovernmental forums that accompanied the conferences became important meeting grounds for networking, strategizing, exchanging ideas, establishing differences, and negotiating common ground.[11]

In contrast to the first wave of the women's movement, the second wave was much broader, involving a huge number of nongovernmental organizations: among the ca. 40,000 women who attended the NGO Forum in Beijing, 4,035 represented officially accredited NGOs, reflecting the broad level of institutionalization within the movement.[12] Also in contrast to the earlier women's movement, the second wave was much more diverse. It comprised not only many more women from Asia, Africa, and Latin America, but also women whose feminism included an identification along national and racial lines, or who represented certain socioeconomic groups. Feminists from Asia, Africa, and Latin America pushed into the foreground issues relating to women and development, the status of women in the international political economy, and the differential impacts of structural adjustment policies on women. Many were particularly concerned about women workers in the informal sector, and many shared the understandings of the microenterprise movement, considering women's work in the sector as ingenious survival strategies that had the potential of lifting families out of poverty.

In the 1990s, the microenterprise movement gathered a diverse range of supporters including "right-wing romantics, conservatives eager to break the influence of labor, and leftist proponents of the 'little guy.' "[13] But its origins lay in the work of nongovernmental organizations that had found the provision of credit an effective way to strengthen the economic activities ("microenterprises") of the poor. Unlike many earlier development interventions, those focusing on microenterprise were not designed to introduce new occupations into poor regions, but to support the activities the poor already engaged in. Rather than constituting comprehensive interventions in one geographical area, they focused on a single missing ingredient—credit. Banks usually are not interested in lending small amounts because of the disproportionate administrative costs involved, because they perceive such loans as risky, and because governments often require them to keep interest rates low. Acknowledging the barriers that poor and often illiterate people faced to obtaining formal credit, microenterprise programs made access to credit easy and "convenient." They offered loans at affordable (though not necessarily below-market) rates. Loan officers helped borrowers complete their paperwork, and application and disbursement procedures were quick and simple. Because many poor people lacked collateral, the programs applied social group pressure and the promise of future loans to guarantee repayment.[14] Microenterprise programs became extremely popular because they succeeded in stabilizing the incomes of their beneficiaries while ensuring high repayment rates which made some programs entirely self-sufficient.

In the 1970s, the approach found support within the U.S. Agency for International Development (AID) which over the years exerted "more influence on the evolution of small enterprise and microenterprise work than all other donor institutions combined."[15] AID financed studies of NGO projects to document the effectiveness of the microenterprise approach.[16] In part as a result of these studies, donor agencies increasingly funded NGOs that provided credit to microentrepreneurs. By 1998, groups offering credit to people that pursued various small economic activities had mushroomed to an estimated 3,000 world-wide,[17] and many succeeded in raising the earnings of their clients. They linked themselves in networks such as Accion International and FINCA, which operated mostly in the Americas, CASHPOR with affiliates in the Asia-Pacific Region, Women's World Banking and the Microfinance Network, both of which operated globally.

The debt crisis and the new economic orthodoxies of the 1980s, often summarized under the label of neoclassical liberal economics, boosted the movement. Supporting microenterprises was compatible with free-market principles and emerged as a social policy to cushion the adverse effects of austerity measures. Microenterprises also became a *cause célèbre* among neo-liberals with a romantic streak, such as the Peruvian Hernando de Soto who argued that microentrepreneurs were the true entrepreneurs, the problem being "mercantilist" states with excessive regulations that benefitted primarily monopolistic firms. From de Soto's point of view, the expansion of the informal sector constituted a revolutionary movement, an uprising of the popular sector against a suffocating state.[18]

The popularity of the microcredit strategy propelled the global movement to work toward making such credit available to poor people all over the world. Advocacy groups and networks such as the International Coalition on Women and Credit and the RESULTS Education Fund promoted the idea of microenterprises in policy circles. The Microcredit Summit held in Washington DC in February of 1997 marked a high point in efforts to mainstream the approach, bringing together leaders of governments and development organizations, and launching "a global campaign to reach 100 million of the world's poorest families, especially the women of those families, with credit for self-employment and other financial and business services, by the year 2005."[19] Increasingly, development agencies were making microenterprise programs part of their tool chest, and although many remained skeptical, some agencies, including the UN Development Program and U.S. AID, came to see microenterprise development as the "key instrument" for poverty alleviation.[20]

Feminists working in development organizations found that poor women were particularly unlikely to have access to formal credit. They shied away from the paperwork and the travel costs involved, and they were more likely than men to be illiterate and to lack the collaterals that most banks required.[21] Thus microenterprise programs benefitted women disproportionately, and feminist development practitioners became passionate advocates of the approach. Important sections of the women's movement came to overlap with the microenterprise movement as feminist development organizations adopted the provision of credit as a crucial strategy to reaching poor, unorganized women. Many used the microenterprise approach to deliver messages about health care and education, to fight dowries and communal violence, or to support widows or wives with abusive husbands. Such organizing activities were especially prevalent in South Asia. Attacks on rules of the family combined with attacks on rules of the political economy in the interventions of these organizations and contributed to undermining divisions between home and work, public and private, modern and traditional in global debates.

The Informal Sector: Feminine Survival Activities, Masculine Dynamic Enterprises

In the early 1970s, under the umbrella of the World Employment Programme (WEP), the ILO sent teams of experts on advisory missions to various countries, formed national and regional employment teams, and engaged in a large-scale research effort to probe venues for employment creation.[22] Concerned initially with high levels of urban unemployment, ILO experts soon realized that the notion of unemployment carried little meaning in Third World societies. Male, breadwinning workers that benefitted from welfare protection were a minority here. Without insurance to fall back on, poor people could not afford to be unemployed and instead took up various survival activities in what came to be known as the informal sector. ILO studies emphasized that, far from being only marginally productive, the informal sector was "economically efficient and profit-making." They recommended that the sector be fostered as an engine of growth.[23] In both urban and rural areas, small enterprises emerged as an acclaimed source of employment, as enabling equitable income distribution, and as producing "unsophisticated low-cost goods" meeting the basic needs of the population.[24]

The emphasis on the activities of the very poor constituted a significant change from earlier writings about small industry. They signaled a retreat from efforts to convert small industries into large factories that offered jobs with family wages, legitimizing instead support for small productive entities and even home-based work. Staley and Morse had defined small industry as firms employing one to ninety-nine workers and dropped consideration of all units with fewer than ten workers because of data problems. They legitimized this procedure by arguing that the very small industries probably were home-based and therefore something to be overcome, certainly not relevant for modernization.[25] The research on the urban informal sector challenged this dismissive treatment of very small industries. Small enterprises (rural and urban) increasingly appeared as the core of "Third World" economies. In many countries they were said to contribute "from 70 to 96 per cent of all manufacturing employment," adding "more than one-third of the manufacturing industrial value."[26]

The ILO's Kenya report suggested that "women's employment would . . . be assisted by the development of the sector,"[27] and the language of equity and justice wove into arguments for supporting the informal sector. But as the sector increasingly emerged as feminine in subsequent writings, the celebration of its virtues mutated into sober descriptions of its supplemental, secondary, and exploited status. In the academic debate over the relationship between the formal and the informal sector, Marxists and liberals clashed, but agreed in constructing the informal sector as subordinate and feminine. Those who considered the relationship benign saw the informal sector to provide services to the formal sector in the same way housewives provided services to breadwinners: "Most of the exports [from the informal to the formal sector] are service activities—commerce and domestic services—which are complementary to formal production."[28] Those who considered the relationship exploitative argued that activities in the informal sector should be understood as "petty commodity production" which was subordinate to capitalism. Like women in Marxist analysis petty producers had two functions: they constituted an army of reserve labor, and they supported the low-cost reproduction of masculine-identified formal sector labor.[29]

But the simple gendered opposition between formal and informal sectors soon proved unsatisfactory. A number of researchers, including those affiliated with the ILO, insisted that the informal sector was very heterogeneous, including "direct subsistence, small-scale production and trade, and subcontracting to semiclandestine enterprises and homeworkers."[30] To capture heterogeneity, the informal sector ramified into two gendered subcategories, repeating the bifurcation that modernization researchers had sculpted onto the crafts sector. Concerned with its growth potential, William House distinguished a dynamic and a stagnant subsector. The first he labeled "the intermediate sector" (i.e., intermediate between formal and informal), the second he named "the community of the poor." The two subsectors resembled earlier distinctions between "a small-scale family-enterprise sector where incomes show great variability and some capital accumulation takes place [and where male heads of households presumably run the business] . . . and an irregular or 'street' economy where low-status, low-skilled trading and service activities abound and where existence is essentially at subsistence."[31] Similarly, Victor Tokman of the ILO insisted that it was necessary to differentiate activities "using additional labor" from those "performed only by one person, and activities which require capital from those in which income constitutes largely remuneration for labor: Some activities, like domestic services or street vending [both heavily female], require little or no capital. Others, like driving a taxi [heavily male] or keeping a small shop [the most profitable ones usually male], require more."[32] Describing the informal sector as heterogeneous meant separating the masculine from the feminine by separating entrepreneurs from dependent workers, masculine-identified from feminine-identified occupations.

Empirical data mirrored the gendered metaphors of these characterizations and showed that women did concentrate in informal activities, especially in "marginal microenterprises" or the "survival economy." First, women did make up a disproportionate number of those in the informal sector. In some countries, such as India, they comprised as much as 50 percent of the urban "unorganized sector,"[33] and in some the percentage of women workers in the informal sector was considerably higher than that of male workers.[34] But on average, studies showed that women owned or operated about a third of all informal sector businesses.[35] Yet, typically their proportion in the informal sector exceeded that in the formal sector. In manufacturing, they accounted for a much higher share of the self-employed than the total labor force in five out of six countries studied in the 1980s.[36] The economic crisis of the 1980s pushed even more women into unregulated employment in countries around the world.[37]

Second, women evidently occupied the lower ranks of the informal sector. NGOs found that women predominated among those whom House called the community of the poor.[38] Berger estimated that more than 90 percent of women's informal businesses had only one worker, the owner herself.[39] A UN survey concluded that "the great majority of women in the informal sector are engaged as paid or unpaid workers" and not entrepreneurs.[40] And women's informal sector activities on average tended to be less profitable than those of men. According to Portes et al., women in Uruguay were about twice as likely as men to hold low-paying casual jobs in the informal sector and less than half as likely as men to be informal employers: "There is a clear separation between informal sector workers and informal employers in terms both of individual characteristics and the economic effects of their respective positions. . . . [And] it is sex which most clearly differentiates between these employment situations."[41] A vast number of case studies from cities around the world confirmed these contentions.[42] Moreover, the home-based character of informal sector activities apparently had different outcomes for women and men. In Lima, Peru, home-based enterprises that sold only in the neighborhood, mostly stores and cafes run by women, had much lower incomes than those which sold city-wide or to businesses. If a woman instead of a man operated any home-based business, income dropped by an average of $51.20 per month.[43]

These studies participated in creating gendered instruction-rules about the informal sector that came to influence the projects of NGOs, governmental, and intergovernmental aid agencies. AID identified three approaches to supporting microenterprises: enterprise formation targeted the "pre-entrepreneurial" population in the survival economy, enterprise expansion provided credit to stabilize the businesses of existing microentrepreneurs, and enterprise transformation sought to "graduate" microenterprises into small enterprises. Women predominated in the first two approaches: "The majority of the enterprise formation programs reached a large proportion of women, both through explicit targeting and through focusing on the neediest groups in the program communities. Programs following the enterprise expansion approach, by virtue of their orientation toward commercial activities, tended to have a high proportion of women beneficiaries. Transformation programs, except when specifically targeted, did not reach a high proportion of women."[44] The activities of women apparently showed little potential for growth: those who engaged in survival activities demanded comprehensive welfare interventions, and the traders who received credit could not be expected to significantly expand their enterprises.

In a replication of modernization themes, there was a clear bias toward supporting businesses that could grow and create employment. Although some NGOs, such as Save the Children, consciously held on to the ideal of reaching the very poorest, many programs targeted microenterprises that showed promise of graduating into small enterprises and neglected women's survival activities.[45] Practitioners found that it was especially difficult to promote the "very small micro-enterprises," mostly run by women: "They do not perceive themselves as entrepreneurs, nor do they conceive of their moneymaking activities as 'business opportunities.' Their activities lack the systematic qualities of enterprises at other levels, especially planning and scheduling."[46] Many economists insisted that support for microenterprises in AID's first two categories distracted from the task of making economies more efficient. They contended that "one-person enterprises were not economically viable" and that those operating "outside of the home were more economically efficient than those in the home." Helping microentrepreneurs in the end required building large firms: "An efficient large-scale sector" was crucial for the growth of microenterprises.[47]

In a sense then, the debate on the informal sector replayed the gender rules of modernization rhetoric. It redefined the boundary between efficiency and inefficiency to expanded gendered constructions of the economy to the very small enterprises and home-based workers that earlier modernizers had dismissed. Whereas the previous cutoff point was the small firm with ten workers, it now was the one-woman microenterprise. Gender reproduced vividly in dualistic categories that opposed the formal and the informal sector, dynamic enterprises, and the survival activities of the poor. Femininity again emerged as a sign of supplementality and secondary status, but also came to signal exploitation and hopelessness. The interventions of the feminist movement began to destabilize the gendered oppositions of modernization rhetoric by undermining the home–work, production–reproduction dichotomies that buttressed these oppositions.

Women in Development: Changing the Meaning of Home-Based Work

In the 1970s, feminist scholars, practitioners, and activists argued that women should receive equal attention in development planning and projects, launching the women in development (WID) movement. The preoccupation with basic needs and with the informal sector provided an auspicious environment for their arguments. WID researchers and activists emphasized the productive nature of women's work and its crucial contribution to family wealth and welfare. They fundamentally revalued women's supposedly marginal activities, portraying them as key to poverty alleviation, and sometimes celebrating them as an alternative approach to organizing the economy. In the process they reversed the rules of modernizers to construct home-based workers as nurturant entrepreneurs who ensured communal well-being. In documenting the breadth of women's home-based economic contributions, the WID movement also destabilized oppositional constructions of home and work, production and reproduction, and in this way prepared the grounds for new instruction-rules on gender.

Critical of the optimistic view that development benefitted all, WID practitioners, scholars, and advocates insisted that supposedly gender-neutral economic policies had hurt women. Colonial policies as well as contemporary development interventions had tended to ignore women's work. Censuses and employment surveys did not count such work, making women's economic contributions invisible, in part because women often worked at home.[48] Development planners often considered women's work not to be "real work," ignored it in their planning, and introduced new technologies and modes of work organization that displaced women and destroyed their sources of independent income. Agricultural extension agents targeted men to promote cash crops, ignoring women's subsistence production and their labor contributions to men's farming. Cash crops often increased demands on women's labor, and family nutrition suffered as a result. Cooperatives often excluded women and paid men for the goods their wives or daughters produced. Equity considerations demanded that women's activities received equal consideration in development planning, that women be "integrated" into development.[49]

WID researchers set out to make women's work "visible" and to destroy the construction of women's work as secondary. The distinctions between home and work, between productive and reproductive activities became meaningless in their descriptions. Using ethnographic methods, case studies, and time use surveys, they documented that women engaged in vastly diverse kinds of work. Women farmed for subsistence, raised livestock, processed food for consumption and for sale, fetched water and fuel. They produced crafts and assembled goods for household use as well as for subcontractors. They sewed and embroidered clothing, crocheted lace, knit sweaters, and wove carpets and shawls. They made pottery, baskets, batik, mats, and hats. They kept cows, goats, and poultry, sold milk, eggs, meat, manure, dung cakes, and animals. Some of their activities were paid, some unpaid, but all, WID researchers insisted, had economic value. In attaching value to the "reproductive" activities of women, WID researchers destroyed the image of the idle housewife. Time use surveys showed that rural women in particular worked long hours, typically much longer than the men whom global talk had created as breadwinners.[50] Once the artificial distinction between production and reproduction, between domestic work and real work, was destroyed, women emerged as family providers even more than men.

The WID movement brought women's home-based work within the orbit of development planning. A large number and often the vast majority of women's work that WID researchers described took place at home.[51] In rural areas this included the bulk of women's manufacturing work as well as their work on farms (including food processing and animal husbandry). In urban areas women's manufacturing or assembly work took place in homes or in small workshops attached to homes; women traders generally operated at or close to their homes and many female street food vendors produced their goods at home.[52] Within the rich documentations of women's work in WID research the meaning of home-based work expanded: Paid and unpaid work, productive and reproductive activities, merged. Petty vending, agricultural processing, and services added to manufacturing and crafts production to configure a new problematique of home-based work.

The early WID literature largely drew on liberal economic premises and failed to see the significance of women's work being home-based. Socialist feminists criticized liberal WID research for remaining within the economic parameters of the modernization perspective and for implying that—if done the right way—modernization could benefit women. They argued that the liberal perspective lacked a systematic account of women's subordination and failed to analyze the way in which capitalist development and certain constructions of gender went hand in hand.[53] More attuned to economic exploitation, socialist feminists, some with support from the ILO's Programme on Rural Women, made the home-based character of women's work an explicit topic of debate, emphasizing that women's definition as "housewives" facilitated their subordination to merchants, subcontractors, and employers.

During the 1980s, the Programme sponsored a series of studies on subcontracted home-based work that documented exploitative practices and revived the concern about low wages that had preoccupied global debates about industrial homework in the early part of the century. But they added a new element as well: the extent to which international demand and inequalities in the organization of global capitalism enabled the new subcontracting relationships. The studies affirmed that women's domestic role and their role in the labor market were tightly interwoven, and they sometimes described a functional link of gender ideologies to global capitalism thereby providing an explanation for gender subordination. Maria Mies expressed the connection perhaps most systematically. "Ideologies" that constructed home-based workers as nonworking housewives legitimized their superexploitation as workers and in this way facilitated capital accumulation for merchants. But they also created women as unpaid subsistence producers (housewives and subsistence farmers) that, by ensuring family survival, enabled the big landowners that employed the men to pay less than living wages. Women's subordination enabled capital to appropriate value produced through both women's paid and unpaid work.[54]

Much of the evidence documenting these relationships came from India where subcontracting arrangements frequently tied women to traders and employers in the garment and textile industries, as well as in the areas of food processing and livestock rearing. In the Narsapur district, women formed the backbone of the lace industry, crocheting lace at home which their husbands and middlemen marketed. Much of the lace was exported and the women earned puny wages. Census enumerators did not count lacemakers as workers; the general perception was they were nonworking housewives. In Allahabad, women rolled cigarettes for contractors, making significant contributions to household income and shattering the image that secluded women did not work. A study of rural women in Turkey found carpet-weavers working in quasi-independent production as well as in putting-out systems. Even though they were the main weavers, their work was not counted in national economic statistics and typically their male relatives held control over the income.[55]

Academic work supported the findings of these ILO-sponsored studies. An investigation of Hausa women in Nigeria challenged the image of passive secluded women showing that they were "very active economic entrepreneurs."[56] Comparable evidence emerged from an analysis of women's work in the walled city of Lahore where many observed rules of seclusion yet engaged in various types of home-based work to contribute to household incomes.[57] Studies of carpet weavers in Iran, and of garment homeworkers in Indonesia and Thailand documented the way in which patriarchal ideologies suffused the organization of production.[58] In Latin America, researchers explored the "crossroads of class and gender," i.e., the way in which firms took advantage of women's weaker labor market position, the impacts of home-based work on women's status, and its relationship to the life cycles of families. Others analyzed differences between feminine and masculine home-based work, documenting the spatial integration of women's work into kitchens and men's tendency to create workspaces away from children and from spaces dedicated to reproductive tasks. They also showed that men often took over an enterprise when it became profitable. Studies of Middle American artisans described their insertion into dependent capitalist economies, the effects of industrial restructuring and export-oriented development strategies on these artisans, and the extension of subcontracting networks into rural areas. They linked these processes to changes in household divisions of labor and in the status of women.[59]

In sum, studies on home-based work contributed to making women's work visible and to establishing women's contribution not only to household economies but as well to capitalist accumulation. Furthermore, in linking home-based work to gender divisions of labor and to patriarchal ideologies that facilitated and mystified exploitation, they proposed an explanation of women's subordination. The effect was to destabilize instruction-rules of women as idle housewives or secondary earners. Women's income, far from being merely supplemental, ensured the survival of poor families. Women were not housewives but "women workers," "producers," "income-earners," "economic providers," "entrepreneurs," "semi-proletarians," and "disguised wage workers."

From the debates on women in development, women and their work thus emerged changed. In a redefinition that destabilized the boundary between home and work, home-based work broadened to encompass diverse types of subsistence production and production for the market in addition to reproductive service activities. In addition, WID researchers effectively reversed the rules that had guided global talk about the formation of welfare states and about nation-building, substituting the images of the worker, entrepreneur, and economic provider for that of the supplemental income-earner or the mother that should be shielded from work. In WID research, motherhood no longer defined womanhood. It limited women's work options but became a secondary characteristic that no longer dominated their identities. However, maternalist arguments that appealed to women's distinctiveness formed an undercurrent of WID rhetoric and emerged in arguments to justify support for women's economic activities against efficiency-oriented development institutions.

Integrating Women Into Development: From Nation-Builders to Nurturant Entrepreneurs

Demands to integrate women into development preceded the second wave of the feminist movement. Indira Gandhi had suggested as early as the 1950s that "women today have a twofold responsibility—one domestic and the other of developing the country."[60] She was not alone. Two resolutions at the 1964 International Labor Conference, stressed the "urgency . . . of integrating [women] more closely and effectively into the whole process of developing human resources," and proclaimed that "their work is necessary to the development of productive forces of their countries."[61] The terms of that integration consisted of instruction-rules that connected to nation-building rhetoric and defined women as mothers. U.S. Assistant Secretary of Labor Esther Peterson, who introduced the resolutions to the Conference, stressed that "as a country develops," women, like any citizen, should be trained for "productive employment of the kind the country will need *while giving due consideration to the I.L.O. standards for her traditional role as mother and home maker.*"[62] The government delegate from Cyprus spelled out the agreement even more clearly: "The point is to devise ways and means and to plan ahead for a smooth, orderly and economical integration of women into the labour force without too much disruption of the traditional family structures and without detriment to a woman's responsibilities and duties vis-à-vis her family and her children."[63] The attitude was that they "could do a lot more than just being in the kitchen."[64]

In the 1960s home-based handicraft production appeared as the most effective way to achieve this integration without disturbing women's home duties. Jasleen Dhamija, an ILO expert on handicrafts, proposed that "both society and the women themselves benefit when the latter participate in economic activity, and . . . in rural societies handicrafts are the most suitable means of enabling them to do this while continuing to perform their vital role in the home."[65] Others concurred, "through handicrafts and small-scale industry the full participation of women in the economic and social development of their countries can most easily be achieved," allowing women to assume their "rightful role in the battle for development."[66]

By the 1970s, explicit references to women's housewifely identities had virtually disappeared. But instruction-rules defining women as housewives lived on as development agencies continued to promote crafts production together with other "income-generating activities." Adopting feminist rhetoric, Dhamija now argued that developing these activities would not only "contribute to the economy of the country," but also "raise the status of women in society as a whole."[67] The objective of crafts projects was to draw women into market-oriented production by teaching them new skills, providing them credit, and often forming producer groups. Most projects were small and targeted women in a particular geographical area. NGOs, often with financial support from donor agencies, implemented the projects. Animal husbandry, bee keeping, raising silk worms, sewing, vending, and various forms of food processing joined handicrafts production as the favored income-earning opportunities to be promoted.[68]

But handicraft projects soon came to epitomize what was wrong with these localized efforts to introduce new income-earning opportunities, and they became increasingly controversial. Critics attacked their implicit definition of women as nonworking housewives: projects operated on the assumption that women's time was free, and that women would be idle if they did not produce handicrafts. Projects often faltered because there was no market for the goods produced. Rather than helping women, they ensnared them in activities that required long hours of labor and fetched very little income. The projects created women as supplemental income-earners, reproducing a division of labor in which women were relegated to the least remunerated and least respected jobs.[69]

WID advocates increasingly challenged the instruction-rules about women that informed these income-generating projects. Dhamija, an enthusiastic promoter of handicrafts for women in the 1960s and 1970s, sounded the death knell for this approach in the 1980s: "In most instances . . . crafts production concentrates women in an area that is labor intensive and exploitative, providing a meager income for long hours of work."[70] Advocates increasingly realized that many women's projects "tend[ed] to be confined to those home-oriented activities such as embroidery and sewing, which [did] not necessarily lead to profitable employment,"[71] and they argued that projects should allow women to earn a decent income and thus gain them a measure of economic independence and a higher status in society.[72] Recognizing that African women did not conform to the stereotypical nonworking housewife but were active in many production and marketing activities, participants at a 1978 workshop on handicrafts for women in Francophone Africa forcefully argued not to direct women into low-productivity areas and not to limit promotion to "feminine crafts" like sewing and embroidery.[73] Many questioned whether it was desirable at all to support activities which often became embedded in exploitative putting-out systems: "Were such income-generating schemes the answer for women?"[74]

Demands for new strategies reflected the new instruction-rules implied in these criticisms of income-generation projects: women no longer were mothers and nonworking housewives but workers and income-earners. Consequently, alleviating women's excessive work burden, reducing the "drudgery of their day-to-day life," giving women equality with men in legislation, and providing child care facilities all became themes in the debate about such projects.[75] There even was talk about organizing women so they would be able to "approach governments for assistance and information with a stronger voice."[76] In this context the microenterprise approach gained prominence in WID circles, increasingly fostering a definition of home-based workers as entrepreneurs.

In the 1980s, S. V. Sethuraman, an ILO researcher, still had cautioned that it was misleading to label small-scale economic activities in the informal sector "enterprises,"[77] but by the 1990s "promoting female entrepreneurship and micro-enterprise development" had become an integral part of women-oriented development.[78] For the new feminist bureaucrats whose mandate it was to integrate women into the activities of development agencies, microenterprise development became a key strategy. Not only was it one of the few interventions that actually did make a difference for poor women, but it also fit within the emerging talk about strengthening the private sector that had dominated development circles since the 1980s. It became the task of WID technocrats to turn women's "riskless activities, some of which are not necessarily profit-motivated"[79] into small enterprises, teaching crafts producers and home-based workers the tools of management and the trade of capital accumulation. But they also had to justify their activities in the context of a broadening understanding that women's home-based activities tended to be inefficient and had little potential for growth. A revival of maternalist themes helped them make the case.

One strand of WID technocrats responded to economists' pessimistic assessments of women's economic activities by chiding them for their obsession with growth and efficiency and for not recognizing the economic significance of women's incomes. Even though women's microenterprises did not tend to grow or create additional employment, they clearly stabilized the incomes of poor families and in this way helped families reduce poverty. Furthermore, women who engaged in economic activities often gained status within households, in addition to increased self-confidence and a greater voice in decisionmaking.[80] Thus, supporting women's economic activities did make sense from a feminist point of view; giving poor women credit could become a source of empowerment.

A second strand of WID arguments employed maternalist themes, constructing women's entrepreneurial strategies as creating a more humane economy that valued nurturance. Advocates contrasted the unselfish inclinations of mothers to the economists' assumptions of self-interest and touted women's key role in alleviating the impacts of poverty on their families. Many saw in the activities of poor women an alternative to capitalism, a source for the renewal of a corrupt world. WID practitioners confirmed that women spent their income in an altruistic and responsible fashion, and WID researchers found that women microentrepreneurs were less interested in profits and growth than in paying school fees for their children: "Women consistently devote a higher proportion of their income (nearly 100 percent) to family needs than do men."[81] For them nurturing the family took priority over the individual pursuit of profit. Accordingly, if their businesses were successful, they often set up a relative in a parallel enterprise, initiating an "amoeba-like pattern of growth" rather than enlarging their own businesses.[82]

This type of behavior did not mean that women were worse entrepreneurs. On the contrary, WID advocates often exalted women's entrepreneurial qualities. This was most evident in the impressive loan repayment rates of women borrowers. It became general wisdom that "women borrowers are reliable and have high repayment rates,"[83] and therefore were a good credit risk. WID advocates also trusted women more than men to responsibly manage money: "Women are more thrifty and are better at foreseeing tomorrow's needs than are men. Furthermore, they are better at keeping and managing money saved for family purposes—e.g. to spend on food, clothing and the health and education of children—whereas men do not in many cases bring home their savings."[84] Motherhood meant not only nurturance but also savvy entrepreneurship.

This tendency to construct home-based women workers as nurturant entrepreneurs was even more pronounced in some NGOs that worked predominantly with women. For Muhammad Yunus, founder of the Grameen Bank, the celebrated model for village banking in Bangladesh, poor entrepreneurial women provided the vision for overcoming a capitalist world in which "a greedy (almost bloodthirsty) person . . . play[s] the role of profit-maximizer."[85] Ninety-four percent of the Grameen Bank's borrowers were women and their work home-based.[86] Yunus imagined "a world where every human being is a potential entrepreneur, . . . a system to give everybody a chance to materialise his/her potential." He dreamt of socially conscious entrepreneurs that created an egalitarian economy designed for poor women working out of their homes: "Home-based production based on self-employment can be as mass-scale as in a single roof wage-based factory system. The more we can move towards home-based production by the self-employed masses, the more we can come close to avoiding the disasters of capitalism."[87] His vision echoes in the words of Noeleen Heyzer, Executive Director of the United Nations Women's Fund (UNIFEM): "Instead of just bringing women to struggle against the mainstream, or admit them as part of the economic mainstream, [the goal is] really to use them to change the economic mainstream. Women can play the lead in transforming businesses so that they become ecologically and socially accountable."[88]

This rhetorical appropriation of motherhood resembles nationalist rhetoric in constructing women as an antidote to capitalism, maintaining values such as altruism, reliability, and a sense of responsibility for others. Womanhood here emerged as the wellspring for a better world, for an alternative to exploitation, inequality, and poverty. While reviving instruction-rules about womanhood as motherly, motherhood no longer meant being economically inactive or marginal. Motherhood included breadwinning. Indeed, motherly women could do better than men in providing for their families. The mother's duty was the economic development of the country as a nurturant entrepreneur. Women workers in this argument were not like male workers; instead women could do everything that men could and more. The combination of motherhood and income-earning, home and work, emerged as necessary and desirable.

The WID movement was significant because it destabilized instruction-rules that variably created women as marginal earners, such as the motherly woman of the nationalist rhetoric or the traditional and pregnant woman of modernization rhetoric, rules that effectively cemented the subordinate status of women. Together with the microenterprise movement, it effected a reversal of values attached to womanhood and home-based work. Where modernizers saw traditional and backward crafts producers, microenterprise developers found creative entrepreneurs whose ingenuity created a better world for families and countries. Where economic planners perceived idle housewives, the WID movement revealed overworked women engaged in a broad range of paid and unpaid activities of high economic value. Where development economists and some microenterprise practitioners saw survival activities of the poor without growth potential, WID advocates spotted enterprising women who reduced the impacts of poverty and who operated according to the values of a "human economy."[89]

Much of the critique of WID activists entailed a reversal of dichotomies, constructing supposedly nonworking housewives as working breadwinners, and supposedly exploited dupes as entrepreneurs creating a better future. While this reversal kept the dichotomies themselves intact, WID critique also began to destabilize the opposition between home and work and debates in the 1990s carried this even further.

5   Fordist Gender Rules at Issue: The Debate Over the ILO Home Work Convention

In June of 1996, almost ninety years after the Swiss Home-worker Congress of 1907 had called for international agreements, the ILO adopted a convention on homework. The convention requires ratifying states to "adopt, implement and periodically review a national policy on home work." It sets as the crucial guiding principle for such a policy "equality of treatment between homeworkers and other wage earners." The convention extends labor rights that had become global standards for factory and office workers to those working at home for pay. These include rights of association, rights to protection against discrimination, rights to occupational health and safety, access to training, and maternity protection rights. In setting home-workers equal to other workers, the convention reversed definitions of worker that had dominated ILO debates in the early part of the century.

But the issue had become much larger than defined in the Euro-centric debates at the beginning of the century. The home-based producers of Asia, Africa, and Latin America loomed large in the debates of the 1990s, as did "teleworkers," freelancers, and independent contractors. The convention constituted an effort to regulate labor relations in a globalized economy that increasingly relied on subcontracting and flexible employment. In seeking to regulate a section of the global labor force that uniquely served new flexible production methods, the convention expanded the concept of worker and implicitly challenged the gendered constructions of labor relations in welfare states. These challenges became explicit in the discussions of the convention, making them, in the judgment of some ILO officers, the most contentious they remembered.

In the 1970s, high inflation, surplus capacities, mass unemployment, decreasing real wages, low growth, declining productivity, and low rates of investment signaled a crisis in the global economy.[1] Companies sought to reverse declining rates of profit and many relocated production to the economic periphery, taking advantage of low cost labor and increasingly "globalizing" production. Assembly workers and industrial homeworkers employed in footloose manufacturing industries in the core often lost their jobs to a largely female factory work force in the free trade zones of Asia, Latin America, and North Africa in the 1970s.[2] As the need to quickly respond to changes in demand joined imperatives for increased earnings and cost savings, companies met rising global competition not only by cutting direct labor costs, but also by becoming more flexible. They increasingly subcontracted labor-intensive production and service work to small firms and employed "contingent workers," including home-based workers, who could be easily hired and fired. In this way they did not have to pay wages when they had no orders, and the wages they did pay contingent workers were usually lower than those of full-time factory workers. Furthermore, resorting to subcontracting and contingent workers allowed firms to circumvent unions, the high costs of negotiated wages and employment guarantees. New information technologies facilitated flexibilization, and global competition encouraged the spread of the new "just-in-time" production strategies.[3]

A "globalization of states" accompanied this globalization of production. States no longer served as buffers for the impacts of market forces but increasingly adjusted domestic regulatory structures to the demands of global capital.[4] Changes in economic orthodoxy legitimized changes in government policies, and the supply-side interventions of neoclassical economic liberalism replaced Keynesian strategies of demand management. According to neoclassical liberalism, the industrial and social policies of the post-World War II era constituted "structural rigidities" that impaired the free play of market forces and were responsible for the economic crisis. The solution was to eliminate these rigidities through the deregulation of both product and labor markets.

States integrated neoclassical understandings into their policymaking in different ways, some pursuing hyperliberal strategies aimed at destroying corporatist forms of interest intermediation (e.g., the Reagan and Thatcher governments), others following a more consensus-based process of adjustment. Regardless of which path governments pursued, however, fighting inflation increasingly took priority over fighting unemployment in the North. In contrast, industrializing neomercantilist states in Latin America, Asia, and Africa often postponed the impacts of the global economic crisis by borrowing heavily in private financial markets only to face difficulties repaying their debts in the 1980s.[5] For countries intent on regaining economic growth, the World Bank and the International Monetary Fund (IMF) adopted neoclassical liberal prescriptions at the international level and imposed them through structural adjustment and stabilization programs. Such programs often discouraged bargaining between workers and employers and prescribed cuts in welfare programs. In response to pressure from international institutions, but also in order to create an investment climate conducive to foreign capital, governments in the South deregulated their economies and dismantled existing labor protection. Some pursued active policies to encourage subcontracting, on the one hand enticing local companies that produced for domestic markets to draw on rural-based small firms and home-based workers, on the other hand fostering arrangements under which home-based workers produced for an international market.[6]

Home-based workers became ideal workers in a restructured global economy, providing flexibility and costing little. In industrialized countries the decline in the number of home-based workers slowed and sometimes even reversed during the 1980s. Homework increased in Germany, the UK, France, Italy, Greece, the Netherlands, Spain, Switzerland, the US, and Canada.[7] Case studies from Latin America and Asia similarly indicated an increase in the phenomenon. In Latin America and Africa, the economic crisis of the 1980s and monetary stabilization policies forced even more women into unregulated employment.[8] Taiwan and Hong Kong seemed to provide the model for a new organization of manufacturing that treated living rooms as factories.[9] Home-based work and microenterprises no longer provided a romantic alternative to global capitalism, but became an integral part of domestic and global production chains.

The salience of contingent workers in the new world economy constituted a challenge for the ILO. These workers typically lacked rights and did not fall under the umbrella of the international labor code formulated with male factory workers in mind. In the 1990s, the ILO initiated efforts to change this. The International Labor Conference discussed the issue of self-employment in 1990; in 1994 it passed a convention on part-time work, and in 1996, the Home Work Convention. Contract labor was on the agenda of the 1997 Conference, and the organization initiated a campaign for the equal treatment of migrant laborers.[10] From the perspective of the ILO, these actions extended labor protection to previously excluded groups; but they also involved a renegotiation of gender rules that had dominated global debates throughout the twentieth century. Women were disproportionately represented among contingent workers, a condition that brought gender to the foreground of the debates.

Rules

Writers in the tradition of the French regulation school have described the reorganization of production in the last quarter of the twentieth century as a move from a "Fordist" to a "Post-Fordist" regime of accumulation. Regimes of accumulation are historically specific ways of relating production and consumption, i.e., ways to redistribute the social product. Particular modes of regulation—institutional forms or sets of rules—accompany every regime of accumulation. They help realize a regime of accumulation by ensuring that the behavior of workers and consumers conforms to the regime. Fordism combined mass production and mass consumption as the basis of an ideal-typical regime of accumulation, most closely realized in the industrialized countries of Europe and North America. The factory was the productive center of this regime. Here semi-skilled operatives subject to detailed supervision mass-produced standardized consumer goods. The accompanying mode of regulation consisted of institutionalized bargaining between employers and unions, social welfare systems providing a safety net, and Keynesian demand management. These institutions helped realize Fordism by securing factory workers the means to buy the consumer goods they produced.[11]

While writers in the regulation school have focused on national modes of regulation, they have conceded the possibility that there may be international modes.[12] The international monetary regime and the international trade regime were part of a global mode of Fordist regulation, and they changed significantly in parallel with the restructuring world economy. But so was the international labor code, comprising instruction-rules about the identities and statuses of workers, employers, and states; directive-rules assigning tasks to the ILO, states, and employers; and commitment-rules defining the rights of workers, obligating governments to incorporate international rules into national law and practice and employers to abide by these rules. The ILO provided a forum for the negotiation of such rules.

In the second half of the twentieth century, international development institutions, including the ILO, were crucial vehicles facilitating the expansion of the Fordist regime and its mode of regulation. The modernization perspective and the strategy of import-substituting industrialization included the rules of Fordism. Governments, often with support from the ILO, introduced labor codes and social security systems (including all three categories of rules) modeled after Western welfare states. They also reproduced global gender constructs that were embedded in the rhetoric of modernization and import-substituting industrialization, implying the need to create jobs for male breadwinners.

As I show in chapter 2, the struggle to create Fordist welfare states entailed a global debate that constructed women as motherly and men as breadwinners. The need to humanize factories legitimized restrictions on women's work, including policies to ban industrial homework. Regulating the labor of women, constructed as dependents, established the principle of state intervention in labor relations. Although gender constructions shifted in different geographical and historical contexts throughout the twentieth century, oppositional constructions of masculine and feminine became an integral part of global Fordism, enabling practices such as unequal pay, occupational segregation, restricted pension rights for married female workers, or the concept of the family wage. Furthermore, femininity denoted that which Fordism did not fully encapsulate: home-based work, the informal sector, crafts production. Constructed as secondary, supplemental, and feminine, these forms of production were either marginally integrated or remained outside the regulatory edifice of Fordism.

In generalizing Fordist gender rules that opposed home and work, housewife and breadwinner, modernization strategies participated in creating a large group of workers without rights, lacking job security, and never sharing the fruits of industrial growth. According to one estimate, the international labor code applied only to about nine percent of the world's labor force in 1972,[13] excluding for example subsistence farmers, the self-employed, informal sector workers, housewives, and most home-based workers. Gender constituted an unspoken subtext of such exclusions as women, in addition to young people, immigrants, and minorities, accounted for a significant portion of the unprotected workers.[14] Industrial homeworkers were marginally integrated in the international labor code. A small number of commitment-rules define their rights: The Minimum Wage Fixing Machinery Convention of 1928 commits governments to establish legal mechanisms to set minimum wages in areas where there is no collective bargaining, "in particular in home working trades." The Convention Concerning Sickness Insurance of 1928 stipulates that there should be compulsory sickness insurance for "manual and non-manual workers, including apprentices, . . . out-workers and domestic servants." And the revised Maternity Protection Convention of 1952 applies to "women in industrial undertakings and in non-industrial and agricultural occupations, including women wage earners working at home."[15] Many of these conventions include a "flexibility clause" which allows governments to exclude homeworkers if national conditions pose problems of application. The fact that these conventions specifically mentioned industrial homeworkers attests to their marginal integration: It was unclear whether ILO conventions covered industrial homeworkers if they were not specifically mentioned.[16]

Since the 1980s, post-Fordist labor relations, in global and local contexts, increasingly valorized forms of production previously constructed as marginal. In parallel with the women's movement, post-Fordist labor practices increasingly defined women as workers. Initially, the globalization of production and the creation of a female work force in world market factories perpetuated the housewife–breadwinner dichotomy. The global conversations of multinational company executives and of governments seeking to attract foreign direct investments often drew on definitions of women as housewives and mothers. This led them to favor young and unmarried women whom they defined as nimble-fingered, docile, and suited to tedious, repetitive, and monotonous work. Their potential to bear children and the expectation that they would quit work once they got married defined their secondary status in the labor market and justified their low wages.[17] But increasingly managers undermined such constructions and favored married women and mothers. They no longer saw domestic commitments as an obstacle to income-earning, but considered married women and mothers more reliable, mature, and responsible.[18] New employment practices not only challenged instruction-rules that defined motherhood and breadwinning as contradictory, but also undermined the attachment of mothers and housewives to homes.

This change of instruction-rules about gender destabilized as well definitions of what it meant to be a worker. With workers no longer delineated as masculine breadwinners, demanding worker rights became legitimate for motherly and home-based workers. Debates on the homework convention constituted an effort to extend rights to these newly defined workers, to broaden commitment-rules specifying relationships among home-based workers, their work givers, and governments. The debates made clear the interaction between instruction-rules and commitment-rules, the way in which identities enabled rights while demands for rights impacted identities.

Negotiating the Home Work Convention was contentious in part because participants brought to the table very different understandings of what home-based workers were. Clearly, the old rules were under attack and needed modification to account for new practices. But there was little agreement on the new identities of workers, women, or men under conditions of flexible accumulation. Next to conceptualizations of identity that revived the old image of exploited mothers (the unions' perspective) appeared those that suggested home-based workers were the maternal source of economic development (the Third World government perspective), and those that reversed the dichotomy and described home-based workers as resilient and resourceful family providers (the homeworker advocates' perspective). But there were also those (the Western employers' perspective) that de-feminized home-based work and created an androgynous worker flexibly integrated into a new, technologically enabled circuit of production. Without agreement on identities, there was no agreement on rights.

Movements

Capitalism is not merely a system but a social construction. Seemingly unsocialized self-interested action is social action; modes of regulation and economic institutions are social institutions that circumscribe economic practices. From this perspective, the Fordist crisis of accumulation may have resulted from contradictions inherent in capitalism, but these contradictions emerged because capitalists, workers, and consumers followed certain rules. Global restructuring then was not only a functional solution that imposed itself but also the result of rule changes. From a constructivist perspective, these rule changes required the articulation of arguments that challenged the Fordist regulatory structure. Neoclassical economic liberalism provided these arguments including new instruction-rules describing the way the global economy worked. In this way, neoclassical economic liberalism constituted a social movement. It contested the rules of Fordism and worked to institute a new global mode of regulation that undermined the Fordist mode of accumulation. Like other social movements treated here, it challenged established practices, its arguments reached globally and its impacts were dispersed. Unlike other social movements treated here, its arguments became those of the powerful, i.e. of those that benefitted from the ruled distribution of privilege in capitalist societies.

The central instruction-rule of neoclassical economic liberalism is that markets work best without state intervention. Prescriptions for economic policy and conduct follow from this central rule. Many economists, conservative politicians, technocrats, and capitalists adopted the rule as a new credo and realized it through their practices. So did "central bankers, finance department officials, investment fund managers, securities regulators, insurance executives, money traders, commodity brokers, bond raters and countless other obscure but important figures in the private and public sector [who] were involved in developing the consensus about what had to be done [about the economic crisis]."[19] Organizations such as the Trilateral Commission, the Bilderberg conferences, the Club of Rome, and the European Business Roundtable were movement organizations that contributed to spreading a neoclassical liberal consensus and advocated the creation of free markets as the best response to overcoming the global economic crisis.[20]

If neoclassical economic liberalism achieved ideological hegemony in the 1980s, sections of the women's movement emerged as its fierce critics. Feminist scholars castigated the disempowering effects of neoclassical economic strategies on women and the lack of value such strategies gave to women's unpaid work. They described the way in which private patriarchy became public patriarchy for women workers in world market factories. They chronicled the impacts of structural adjustment policies on women: their loss of jobs in the public sector, traditionally a bastion of female employment; the long additional hours they spent providing care that governments no longer afforded and preparing goods that were too expensive to buy in a processed form. Locally and globally women organized against the devastating effects of debt crises and austerity policies, participating in bread riots, forming support networks for the exchange of goods, services, loans, and child care, establishing popular canteens, and organizing in unions. In some countries, the latter drew thousands of home-based workers. In OECD countries women gained visibility in (albeit weakened) unions, fought the efforts of firms to lower labor standards and to relocate. In Britain, the Neth-

erlands, Canada, and Australia union women advocated on behalf of im-
migrant women trapped in informal jobs. Feminist community organizers
in Britain built advocacy organizations for home-based workers.[21]

At the global level, propelled by the prospect of ILO action on homework,
advocates for home-based workers institutionalized a network, HomeNet International. British and Indian organizations played a leading role in the
network. It included organizations from Asia such as the Self-Employed
Women's Association (SEWA) of Ahmedabad, India, representing informal
sector workers. It involved European, North American, and Australian feminists working on behalf of home-based workers either within traditional unions or in separate organizations that ran telephone hotlines and engaged in
public advocacy. Furthermore, the network connected researchers and academics from all over the world with sympathetic women in the ILO, and
with homeworker organizations and advocates.[22] The network showed the
degree to which the feminist movement had become institutionalized in
dispersed sites: in NGOs, in Women's Studies in the academy, in WID
components within development programs such as those of the ILO. In
terms of its material capabilities the network was weak, lacking finances and
relying on soft money, short-term grants and the commitment of its leaders
for survival. But the network succeeded with its agenda because the rules it
championed had become widely dispersed through the feminist movement
and were thus able to support both local and global interpretations of what
needed to be done about home-based work.

The ILO Home Work Convention: A Feminist
Movement Victory

The ILO is unique among international organizations because of its tripartite structure. Unions and employer organizations participate in its annual
meetings, the International Labor Conference, in addition to governments;
and they have a vote at these meetings. In practice, the votes of unions and
employer organizations often cancel each other out, leaving governments to
decide issues. However, unions and employers fully take part in deliberations, and the International Labor Office routinely consults unions and employer organizations on various matters outside the conference. Some other
international NGOs have observer status at the ILO. They are invited to sit
in on conference proceedings and in some cases to make statements.
HomeNet International had observer status during deliberations of the con-

vention on homework. But, while HomeNet members provided extensive background information to the International Labor Office, they were not allowed to speak at the conference, creating the ironic situation that those most representative of the workers under consideration remained on the sidelines. But HomeNet members used the special relationship they had built with unions in advance of the conferences to get their arguments on the floor.

In contrast, those advancing neoclassical liberal arguments had an unmediated voice in the employer representatives of the conference who fiercely opposed the convention. Under Fordist rules, employers and unions at the ILO negotiated in a typically nonantagonistic fashion to formulate ILO standards. Apparently this style of engagement progressively disappeared in the course of the 1980s. At the 1996 International Labor Conference, employers went so far as to refuse to participate in the drafting of the convention and silently sat through debates in the Committee on Home Work while unions and governments hammered out language. To anybody's memory this had never happened before, and governments deplored the employers' tactics as undemocratic behavior, "a threat to ILO procedure and the spirit of tripartism."[23] From the neoclassical liberal perspective that the employers championed, standard-setting had become a dubious activity: setting standards for flexible workers contradicted the post-Fordist regime of flexible accumulation that had pulled capital out of crisis.

It was a measure of the power of feminist arguments that the convention passed against this fierce opposition and even though home-based workers lacked direct representation in debates at the Conference. The passage of the convention marked a shift in basic instruction-rules that validated women's labor and challenged the housewife-breadwinner dichotomy. Because it was a movement victory, no one organization can claim credit. Feminist rules had invaded even those organizations that held the highest stakes in a Fordist mode of labor regulation: unions and the International Labor Office. Together with organizations that identified themselves as feminist they accomplished the passage of the homework convention.

The International Labor Office

The idea for the ILO convention on homework grew out of the activities of the ILO's Programme on Rural Women. Programme-sponsored research in the 1980s documented the exploitation of rural women in Asia involved in subcontracting relationships and informed ILO projects for home-based workers.[24] A series of projects in the late 1980s and 1990s sought to gain home-based workers access to labor rights. The ILO collaborated with SEWA to conduct legal camps and workers' education classes for home-based *bidi* (cigarette) rollers in India, teaching them about their legal position, minimum wage laws, and entitlements to welfare benefits.[25] It launched a project to promote the welfare of home-based workers in rural Indonesia, Thailand, and the Philippines by creating organizations of home-based workers that would fight for legal rights as well as empower these workers economically.[26] In the Philippines the project fostered the formation of a national umbrella group and local organizations of home-based workers. In Thailand, it succeeded in creating an economic support network gaining home-based workers easier access to market outlets, credit, raw materials, and technology.[27] In Indonesia, government interference limited activities to a local action project geared toward improving the health of home-based workers in one village.[28]

In parallel to these projects, feminist staff in the Programme on Rural Women began to float the idea of an international labor standard within the International Labor Office, the ILO's secretariat in Geneva. An interdepartmental task force, formed in 1984, considered the feasibility and advisability of creating such a standard. The task force found that too little was known about homework to justify placing it on the agenda of the International Labor Conference and recommended further study. Talk about studying homework also had emerged periodically from the ILO's industrial committees (tripartite bodies representing certain industries that met irregularly) and technical meetings especially in the textile, garment, leather, and footwear industries.[29] Starting in 1986, homework appeared as a separate item in the ILO budget. The Labor Law and Labor Relations Branch allocated funds to collect, synthesize, and distribute information on legislation in different countries.[30] The Conditions of Work and Welfare Facilities Branch commissioned monographs on homework in six countries, sent questionnaires to governments, employer organizations, unions, and other NGOs to collect information on homework, and published the summarized information.[31] Two regional tripartite seminars, one held in Manila in December 1988 and one in São Paulo in October 1990, raised the issue and gathered sentiments in Asia and Latin America. Finally, the ILO convened an international meeting of experts in October 1990 in Geneva to advise its Governing Body how to proceed in dealing with homework.

In the early 1990s, the Governing Body decided to put the issue on the official agenda of the 1995 International Labor Conference as a possible item for standard-setting. In preparation, the Office circulated to governments a questionnaire to probe what kinds of standards employer organizations, unions, and governments found acceptable.[32] Responses provided the basis for a first draft of an international standard, in this case (typical for the ILO) combining a convention that governments could ratify and then had the obligation to incorporate into national law with a less formal recommendation. When the Conference discussed the draft in summer 1995, there was fierce opposition from employers that would continue throughout the discussions. Most centered around the definitions of homeworker, intermediary, and employer. The Office incorporated into the draft text changes to which the parties had agreed at the Conference, and circulated it again to governments with requests for comments and amendments.[33] After adjusting the text for such suggestions, the Conference discussed the draft convention and resolution a second time in summer of 1996. Contentious exchanges with employers seemed to threaten passage, but the convention won the support of the European Union (EU) ensuring a positive vote from virtually all EU member states. The conference passed the convention and the recommendation with employers abstaining. As of September 1998, no state had ratified it, although the Commission of the European Union recommended ratification to its member states in May and the United Kingdom indicated its intention to ratify in December 1997.[34]

The contentiousness of debates around the homework convention together with states' hesitation to ratify signaled the degree to which rules about labor relations were in flux. In the end, the convention may have been significant, not so much for the legal changes it may have occasioned in ILO member states, but for having initiated a global debate about regulating flexible labor. The activities of the Office and the debates at the International Labor Conference articulated homework as an issue that needed attention. It mobilized research activities at local levels and created a reason to talk about homework. Thereby it provided a chance to argue the rules that should define not only the identities and rights of home-based workers, but also of workers in general. While talk around the convention no longer defined home-based workers as nonworkers, there was no consensus on the new meanings of class and gender. Instead, speakers employed the rules of informal sector debates and WID rhetoric, nationalist themes that celebrated home-based work as a fount of wealth for the nation, and the interpretations of neoclassical economic liberalism.

Movement Organizations

Among homeworker organizations, SEWA was the most important in lobbying, networking, and advocating for an ILO convention on homework. A self-defined "union of the self-employed" with a membership of 46,000 informal sector workers in 1994 (including vendors and casual laborers in addition to home-based workers) SEWA saw itself part not only of the feminist movement but also of the labor and cooperative movements. For the organization an ILO convention was part of a larger agenda to gain rights for informal sector workers that Fordist labor rules marginalized, many of them women. The struggle was to ensure, in the words of SEWA's Secretary-General that "those who have been marginalized are now entering the mainstream."[35] SEWA considered the convention a tool with which it could improve the lot of home-based workers in India. Years of lobbying the Indian government for a law on homework that would establish tripartite wage-setting and supervisory boards had borne no fruit. SEWA's homeworker protection bill was stalled in the Indian parliament, and SEWA saw an international standard as a way to propel the Indian government toward action.

While feminist allies moved the issue in the ILO, SEWA helped build HomeNet International, institutionalizing a global network of homeworker advocacy organizations. Among the network's core members were the National Homeworking Group of Great Britain (an organization that increasingly built connections with homeworker advocates in the European Union), the Association for the Establishment of a Self-Employed Women's Union of South Africa (which recruited 1,000 members in 1996, its first year of existence), the International Ladies' Garment Workers' Union of Canada (which organized homeworkers in Toronto), Homework Support Centers, and the Clean Clothes Campaign in the Netherlands. Other affiliated organizations were the PATAMABA (a national network in the Philippines with 5,000 members in 27 provinces that was created with support from the ILO), and a Portuguese union with a long tradition of organizing the embroidery homeworkers of Madeira. The network loosely institutionalized with a newsletter and headquarters in Great Britain. HomeNet coordinated the activities of homeworker advocacy groups in preparation for discussions at the ILO, facilitated the exchange of information, and functioned as a clearinghouse. HomeNet members sought support from their own governments and unions for an ILO convention, and gave international visibility to the issue by participating in feminist conferences and writing in feminist publications.[36]

SEWA also lobbied international union federations, gaining resolutions in support of home-based workers from the International Union of Food and Allied Workers (IUF), the International Textile, Garment and Leather Workers Federation (ITGLWF) and, most importantly, from the International Confederation of Free Trade Unions (ICFTU) which the ILO considers the most representative federation of trade unions at the international level. The ICFTU provided crucial support and advice in the lobbying activities during the International Labor Conferences that discussed the convention on homework. Homeworker advocates' savvy coalition-building, together with the increasing salience of home-based work within new economic structures, helped thrust the issue into the mainstream of international deliberations. Feminist rules shaped the course of deliberations.

Post-Fordist Identities

The ILO convention on homework was an effort to create rights, i.e., commitment-rules, for home-based workers. What types of rights these workers should have crucially depended on the understanding of who they were. Arguments about definition—about instruction-rules describing the identities of homeworkers—dominated debates around the convention. Employers, unions, and homeworker advocacy groups had very different understandings of what homeworkers were. Unions most closely retained the language of Fordism and the gender rules that supported it, portraying homeworkers as victims of unscrupulous employers. But others pushed beyond such rules. The themes of the informal sector and of nurturant entrepreneurs as a source of national wealth inspired the language of employers and governments from the South. Heroic womanhood informed the language of homeworker advocates, albeit wrapped in the realities of post-Fordism that had transformed microenterprises and women's work from virtuous occupations to efficient entities in the new machineries of capital. Futuristic visions of a new technology-based flexible economy led employers from the North to de-feminize homeworkers: in their scenario of the future, everybody was a potential homeworker.

The Union Argument

As they came to acknowledge the importance of organizing workers in the informal sector and as feminist voices asserted themselves within the union movement, unions put aside their traditional hostility toward home-workers.[37] At the 1996 International Labor Conference, voices portraying homeworkers as outside the working class, "competing with organized labour, organized work places, and avoiding payment of just taxes to the State" were not contradicted, but were not very loud either.[38] International union confederations, including the ITGLWF, IUF, and the ICFTU, had changed their policies at the end of the 1980s, from a preference for banning home-work to calling for regulation and expressing their solidarity with home-based workers.[39] At the 1996 International Labor Conference unions allowed homeworker advocates full access to their daily caucus and were keen to receive the input of advocates. Although some union leaders grumbled about the prominent role allowed to HomeNet, they had to give in to the feminist supporters of HomeNet within their own ranks, some of whom were HomeNet members. Unions suggested that Ela Bhatt, General Secretary of SEWA, be allowed to address the Conference and deplored that employers opposed this.

Although homeworker advocates and unions were thus united in their strategy and in demanding worker rights for homeworkers, they justified their demand differently. In the union arguments themes from the debate in the early part of the twentieth century resurfaced. While unions no longer sought to preserve the home for motherhood, they were far from according home-based workers historical agency. Representatives of unions portrayed homeworkers as "invisible, marginalized and isolated" with "few or no skills," many being immigrants or members of ethnic minorities.[40] They considered homeworkers passive victims of unscrupulous employers who denied them minimum wages and legal benefits. Homework had advantages primarily for employers because it allowed them to evade labor laws. Homeworkers did not choose this form of employment, but were left with no alternative because of a lack of child care, illegal immigration status, or because of racism and sexism in society. Thus, in the words of the union member from the Netherlands, "if you offered women a choice, they would choose factory work" over homework.[41] Homework in this view existed because of the specific disadvantages women faced in society. Unions would organize home-workers. But efforts failed because homeworkers were so dispersed and isolated. The only way homeworkers could achieve justice was through legal protection.

The Feminist Argument

Homeworker advocates, in contrast, challenged the conception of home-workers as victims, passive, dispersed and difficult to organize. The difference became clear during the 1995 International Labor Conference when conflict arose over a photo exhibit which HomeNet had organized and displayed at the entrance to the meeting room of the Conference's Committee on Home Work. Australian union representatives criticized the exhibit as "too pretty" because it showed British homeworkers in tidy homes, Indian homeworkers in colorful saris working together in front of their houses, and Philippine homeworkers collaborating on decorative craft items. The Australians added their own images of homeworkers: black and white photos showing tired immigrants at sewing machines in dilapidated houses. HomeNet representatives defended their pictures, insisting that it was necessary to get away from the image of homeworkers as victimized dupes who had no power to change their own situation.

Advocates conceded that homeworkers were exploited, but insisted that they could take fate into their own hands, that they had the power to act. Renana Jhabvala, a leader of SEWA, characterized homeworkers as follows:

> Vulnerability makes it very difficult for her to organise. But the extreme pressures have in some ways made such a woman strong. She is able to survive under such crushing conditions only because of her deep faith, her courage, her love for her family and her indomitable will. She is weak, but her weakness is due to the pressures of society. She is weak as a social being in her relations to others, as a political being and in her social status. However, as a person she is strong, for her very social weakness requires that she be strong internally. In order to survive in a desperate struggle as the weakest in society she must develop internal resources of courage and strength. It is these strengths she draws on in the rare cases when she tries to fight back, to organise.[42]

And with some help she did organize, resisting isolation, low wages, and exploitation. Far from being passive victims, homeworkers here emerged as strong and courageous survivors who could fight back.

Using the language of Women in Development, advocates argued that homeworkers made a crucial contribution to family survival. They found that women's home-based work was at least as important as that of male income earners, especially when homeworkers were heads of households. Homeworkers were workers and breadwinners, and it was a matter of justice that an ILO convention recognize this and treat homeworkers as part of the working class. According to Ela Bhatt of SEWA, homeworkers were "not demanding charity but their rightful place in the labor movement."[43]

The Neoclassical Liberal Argument

For employers and governments preaching neoclassical liberal economics, however, post-Fordist society was not (or no longer) organized into antagonistic classes and the labor movement that homeworkers wanted to join a relict of the past. Employers identified four types of homework: pre-industrial, industrial, telework, and mobile professionals. The homeworkers of interest to employers from the North, who dominated in the employer group at the International Labor Conference, were mobile professionals and teleworkers who took advantage of new communications technologies in order to work at home. Telework, the management literature showed, had many advantages: reduced expenses for clothing and meals, reduced travel time and an increase in productivity.[44] According to employers, telework was widely studied but not yet very common. Therefore, it was "premature and inappropriate" to regulate this type of homework which was "dynamic and constantly changing."[45]

In the neoclassical liberal view, teleworkers and professional homeworkers were the prototypes of the flexible labor force of the future. They bore little resemblance to the industrial homeworkers of the early twentieth century, the feminine crafts producers of nation-building countries, or to the ambiguously gendered workers in the informal sector. Instead, these homeworkers were androgynous professionals who, freed of bureaucratic labor regulations, constituted a fount of wealth and progress in the post-Fordist economy. Rather than an evil, the U.S. employers' delegate intoned at the International Labor Conference, homework was "an opportunity to spur economic growth, create jobs, eliminate poverty, increase productivity and provide real options to the traditional workplace."[46] Regulation by contrast would be "counterproductive to meeting the preferences of workers, job-creation, a rising standard of living for workers, business growth and competitiveness."[47] Indeed, in the words of the employers' vice-chairman of the Conference's Committee on Home Work, the homework convention "had little to do with home work as a vehicle for job creation and the alleviation of poverty and had everything . . . to do with creating machinery and bureaucracy to hold back progress."[48] Therefore any attempt to regulate homework needed to be resisted with all means available.

The problem for employers from the North was that the ILO debate engaged, in the words of the delegate from the UK, "language from the 1920s," an "old paradigm," to regulate the flexible workers of the new economy.[49] Their "new paradigm" no longer envisioned exploited women stooped over sewing machines in unhealthy conditions, but androgynous professionals who found new freedom by employing advanced technologies at home. The employer delegate from Canada presented himself as an example. "I am a homeworker," he declared. "My office is at home, and at home I am hooked up with all the high-tech equipment that enables me to function effectively. . . . I happen to have a cottage 15 miles by boat out on an island in the middle of Lake Huron. That place will be my workplace for most of the summer, naturally with all the technical equipment I need." He sneered at the suggestion that his type of a homeworker would need an international convention: "Will the inspector come and visit me at this workplace by taxi boat at great expense to the taxpayer? Will the inspector determine that occupational health and safety rules require that my employer get rid of the bears and rattlesnakes? I am also a long way from a doctor and hospitals. Do I contravene the first-aid regulations?"[50]

With the stigma of the weak and exploited female removed, homeworkers became the stars in a futuristic plot of a technology-based flexible economy, transforming the spatial configurations of private and public, masculine and feminine, that defined spheres of work under Fordism. In this plot the home became the home office, and cottage industry became management from the lodge in the country. Technology had made the Fordist separations of home and work place irrelevant, enabling a new understanding of home as the feminine "private sphere" merged with the masculine "private sector." Ruled by neoclassical liberal economic principles, the new home housed a reconstructed worker: a manager-entrepreneur who had transcended the limiting geography encoded in the home-work distinction.

The Neoliberal Maternalist Argument

Whereas the employers from the North and their focus on professional home-based workers dominated in employer arguments at the Conference, the contributions of Southern employers and some governments were concerned with home-based workers in the informal sector. The themes of job creation and poverty alleviation resonated in the interventions of employers from the South who drew on the language of the informal sector and microenterprises. Their main concern was economic development, and they apparently believed that neoclassical economic liberalism provided the right prescriptions. Associating homework with entrepreneurship and self-employment in the informal sector, they saw excessive regulation as a major obstacle to development and therefore opposed the convention. The employers' delegate from Zimbabwe argued that 40 to 90 percent of workers in developing countries were informal sector workers. The provisions of the convention would force these people underground and destroy their "life-style for survival."[51]

Unlike the arguments of Northern employers, those of Southern employers and some governments often merged neoclassical liberalism with maternalist notions of womanhood. In this rhetoric feminine home-based workers nurtured not their families but their nation's economy by gestating home-grown enterprises. Echoing motherly capacities, the employers' delegate from Panama reminded the 1990 ILO Meeting of Experts that homeworkers were "incubator[s] for enterprises." After all many of the largest U.S. entrepreneurs started out in their homes. Domestic metaphors joined neoclassical logic as the Indian employers' delegate celebrated the virtues of homework in nurturing an economy: "Conceptually home work is . . . the cradle and kindergarten of enterprise; it paves the road to and stabilizes entrepreneurship. . . . it is the fountain spring for small and medium enterprises which spring from the spirit which guides home work. To nip home work in the bud amounts to throwing the baby away with bath water." Feminine homework no longer was backward but progressive: "Unbridled, these provisions [i.e. the convention] would interfere with and jeopardize the genius and culture of domestic establishment, particularly involving women workers."[52]

Such rhetoric created an uncanny new definition of motherhood that married metaphors of care with promises of economic growth. Domestic businesses allowed the realization of national aspirations: the growth of a flourishing domestic economy. Like the maternalist WID arguments this rhetoric reproduced an essentialist notion of femininity that saw motherly caring and income-earning as compatible. However, maternalism here was not an antidote to profit-oriented capitalism. Instead, in a way that the maternalist microenterprise argument had not intended, this rhetoric harnessed domestic ingenuity for the purpose of capital accumulation.

Like unions, feminists, and neoclassical liberals, neoliberal maternalists groped for a better understanding of home-based workers in the context of a post-Fordist global economy and thereby participated in a debate about what it meant to be a worker. There were points of agreement and disagreement. Feminists, neoclassical liberals, and neoliberals joined in rejecting the definition of mothers and income-earning as incompatible, but in different ways. Feminists employed WID rhetoric to insist that women, in addition to being mothers, were *de facto* breadwinners and therefore part of the working class. Neoliberal maternalists framed home-based work not as a feminine activity but a preoccupation of informal sector workers (conceivably both female and male) that brought to bear feminine characteristics of nurturance. The domestic here was not a burden but an asset. Neoclassical liberals, in contrast, refused to discuss homework in gendered terms, creating an androgynous homeworker unencumbered by domestic tasks, a worker for whom the mother-worker dichotomy was irrelevant. Only unions held on to the dichotomy, describing motherly and housewifely obligations as constraints, but also expanding the category worker at the margins to admit subcontracted homeworkers.

Although feminists, neoclassical economic liberals, and neoliberal maternalists thus agreed that the mother-breadwinner dichotomy was not useful to describing flexible employment relations, they agreed on little else. The neoliberal materialists' romantic image of the motherly entrepreneur shared little with the feminist image of women's strength in adversity or with the neoclassical liberal image of the androgynous worker transcending the home-work divide. Furthermore, those who employed these rhetorics arrived at different conclusions concerning the need to regulate homework. Those celebrating motherly entrepreneurs and those advocating androgynous workers found a common cause in neoclassical liberalism and opposed the convention. In contrast, the unions that implicitly defended the mother-breadwinner dichotomy allied with feminists who rejected the opposition to fight for the convention.

The diversity of arguments reflected a shakeup of instruction-rules about the identities of women and workers and the lack of agreement about how gender should be redefined. Gender thus inhered the arguments but assumed contradictory meanings. But equally important in the debate about homework was the issue of class. What was at stake was not only what it meant to be a woman or man, but also what it meant to be a proletarian or a capitalist. Indeed, just as the opposition of masculine and feminine, defined as breadwinner and mother/housewife, came under attack, so too did the opposition between employees and employers.

6 Fordist Class Categories at Issue: Are Homeworkers Employees or Self-Employed?

In the course of the twentieth century, gender defined what it meant to be a worker, as I have shown. But so did the legal notion of employment status by creating the category employee in opposition to employers and the self-employed. Gender and employment status interacted to create historically specific understandings of class. Labor law supported exclusionary definitions of home-based workers as housewives, supplemental earners or microentrepreneurs because it often defined them not as employees (i.e., workers) but self-employed. In this way, it denied them labor rights, protections, and access to benefits that arose from commitment-rules defining the relationship between workers and employers under Fordism.

Post-Fordist labor practices have entailed a weakening of such commitment-rules. Subcontracted, temporary, and other contingent workers typically are considered self-employed and therefore rarely qualify for social security benefits (such as health care and retirement benefits) and job protections (such as protection from arbitrary dismissal). Employment status has therefore become a crucial point of contention in talk about post-Fordist labor relations. This chapter explores debates about the employment status of home-based workers. These debates had as their topic the proper understanding of class relations under a post-Fordist regime of accumulation and the types of commitment-rules that should guide these relations.

The self-employed are marginally integrated into Fordist modes of labor regulation. ILO standards extend to the self-employed the right to organize, and there are recommendations to include them in social security, health, and safety provision where practicable. But in both national and international practice the rights of the self-employed hardly match those of employees. Minimum wage legislation and social insurance schemes rarely include the self-employed; in addition they lack protection against discrimination, job security, and draw few benefits. While some ILO standards acknowledge the desirability of promoting self-employment, they refer primarily to minority populations such as older workers, young people, the disabled, indigenous and tribal populations.[1] Like home-based workers, the self-employed appear as a marginal category within the international labor code. The secular decline in self-employment in the course of the twentieth century may have encouraged such treatment.

In the 1980s, self-employment emerged as part of the new strategies of flexible accumulation and became a new object of state interest. Trends in self-employment reversed in countries that encouraged flexible employment, including the U.S. and the U.K. In addition, virtually all industrialized countries saw a rise in self-employment among women, often concentrated in the service sector. Increased levels of self-employment in developing countries during the 1980s apparently were a countercyclical response to the economic crisis, interrupting but not reversing a secular decline.[2] Yet, they contributed to making self-employment a topic of global talk; the concern with the informal sector and microenterprises added urgency to the matter.

The question whether home-based workers were employees or self-employed lay at the heart of the debate about the Home Work Convention. It also was a matter of contention in ILO technical assistance programs that targeted home-based workers. Frequently the relationship between home-based workers and their work givers is ambiguous. Those who wanted to gain home-based workers Fordist rights and protections, and those who favored union organizing techniques, argued that home-based workers should be defined as employees. Those who saw Fordist rights and protections as an obstacle to economic growth argued that home-based workers should be thought of as self-employed. Many homeworker advocates argued that the distinction between employee and self-employed was itself problematic. Because the International Labor Office's draft convention suggested that homeworkers be treated as employees, the definition of who was a homeworker, i.e. what types of home-based workers should be considered employees, became the major point of contention. Various arguments challenged not only what it meant to be a worker but also what it meant to be an employer or self-employed; they redefined the meaning of class in post-Fordist modes of regulation.

Rules

In 1977, Robert Cox described the organizational ideology of the ILO as "tripartite corporatism," influenced by U.S. managerial ideologies that considered labor relations not as inherently conflictual but favored cooperation between workers and management.[3] Tripartite corporatism championed bargaining between employers and unions and positioned states as mediators. In constructing class oppositions as basically harmonious, it created a condition of heteronomous rule under which workers acquiesced to their own subordination.[4] Indeed, from the perspective of workers, subordination became something to be desired because, by conveying employee status, it offered access to rights. In seeking to create comparable working conditions around the world, employers and unions collaborated in globalizing a tripartite corporatist understanding of class relations based on instruction-rules that defined class as a binary opposition between employers and employees and on commitment-rules that formulated rights and created labor relations as heteronomous rule.

Tripartism built on a constitutive instruction-rule that constructed employers and employees as oppositional. The rule not only described the universe of those who should be the object of the international labor code — industrial workers and their employers — but also defined what workers and employers were: Employers were those who employed workers, and workers were those who subordinated themselves to employers. The liberal legal tradition provided the basis for this definition. It modeled the opposition between employers and employees on the opposition of masters and servants that characterized labor relations in patriarchal household units of the eighteenth century.[5] But masters and servants did not exhaust the universe of labor relations at the time. In seventeenth-century England, multiple employment categories, such as "artificers," "laborers," and "servants," were common; and, when industrial production spread in eighteenth- and nineteenth-century England and America, employers and employees coexisted with the category own-account workers who were conceptualized as owning both means of production and their own labor power. However, labor law increasingly allowed only two categories: employers and employees.[6] Unlike Marxist class categories (ownership of means of production can be depicted on an ordinal scale), the categories employer and employee were binary, mutually exclusive, and created each other. Twentieth-century Fordist labor law, including the international labor code, regulated conduct between employers and employees, and tripartism institutionalized negotiations between representatives of the two. Home-based workers, housewives, farmers, or informal sector workers had no place in this regime. They fell outside its discursive boundaries, and their interests were not represented.

As the opposition between employers and employees came to dominate talk about labor relations, there was a tendency to subsume the self-employed under the category employer. Like employers, they were regarded as autonomous and independent agents who reaped profit from investing their own capital; they differed from employers only in that they also applied their own labor.[7] At the end of the 1940s, the International Conference of Labor Statisticians and the Population and Statistical Commissions of the United Nations asked governments to distinguish four categories of employment status: workers, employers, own-account workers, and unpaid family workers. But governments rarely counted the self-employed separately. Reflecting the primacy of the employer-employee dualism, statisticians found it "not always easy to draw the line between an employer and an own-account worker" who may hire "a charwoman to sweep out his business premises," but acknowledged as well difficulties in distinguishing "between an own-account worker and an employee where, for instance, the individual works on a commission basis or when he [sic] is employed by the day or for a particular task in the home of another person."[8] But government statistical agencies apparently ignored the second problem (finding a way to distinguish between the self-employed and employees) and solved the first problem of distinguishing the self-employed from employers by lumping them together. Changes in legal understandings of firms encouraged the practice. As establishments grew into corporations and even small enterprises increasingly incorporated, employers became employees of corporate entities. Individual employers disappeared, or at least their numbers became statistically insignificant, and the self-employed took their place in labor statistics.

While the research focus on enterprises within the informal sector and on policy interventions for microentrepreneurs furthered an identification of the self-employed as capitalists, home-based workers, informal sector workers, and crafts producers raised the question of the self-employed in a new fashion. These workers did not fit the Fordist categories that interpreted class status as an opposition between employers and employees, and that approximated the self-employed and employers. Global debates on the informal sector increasingly acknowledged that self-employment entailed exploitation in addition to independence and opportunity, and the interventions of homeworker advocates sought to redefine the self-employed as employees. The meaning of self-employment thus became a contested terrain on which to argue the nature of post-Fordist class relations and the proper regulation of post-Fordist labor practices.

Movements

During the ILO debates about homework employers found a common cause in the arguments of the neoclassical liberal movement. Their positions can be interpreted as efforts to institutionalize neoclassical liberal principles that defined economic agents as equals who pursued their optimal interest in an unregulated market. Unaffected by government labor regulations, the self-employed most closely resembled these free agents. In contrast, unions sorted economic agents into Fordist class categories, employers and employees. These agents held unequal positions, and the subordinate position of workers made it necessary to establish rules for their protection. In the view of unions, many self-employed and most home-based workers, were actually disguised wage workers who resembled employees.

Feminist contentions supported union arguments to a certain extent but also differed from unions. Differences derived in part from divergent positions within the tripartite mode of labor regulation. Unions had a role and a high stake in a regulatory structure that they had helped build. Over the course of a century, they had fought for rights which were legitimized by the understanding that unions represented "dependent workers." To be a dependent worker conveyed rights; in the words of an Italian union leader, "to be a dependent worker is not a bad thing."[9] In contrast, legal definitions of dependency and rules regulating wages, working hours, and social security often neglected homeworkers; they were defined as outside the institutional structures of tripartite corporatism and had no voice within these structures. Feminists doubted whether homeworkers could simply be added to existing categories without transforming these categories and, at least for homeworker advocates from India, the debate about self-employment provided the terrain to initiate such a transformation.

Drawing on Gandhi's vision of a rural society based on cooperatives and village industries, SEWA leaders saw in self-employment an ideal to be achieved rather than a dead-end, as union leaders tended to think. While self-employment promised independence, self-sufficiency, and dignity, SEWA leaders understood that the self-employed needed legal protection. Their position in the economy made them vulnerable. They were not like employers, but neither were they subordinate workers, nor did they aspire to subordination. SEWA implicitly rejected the rules of tripartism and the heteronomous rule they implied. In the organization's view the separation between employees and the self-employed was artificial and inappropriate. SEWA organized all informal workers regardless of employment status, including home-based producers, casual workers, and petty vendors. Some were in subcontracting arrangements, some catered to final consumers, and some took jobs from large clients as available. All worked under extremely adverse conditions and in situations with little negotiating power. At the ILO Meeting of Experts, SEWA's Secretary-General advanced a new understanding of class when she pleaded that the definition of a worker should include "whoever contributes to the economy of the country or the household."[10]

Homeworker organizations in Asia typically combined union organizing techniques with microenterprise development to improve the economic position of home-based workers. In Europe, many homeworker advocacy groups followed unions in considering home-based workers disguised wage workers. But some, such as the West Yorkshire Homeworking Group, came to accept microenterprise development as an appropriate strategy for homeworkers through their international contacts, and began to support homeworkers who wanted to set up businesses and cooperatives. The combination of union organizing with microenterprise development denied Fordist constructions of class relations as oppositional, treating self-employment and worker status as compatible.[11]

Homeworker advocates rejected not only the opposition between employees and the self-employed, but also the home-work dichotomy that sustained it. This affected, for example, the development interventions of SEWA. Most cooperative banks gave loans for productive purposes but not for consumption, including housing. In contrast, SEWA recognized that the houses of women in the informal sector often were workplaces, so that investing in housing was productive investment. Indeed, housing loans were the most common type of loan the SEWA Bank extended to home-based workers.[12] Home-based employment and self-employment thus required policies and interventions that ruptured oppositional Fordist instruction-rules.

Commitment-Rules, Class, and Gender

Demanding rights for home-based workers revealed the degree to which Fordist commitment-rules enacted a spatial and temporal order that separated work and family, paid work and unpaid work, work and leisure, segregating the sphere of socially regulated labor from private work, the "wage-slave" from the "domestic servant."[13] Labor rights and development practices formulated on the basis of this order made little sense for those who violated the spatial separation of home and work. Speculations about how to gain home-based workers access to worker rights and benefits revealed the obstacles that labor laws and development interventions formulated on the home-work opposition posed for "atypical" workers.[14]

Improving the puny wages of home-based workers was a high priority for all who wanted to regulate home-based work. But how could one ensure minimum wages where payment was usually by the piece? With the exception of states that set up wages boards before the Second World War, few governments prescribed minimum piece rates; minimum wage laws typically set hourly, weekly, or monthly rates. But employers of homeworkers rarely translated piece-rates into time-rates, and trying to do so caused considerable difficulty. Because their "work-time" and their "home-time" interwove, homeworkers did not work in an uninterrupted fashion. Consider the lament of a homeworker in Wisconsin who processed insurance claims and had to keep track of her working time by noting interruptions: "You are working at home with small children, and you are always interrupted for 'Mommy can I have a snack? Can I have this?' You have to write down the time you stop and the time you start up again. I have time sheets a foot long [at] times."[15] Because paid and unpaid work took place in the same space, they also interwove temporally, that is, time spend on income-earning was imbricated with time spent on mothering and domestic work. For most employers of homeworkers, the logical solution was to pay piece-rates. But Fordist wage laws did not account for this reality; they included the presumption that paid and unpaid time, work and home, were clearly demarcated.

The question of homeworkers' wages raised another issue. Their expenses included not only their labor time but also costs deriving from the use of their homes as workplaces. Should homeworkers be reimbursed for these expenses? Should not employers subsidize the rents or mortgages of home-workers whose productivity and quality of work after all was related to the quality and size of their homes? Furthermore, should payments to home-workers cover expenditures such as heat and electricity? If employers shared the cost of maintaining homes, did they gain new rights in relation to their workers' homes? For example, did they gain rights of access to homes for purposes of supervision or inspection?

The question of health and safety regulations, together with the notion of "occupational health" created a series of additional questions. The notion of occupational health presumed a workplace separate from homes that af-fected the health of workers. What did occupational health mean where the home provided the spatial context for the occupation? Did the employers have any obligation toward the health of workers? If so, how was it possible to separate occupational health from other health? For example, SEWA had to struggle with the question whether problems such as backaches, pain in the limbs and shoulders, exhaustion, dizziness, eye problems, and gyneco-logical problems resulted from the occupations of homeworkers or from other circumstances. Did they stem from unfavorable working conditions or unfavorable living conditions?[16] Since the two were the same, SEWA re-searchers argued that "our policy approach should be not that a certain occupation causes certain problems but that women doing this type of work do suffer from a particular range of problems."[17] The job could not be sepa-rated from the person; the whole person had to become the health concern of those interested in the home-based worker.

Fordist regulations about leaves, social and employment security enacted rules that temporally separated home and work by demarcating paid and unpaid time, employment and unemployment. They were problematic for flexible workers whose flexibility meant precisely overcoming the boundary between work and nonwork, to move easily from paid time to unpaid time. How could the law provide employment security and prevent arbitrary dis-missal in a type of work arrangement that built on such flexibility? Would the application of such laws not destroy home-based work itself? Further-more, should homeworkers qualify for unemployment benefits? How would one know when a homeworker was unemployed; after all their work was irregular by definition. Should laws regarding working hours and legal hol-idays apply? How could those be enforced? After all homeworkers were free to work wherever, whenever, and however long they wanted. Should home-based workers qualify for annual leave? How could one ensure that they did not take in homework from another work giver while on annual leave? Should homeworkers qualify for sick leave and maternity leave? But what if the illness or pregnancy started on a day on which the homeworker did not have an order? Or what if the homeworker did jobs for several employers? Who should provide the benefit? Finally, how could homeworkers qualify for social security protection given common requirements that a worker must have worked continuously for a given time period before qualifying for benefits?[18]

Thus, speculations about extending labor rights to homeworkers raised a long list of difficult questions. They illustrated the degree to which Fordist commitment-rules included instruction-rules about spatial and temporal separations of home and work, reproduction and production, unpaid work and paid work. Gender informed these separations, as shown in previous chapters, but they also interwove constructions of class as an opposition between employers and employees. The spatial separation of home and work enabled an understanding of workers as dependent and subordinate employee, and labor law reproduced the separation.

Employees Are to Work as the Self-Employed Are to Home? Space and Class in Labor Law

Throughout the twentieth century, there has been considerable diversity both within and between countries in the ways in which they have distinguished employees from the self-employed. When the International Labor Office researched the question of employment contracts in the 1930s, it found that definitions were often attached to specific social policies and different branches of law, and were formulated in such a way as to meet the intent of such policies or laws. This is still the case today; definitions of employment status are diverse and sometimes contradictory even within countries. For example, in the U.S., the Internal Revenue Service (IRS) typically applies common law criteria (which are discussed below) to gauge whether someone is to be considered an employee for tax purposes, whereas courts, in matters of wages and working hours, follow the statutory definition of the Fair Labor Standards Act (FLSA). The result is that the IRS considers as self-employed some homeworkers who would be employees under the criteria of the FLSA. In Britain, courts have similarly determined that homeworkers are employees according to certain labor laws, while Inland

Revenue has arrived at the opposite conclusion.[19] In the 1930s, the complexity of member state practices led the ILO to abandon the effort to develop general principles that characterized employment contracts internationally.[20]

The diversity of national applications makes it difficult to generalize about the messages included in determinations of employment status. While colonialism spread the European common law and continental law traditions throughout the world,[21] this invariably entailed local adaptations and modifications. Labor law finds its application in national courts and there are many idiosyncrasies. In the absence of a broad global debate about employment status the following discussion draws extensively on U.S. and European literature to investigate the issue of employment status from the particular standpoint of home-based workers. This discussion provides the necessary background to assess ILO debates about defining homework and shows the degree to which legal rules concerning employment status in the West are implicated in the home-work separation.

The ILO survey in the 1930s found that states commonly relied on two tests of employment status to determine whether someone was an employee or self-employed: the test of "technical dependence," and the test of "economic dependence."[22] These apparently are still the most common tests of employment status today. In cases of dispute, they rarely provide hard and fast decisions but their application (often in combination) offers guidelines. Because they are designed to identify a worker as either an employee or self-employed, they realize the rule that defines the universe of Fordist labor regulation around the dualistic relationship between employer and employee. Not surprisingly, the tests are problematic for those who violate the home-work dichotomy that buttresses understandings of what it means to be an employee.

Under common law, the test of technical dependence is generally known as the control test. Throughout most of the twentieth century this test was overriding, in both the continental and common law traditions. It stipulates that a worker is an employee if she or he is under the control of an employer. Judges ask whether an employer directly supervises the worker, whether the employer controls hours of work, place of work, and the manner in which a worker organizes the work process. Because those who work at home are not under the direct supervision of employers and because such supervision is possible only in an office or factory situation, the control test has often failed home-based workers.[23] In contemporary contexts, where home-based workers are globally defined as marginal workers, application of the control test has led judges and agencies to call them self-employed. In the 1930s, when home-based workers were defined as outside the working class, the ILO researcher who surveyed employment contracts suggested that "the protection of workers of this kind [i.e. homeworkers] lies outside the scope of the statutory regulation of the contract of employment and is a special social task carried out by special methods."[24] Home as the location of work prevented an identification as employee.

The control test does not inevitably lead to a definition of home-based workers as self-employed. Some have argued that employers may not directly control home-based workers, but do have the *right* to control them; therefore these workers are employees.[25] This criterion overcomes the spatial requirements of the control test by realizing the power that a work giver has over a homeworker. A crucial indicator of the right to control is that an employer can withhold future work. Furthermore, the continental legal tradition adds to the control test the criterion of direction, i.e., whether a work giver provides direction about the manner in which an item should be produced. Industrial homeworkers clearly are under the direction of their work givers; but the issue is ambiguous in the case of skilled subcontracted workers employed in a post-Fordist setting as well as of artisans who use traditional skills but also may depend on a merchant.

For the ILO of the 1930s, economic dependence merely provided the background to technical dependence. But where homeworkers are concerned today, lawyers and laws frequently employ tests of economic dependence in addition to technical dependence. The U.S. Fair Labor Standards Act takes economic dependence as the main indicator of eligibility for coverage. It thereby overcomes the gendered notions of space in the control test. Courts have interpreted FLSA to apply to all workers that are economically dependent as judged by a number of criteria including "skill, capital investment, opportunity for profit or risk of loss [footnote deleted], degree of control by the employer, performance of work as part of integrated unit of the employer's business, and permanency and exclusivity of the relationship."[26] Legal rules in various other countries deem homeworkers to be employees or have employee-like status if they invest little capital (Germany), do not provide raw materials (France), have a relatively permanent relationship with the work giver, do all the work themselves, take risks, have the chance to profit or lose, or do work which is part of the regular business of the work giver (Britain, Israel, India).[27] When several of these criteria are combined, the test typically identifies as employees industrial homeworkers as well as most artisans, micro-entrepreneurs, and independent contractors. It is thus more likely than the control test to gain home-based workers labor rights.

But the economic dependence test is problematic for another reason, one that reveals the oppositional construction of employees and the self-employed itself as untenable. The test lacks logical rigor and potentially defines everyone as an employee: "By providing no plausible stopping point, the test potentially opens the way to proclaiming the existence of universal dependency in the guise of universal interdependency."[28] Judges and lawyers therefore have used the economic dependence test primarily to complement the control test. But universal dependence may indeed be the best way to characterize conditions of work in a global economy where the concentration of capital overwhelms any assets even the richest individual may hold, where employers progressively dismantle job securities for their workers, and where even workers who invest no capital increasingly appear as self-employed. In such a context, the main difference in terms of risk-taking between the self-employed and the employee is that one may be guaranteed her wages for a week while the other is guaranteed her wages for a day: "How a buffer of one day's or one week's wages . . . can qualitatively distinguish the employee from the self-employee [sic] is unclear."[29]

Carried to its logical conclusion, the economic dependence test thus unravels the dichotomous class construction formulated as an opposition between employers/self-employed and employees. Where workers who violate the home-work opposition make the control test inapplicable, the determination of employment status becomes virtually impossible. During ILO debates about the homework convention, employers used this insight to argue a neoliberal vision of labor relations in which class had vanished. This vision entailed a full-scale attack on Fordist modes of labor regulation and on the institution of tripartism.

Attacking Tripartism

While the Home Work Convention constituted a clear victory for home-worker advocates and their union allies, their victory was tenuous. The International Labor Conference adopted the convention over the fierce opposition of employer delegates, and two years after its passage no state had either signed or ratified it. Furthermore, the refusal of employers to participate in redrafting the convention constituted an attack on the principles of tripartism. It signaled the degree to which employers, informed by the rules of neoclassical liberal economics, had disengaged from tripartite forms of interest intermediation and from Fordist commitments. Certainly the ILO's Director General understood that the employers' tactics attacked the foundations of Fordist regulations: "It seems to me that if this kind of situation were to occur again, it could jeopardize the very principle of tripartism from which the ILO's instruments draw most of their strength. . . . Perhaps the time has come to put what, with time perhaps, will seem like a storm in a teacup in a broader perspective and undertake a new and thorough analysis of the standard-setting function of the International Labour Organization."[30]

While the Director General was particularly concerned about employer tactics, the employers' arguments should have been equally worrisome, constituting no less a threat to tripartism. Employers did participate in written exchanges between the ILO and its tripartite constituencies, in the various meetings that led up to the 1996 International Labor Conference, and in debates relating to the recommendation that accompanied the convention. In these discussions, the main target of the employers' attack was the definition of homeworker, i.e. instruction-rules about what it meant to be a worker. They insisted that it was impossible to define homeworkers and that therefore a convention would be meaningless.

The convention defined homework as follows:

The term "home work" means work carried out by a person, to be referred to as a homeworker,

(i) in his or her home or in other premises of his or her choice other than the workplace of the employer;

(ii) for remuneration;

(iii) which results in a product or service as specified by the employer, irrespective of who provides the equipment, materials or other inputs used,

unless this person has the degree of autonomy and of economic independence necessary to be considered an independent worker under national laws, regulations or court decisions.[31]

The definition combines aspects of the control test and the economic dependence test. It first specifies the location where homework is taking place as any "other than the workplace of the employer," because an employer can exercise direct control only at a workplace he or she provides. To distinguish homework from home-based subsistence production, it then stipulates that the work has to be "for remuneration." Item (iii) adds the criterion of "direction" which is common in labor codes following the continental law tradition, and adds that a worker may still be a homeworker even if she provides inputs and owns some tools (i.e., means of production); this is commonly the case among seamstresses who own their sewing machines and provide thread needed to assemble precut cloth. The last sentence then introduces the economic dependence test, specifying that only those who are economically dependent can be considered homeworkers.

The problems identified above with these tests reappeared in the arguments of employers to justify a neoclassical liberal agenda. The employers' main problem with the definition, according to their vice-chairperson in the Committee on Home Work, was that it did not distinguish "homeworkers from truly independent workers."[32] The problem lay with the test of economic dependence. The United States Council for International Business, which apparently carried considerable weight in the employers' group, stated the issue quite clearly in its comments to the Office: "Because virtually no one is ever truly autonomous or economically independent, virtually no worker could be considered an independent contractor under the Convention."[33] The U.S. employers' delegate, an IBM executive, warned the Conference that under the definition "many persons and enterprises who have up to now considered themselves customers could find themselves redefined as employers of persons who are in reality employees of their vendors and suppliers" with the effect that "essentially commercial disputes between independent parties" are turned into labor disputes.[34] The employers' adviser from the United Kingdom pushed the argument further: "I know of almost no consultant or professional or even entrepreneur who is economically independent of his or her clients, and has a high degree of autonomy."[35]

While in these arguments employers sought to show that the notion of the employee made no sense in post-Fordist labor practices, they inadvertently acknowledged that true self-employment had become impossible as well. Once the workplace, and thereby certain aspects of technical dependence or control, lost their significance as indicators of subordination, the terrain was open to identify a multitude of other dependents worthy of protection. If legal tests could not show independence, then a convention demanding the protection of home-based workers constituted a first step toward holding capital accountable for an even broader mass of workers than covered under Fordist regulations.

The convention was innovative in another respect: it defined what was meant by an employer. No such definition had been necessary under tripartism because employers were defined by the mere existence of employees. Indeed, one employer delegate argued at the conference, the definition was obvious, i.e. "he or she employed people."[36] In this argument employers existed only under the old regime where there were clearly defined employees. As employees mutated into independent workers in a regime of flexible accumulation, employers disappeared as well. But the convention instead specified that an employer was someone who gave out homework. This definition broadened the responsibility of capital, creating commitments to a new type of worker.

Homework practices introduced another actor that had no identity in Fordist labor regulations: the intermediary. The homework convention acknowledged intermediaries but failed to provide a definition. Employers took this as one more indication that a homework situation could not be defined. The employers' vice-chairman in the Committee on Home Work suggested: "He or she [the intermediary] could be an employer, an employee of an employer, a subcontractor or even a homeworker."[37] Indeed, various governments disapproved of including the term intermediary in the convention because national law differed significantly on the issue: some countries prohibited intermediaries, some gave them the same status as homeworkers, some considered them to be employers. Thus, when applied to what employers saw as a commercial relationship, the terminology of Fordist labor relations led, from the employers' perspective, to a preposterous confusion of sellers, firms, and employers on the one hand and clients, contractors, and employees on the other. Homeworkers and intermediaries stood somewhere in the middle, impossible to categorize.

The employers' fanfare about defining homework was much more than a strategy to block an annoying new regulation. Clearly the issue of homework struck at the core of a new mode of regulation for a global economy based on flexible production. Homework provided employers an opportunity to advance their understanding of class relations under post-Fordism, and that understanding no longer included employees subordinate to and dependent on an employer. Where the gendered home no longer served to identify work, employees and the self-employed could no longer be distinguished, and contracts of employment became an outdated mode of regulating labor relations.

Although they pursued vastly different agendas, some homeworker advocates, especially those representing SEWA, tended to share the employers' doubts about defining home-based workers as employees. While advocates did not voice their qualms about definitions in the international arena, in part so as not to antagonized their union allies, their local practices spoke loudly. In technical assistance projects ILO officers encountered the ambiguous employment realities of home-based workers in Asia and had to struggle with the issue of how to treat these workers. Ultimately, the ILO's projects geared toward home-based workers became pockets where tripartism was suspended.

Technical Assistance: Suspending Tripartism

In the global debate about a new mode of labor regulation, the International Labor Office played an ambiguous role. On the one hand it functioned as a defender of tripartism, especially in its standard-setting practices. On the other hand, there were voices within the Office that questioned the appropriateness of Fordist instruction-rules and were complicit in validating alternative interpretations. These voices emerged in particular in the area of technical assistance. Feminists in the Programme on Rural Women of the Office's Rural Employment Policies Branch instigated projects for home-based workers that were instructive in both regards. While the projects sought to respond to interpretations of reality emerging from the grassroots, they also had to navigate the ideology of headquarters, and instruction-rules about what it meant to be a home-based worker became a source of contention.

The purpose of the Programme on Rural Women was to achieve "sustainable self-reliant livelihood for rural women workers."[38] Even though it was institutionalized within a bureaucracy, the Programme enacted relatively radical feminist movement principles. "One should be under no illusion," Programme officers argued, "that any substantial progress can be made [in the status of women] without some very basic alterations in society."[39] The Programme supported a diverse range of projects from wasteland development to improving cooking efficiency to organizing home-based workers. Projects challenged gendered rules, laws, and prejudices, and aimed at changing power relations within households. Most sought to link women worker activists with government bureaucrats and agents of civil society to facilitate a process of raising consciousness, changing perceptions and social norms.

In line with feminist critiques of the disempowering effects of positivist research and paternalistic welfare projects, Programme officers made participation of poor women a crucial element of the projects they sponsored. They tended to consider rural women not targets of development designed for them by outside experts but members of the women's movement deserving solidarity in a shared struggle against exploitative patriarchal structures. This approach required collaboration with local grassroots organizations that would organize women workers to do their own development "so that the process of development itself can be altered."[40] SEWA was one organization the Programme worked with and that came to define its approach to home-based workers.

In SEWA rhetoric, program officers explicitly encountered challenges to the identities that constituted the tripartite universe of labor relations, in particular challenges to the definition of employees and the self-employed as mutually exclusive categories. SEWA had grown out of the union movement and considered itself a union. But it was an unusual one, combining organizing strategies that yielded strength through numbers with support for economic ventures to increase the level of self-reliance among its members. In the words of its leaders, SEWA combined "struggle and development." Acting like a union, SEWA demanded (often successfully) that labor inspectors remedy violations of labor laws, that governments set minimum wages in certain industries, and that they intervene to stop police harassment of small vendors. SEWA also lobbied for federal legislation that would ensure minimum wages and protections for home-based workers. On the other hand, SEWA acted like a development organization when it sought to strengthen the economic self-reliance of its members, provided bank loans to individual members and formed trade, production, and service cooperatives. It considered cooperatives the basic units of an alternative economic system under the control of workers.

SEWA organizers saw union struggle and microenterprise and cooperative development not as contradictory strategies, one appropriate for dependent employees, the other for the self-employed, but as mutually supporting. When its cooperatives paid higher wages than the traders, they put upward pressure on everybody's wages in the industry. Cooperatives also provided jobs for members who lost work as a result of their organizing activities. They gave access to crucial inside information about changes in the industry that helped in union bargaining. And SEWA leaders found that cooperatives softened the confrontational image of the union, gaining it favor in the public and the press. The cooperatives benefitted from their association with the union because it provided mass support in cooperative demands for government action (e.g., to reserve waste from government textile mills for the quilt-sewers' cooperative) in addition to legal advice and representation. Running a bank allowed SEWA members savings accounts while also putting the organization on a more independent footing. Furthermore, the bank allowed poor women to build assets over which they exercised control, giving them a more secure position within the patriarchal family economy.[41]

Under a project to support self-employment schemes for female heads of household, the Programme on Rural Women provided funds to SEWA in the late 1980s to monitor the application and enforcement of labor laws in India as they pertained to home-based piece-rate workers.[42] It took some prodding to convince SEWA to target "work which has been moved from the formal to the informal sector, i.e. from the factory to the home through a subcontracting system; and . . . small scale piece-rate workers who produce traditional items for middlemen," and to exclude from the project "own account workers who are not dependent on a contract system."[43] This was quite contrary to SEWA's philosophy not to segregate the self-employed and dependent workers because they were equally disadvantaged. But, for an ILO project, it was necessary to remain within the rules of tripartism that clearly distinguished dependent workers from independent entrepreneurs.

SEWA targeted bidi rollers in Indore and ready-made-garment workers in Ahmedabad. It used participatory action research to find out about the employment conditions of homeworkers and at the same time develop links with potential organizers and community leaders. SEWA also conducted legal camps with the purpose of making homeworkers aware that they were employees and letting them know of their eligibility for minimum wages and welfare benefits.[44] The goal was to move homeworkers toward an identity as workers. With that identity they could claim the rights of employees. In restricting its activities under the auspices of the project to a narrowly defined group of subcontracted workers, SEWA avoided conflict with the ILO's rules of tripartism.

But the Rural Women's Programme encountered resistance in some sections of the International Labor Office when it sought to replicate the SEWA approach in other countries. The criticism concerned the distinction between employees and the self-employed. In reviewing a draft proposal on "employment promotion and social and legal protection of home-based workers in Asia,"[45] the Office's International Labor Standards Department found anomalies deriving from the ambiguous status of homeworkers. In a remarkably circular argument the reviewer illustrated the tight boundaries that tripartite rules had created around the field of labor relations and its exclusionary character:

> Even in countries with developed and (relatively) sophisticated trade union systems—and high levels of membership—it has proved quite impossible to establish effective trade union structures amongst home workers. . . . Furthermore, trade union organisation is not an end in itself. Rather, it is a sine qua non of effective collective bargaining. A further essential pre-recognition [sic] of effective collective bargaining is an "employer" or an "employer organisation" with whom the "union" can "bargain." Employer organisations are few and far between in the home-work sector, even in developed economies, and the "employers" are often too small to engage in meaningful collective bargaining in their own right.[46]

In arguing that the purpose of unions was to bargain with employers, the quote affirmed the employer-employee opposition as defining the field of labor relations. This allowed the author to disparage the proposal to create homeworker organizations. Because there were no employer organizations with whom they could bargain, there was no legitimate cause for the existence of homeworker organizations. In a class structure defined by the opposition of employers and employees, creating class organizations for home-based workers was meaningless. Quotation marks indicated the problematic fit of tripartite identities and practices for home-based workers.

Despite these kinds of attempts to discipline, feminists within the Office were able to secure funding for a project on homeworkers in Thailand, Indonesia, and the Philippines, starting in 1988, and entitled Rural Women Workers in the New Putting Out System. The project targeted "poor women workers . . . in domestic outwork on a putting-out basis," that were distinguished from self-employed home-based workers.[47] Like SEWA, implementing agencies would offer some assistance to strengthen self-employment, such as credit, access to raw materials and markets; the assumption was, however, that "only a minority of homeworkers could possibly develop into entrepreneurs and self-employed,"[48] and that therefore it was necessary to emphasize other types of assistance, including awareness raising, improving the legal status of homeworkers, and organizing homeworkers into unions.

The project thus made porous the boundary between employees and the self-employed while holding on to an understanding of home-based workers as disguised employees that could be subsumed under the international labor code.

But the dynamics of the implementation process foiled the planners' intentions. The issue of defining homeworkers haunted the project throughout its various phases. Initial research found that homeworkers in Thailand and the Philippines fell into three groups: labor-only subcontracting; consignment (market-subcontracting); and self-employment/microentrepreneurs. Labor-only subcontractors sold their labor only and were paid by the piece; market subcontractors provided labor in addition to other miscellaneous inputs in the production process; the self-employed constituted the residual category comprising all other home-based workers. Researchers found that homeworkers frequently moved from one category to the other.[49] A technical meeting convened in June of 1989 failed to resolve the issue of definition. Participants agreed that the project should use both the three-way classification introduced by researchers as well as the ILO working definition that distinguished workers in the putting-out system from the self-employed.[50] But the two definitions were contradictory since the ILO clearly opposed the self-employed and home-based workers and was ambiguous with regard to "consignment subcontracting." At a second technical meeting in May of 1991, the issue surfaced again. There was a strong push to include self-employed homeworkers in the project. Organizers from the Philippines, where a vibrant organization of homeworkers had sprung up under the auspices of the project, argued that self-employed home-based workers were highly vulnerable to market forces and should receive protection and support. Yet, ILO officials at the meeting kept reminding participants of the ILO definition, insisting that "there is a distinction between self-employed and homebased work."[51]

Here external forces intervened. An interim project evaluation, while praising the project for having been successful in organizing home-based workers, criticized that there had been no progress on the project's main indicator of success, i.e. an "increase in income and benefits of women engaged in home-based production of commodities."[52] It recommended that project administrators shift focus toward socioeconomic projects, i.e., creating cooperatives and revolving loan funds. National politics in addition encouraged project personnel to put more emphasis on income-generating activities. In Indonesia and the Philippines, there was apprehension over the formation of homeworker unions. The Indonesian government severely restricted freedom of association and put considerable obstacles in the way of the project, from requiring research permits to changing questionnaires of action researchers.[53] Not surprisingly, a study sponsored by the government under the umbrella of the project described home-based workers as "predominantly self-employed" and as having "capital of their own to engage in microenterprises."[54] The NGO which the ILO had contracted to implement the Indonesian project component navigated between these requirements. It initiated organizing activities in East Java, seeking to create on the one hand "a vehicle for collective bargaining" and "develop ideal employer-employee relationship[s]," and on the other hand provide "skills training, revolving funds, and business management tutorials."[55] In the Philippines as well government officials expressed their fear that agitation of workers would aggravate insurgencies.[56] Here the project had been successful in creating an active national organization of home-based workers, the PATAMABA, and the shift toward socioeconomic activities became particularly noticeable.[57]

But the insistence that homeworkers include the self-employed as well as dependent workers was not simply a means to pacify nervous governments. It also reflected the reality of the situation of poor women workers in South East Asia and their particular insertion into a global regime of flexible accumulation. Debates around the project on Rural Women Workers in the New Putting-Out System repeated over and over the instruction-rule that homeworkers were either subcontracted or self-employed and that regardless of status, they were vulnerable. Furthermore, there was a broad understanding that socioeconomic assistance needed to accompany organizing for legal protection and wage bargaining. In effect, the project created a terrain where the rules of tripartism increasingly were suspended; it became a laboratory for experimenting with strategies to empower home-based workers under conditions of flexible accumulation. In this laboratory interventions considered appropriate for Fordist entrepreneurs, such as credit, training, and marketing assistance, mingled with union organizing tactics, efforts to change labor laws and ensure their application. Organizers and project officers held in abeyance the constitutive rules of Fordism as interventions and agitations drew on local definitions of need in the name of women's empowerment.

In sum, feminist contentions in the global debates about homework destabilized constitutive categories of tripartism, the rules defining the opposition between employee and self-employed and those defining the opposition between work and home. The advocates painted home-based women workers as vulnerable, yet organized, members of a productive work force who deserved protection regardless of whether they were employees or self-employed and regardless of whether work and home merged in their workplace, their health needs, or their working hours. Neoclassical liberal employers similarly destabilized the opposition between dependent workers and the self-employed, but they did so in order to argue the counterproductive nature of labor regulation and paint the vision of a future in which workers became suppliers, "independent" contractors, and entrepreneurs toward whom capital had little responsibility. The effect of both arguments was to undermine dichotomous Fordist instruction-rules about what it means to be a worker, employer, woman, or man. Just as the debate on homework was at the core of debates about the creation of the welfare state at the beginning of the century, it has surfaced as the stone that whets arguments in the struggle for new rules to regulate labor under conditions of flexible accumulation. In the process, gender and class will emerge redefined.

7   Studying Global Politics

The purpose of this study was to show that, in the course of the twentieth century, social movements created historically specific understandings of womanhood and manhood in global arguments and thereby enacted a different kind of power politics than that described in state-centric International Relations. The arguments about home-based work in the ILO and in other global fora distributed advantage by constructing gender and class. Movement struggle about identities and rights was a struggle over power that transcended state boundaries. In global understandings, feminine propriety before World War II meant being motherly, maintaining an orderly home, and keeping paid work out of the home. Because working at home disturbed order and motherhood, home-based workers could not be "real" workers or part of the working class and they had no right to paid work. In the 1960s and 1970s, nation-building rhetoric and development practices fostered interpretations of womanhood as domestic and of women's home-based work as marginal in newly independent countries. Home-based crafts production was created as primordial, a source of identity for the nation. The equal rights movement challenged the devaluation of women's work as early as the 1920s, but its interpretations of women as equal in value and capability to men did not gain wide currency until the late twentieth century. Around the issue of women's home-based work, global debates charted a new course of post-Fordist labor regulation where women's equality became a legitimizer for the dismantling of Fordist labor rights.

In broad outlines, my analysis confirms the interpretations of those who have described a shift in the ILO from a concern with protective legislation based on an understanding of women as different to policies that emphasize the rights of women as equals to men.[1] My analysis adds to these interpretations by identifying ambiguities in global debates and locating them in conflicting rules. The equal-rights language common in official United Nations documents since the 1950s obscured the persistence of instruction-rules that continued to define women above all else as mothers and as deserving different treatment. My analysis also contributes to existing interpretations by reaching beyond the ILO, tracing the multiple meanings of difference and equality at the intersection of different social movements operating at the global level. In the conversations of these global networks, gender emerges in diverse and often contradictory ways to support sometimes opposing policies.

Difference meant different things in different contexts. The construction of women as different in the arguments of European and North American reformers seeking the creation of welfare states carried an array of meanings that shared little with constructions of women as different in the arguments of nation-builders in newly independent states of Africa and Asia. While efforts to involve states in regulating the economy fostered an understanding of home-based workers as decrepit in the European and North American debates of the early twentieth century, the rhetoric of nation-building in the Asian and African contexts of the 1950s and 1960s created women and their crafts as representing tradition and the cherished values of the nation, but also, in an ambiguous fashion, as the symbols of backwardness.

One challenge for this study was to develop a theoretical framework that met the emancipatory intentions of my feminist standpoint while at the same time enabling empirical investigation. To remain true to activist concerns, I located constructions of gender in the contentious politics of social movements. I postulated that movement politics were politics about rules and that an understanding of global politics as social construction shed light on global constructions of gender. In the following I assess the promises and shortcomings of this theoretical orientation in light of the foregoing analysis.

The Promise of Constructivism

By focussing on rules, rather than strategies, agendas, and legal outcomes, I was able to move away from the opposition between the domestic and the international to document social processes in a global space. Gender constructions emerged as global in the sense that they arose from the arguments of diverse sets of influentials who "met" (not necessarily face-to-face) as movement activists or as officers of nongovernmental, intergovernmental and governmental organizations. Notions of gender pervaded the rhetoric of reformers demanding state intervention into labor markets in the early twentieth century, of postcolonial leaders seeking to build nations, of technocrats and grassroots activists championing the informal sector, and of activists and neoliberals negotiating a post-Fordist mode of labor regulation. The arguments of these influentials sustained global rules but also challenged them.

Distinguishing different types of rules provided a powerful tool for interpreting movement politics. Movements played a crucial role in challenging and facilitating the institutionalization of instruction-rules—those that defined identities, and it is here that the power of movements was most evident. For example, the failure of U.S. women in the 1940s to achieve ILO action on homework was in part related to the fact that equal rights feminists had destabilized global instruction-rules about women as motherly. Despite its material capabilities and its willingness to direct international politics on homework, the U.S. was unsuccessful in creating directives and fighting instruction-rules that increasingly defined women as equal workers. The feminist movement was powerful, not because of its capabilities, but because it was able to reinterpret what it meant to be a worker.

Disentangling different types of rules helped me offer a rich picture of the way movements intersect. Instruction-rules enabled the formulation of labor rights, i.e., they enabled the creation of particular commitment-rules. Fordist labor rights leaned heavily on instruction-rules of workers as masculine and located outside the home, excluding those who worked at home. In the 1990s, the neoclassical liberal movement as well as the women's movement attacked these Fordist instruction-rules and the labor rights (commitment-rules) they made possible. But while advocates for home-based workers and advocates of neoclassical economic liberalism agreed that instruction-rules separating home and work, and the related concepts of employee and self-employed, were problematic and outdated, they disagreed about the status of commitment-rules. Homeworker advocates sought to expand commitment-rules that defined worker rights while neoclassical liberal employers sought to undermine such rules.

In the relationship between the feminist and the labor movement the issue was reversed. Although feminists and unions united in the fight to extend labor rights to home-based workers, they often employed contradictory instruction-rules. Some union men supported equal rights feminists in their demands for equal pay in the 1920s because they wanted to eliminate competition from workers they considered naturally inferior. These union men believed women workers were less effective than men, so that equal pay laws would reduce the demand for women workers. In contrast, equal rights feminists believed that women workers were as good as men and would therefore benefit from equal pay laws. In the 1990s, the instruction-rules the two movements relied on differed again as unions projected an image of home-based workers as exploited victims while advocates celebrated the tenacity of these workers. Yet they joined in arguing for an international convention on homework formulating commitments toward home-based workers.

The focus on rules allowed me to document the power of activism in global politics. The two waves of the women's movement, the labor movement, the nationalist movement, and the neoclassical liberal movement all surfaced as crucial forces in my narrative of global politics. If global politics are indeed contentions about rules, then movement activists play a much larger role than that of the hopeless utopians or "idealists" that state-centric analysts assign them. Movements are a source of identification and provide a venue for the institutionalization of alternative worlds.

However, there are weaknesses in my focus on movements. Most importantly, it did not provide me the tools to assess why and how certain interpretations came to override others. This was especially troublesome in my analysis of the contemporary debate about a post-Fordist labor regime. Why did neoclassical liberalism carry the day in the 1980s and not the strategies of those who called for a reduction of labor time and the separation of basic welfare rights from the employment relationship? Clearly, to answer this and similar questions, it is necessary to explore systemic forces in the global polity—forces that have their origins in rules but have become so highly institutionalized that they appear to be outside of history and contention.

The focus on movements furthermore skewed my analysis in highlighting politics targeting instruction-rules more than politics involving other types of rules. Directives and commitment-rules often become the focus of politics in more organized settings, including during periods when movement activism is subdued. The two decades after the Second World War constituted one such period. In this context the contentious politics of movements institutionalized and the weight of global politics shifted from movements to organizations. A one-sided emphasis on movements may hide the way in which commitment-rules actualize, i.e., the mechanisms through which workers claim rights in situations that typically are highly institutionalized. Because home-based workers had few rights in the global polity in the course of this century, my focus on movements and instruction-rules was appropriate. But the Home Work Convention signaled a step toward the institutionalization of fundamental rights for home-based workers. Assuring the application of the convention and thereby the rights of home-based workers most likely will take place in courts, government agencies, and through the advocacy of highly organized sections of the homeworker movement, including advocacy groups and unions.[2] A pure focus on movement activism and changing instruction-rules would risk missing these processes.

The Global, the Local, and the Universal

Within the disciplinary frame of International Relations, the sovereign state provides the spatial demarcation of inside and outside, separating "politics" from "relations." Because the state is defined territorially, there are actual locales—capitals and the headquarters of international organizations—containing the practices that count as political in state-centric scholarship. In this way, states create places that facilitate a researcher's task of empirical investigation. Displacing the state as the constitutive concept of international politics opens the view to other places but also raises practical problems. Conversations about home-based work are everywhere and in this sense the spatial image of such politics more appropriately is that of a network of connected individuals than that of states meeting like billiard balls. But such networks are difficult to trace, leaving the analyst to search for venues that reflect debates taking place in these networks.

In this study, instead of tracking a dispersed debate, I took a shortcut by analyzing discussions in the orbit of an interstate organization, the ILO, venturing that they reflected a cross-section of global arguments. There are advantages and disadvantages to this strategy. On the one hand it made my job manageable—rather than surveying the globe, I could focus on materials, texts, and conferences gathered in one geographical location. Furthermore, the vantage point of the ILO allowed an opportunity to explore the intersection of arguments in global movements with those emerging in an interstate organization. On the negative side, my geographical research location at the headquarters of an interstate organization removed the analysis from the experiences of individual home-based workers and limited the degree to which I could investigate the interaction of constructions at different levels. The issue carries deeper implications in the context of feminist debates about epistemology.

Suggestions that both patriarchy and sisterhood are global formed an integral part of the second wave of the women's movement. From the 1960s to the 1980s, feminists grounded universal claims to the global character of patriarchy in various roots of common subordination and oppression including, among others, men's "control over women's reproductive capacity," "men's control over women's labor power," men's "extractive, non-reciprocal, exploitative object-relation to nature," men's "structural capacity to rape," and the "universal, structural opposition between domestic and public domains of activity."[3] The critiques of women of color, Third World women, and lesbians delegitimized this kind of theorizing because it ignored the diversity of women's experiences and the way in which these experiences intersected with class and ethnic positions, racial and sexual politics, and with positions in the international division of labor. Scholars influenced by postmodern and poststructuralist ideas buttressed this criticism, arguing that totalizing feminist theories imitated the meta-narratives of modern philosophy that postured as universal, unsituated and ahistorical truths while hiding their contingent and partial character.[4]

In the context of these criticisms, research on international structures or global gender phenomena increasingly lost its legitimacy. Feminist theorists called for investigations to start from "situated knowledges," to embed research and theory in cultural specificities, and to approach subjects in a "comparativist rather than universalizing" fashion.[5] To the extent that feminists focused on global issues, the point of departure now increasingly was "the local." "The global" revealed itself in "local" practices; and for feminists outside the field of International Relations doing "international" research meant primarily doing comparative research. For example, a recent treatment of feminist activism from a "global perspective" described movements in different countries but ignored the interactions of these movements and the way they met in global spaces.[6] Another collection investigating "feminisms in international politics" reduced such politics to "translations" or "continual negotiations" between Western and other types of feminisms, which had local effects but apparently did not produce any global rules.[7] Along with this disregard for global effects, some scholars have been vocally hostile toward feminist politics engaging processes of international organization and global governance, for example characterizing the Beijing Women's Conference as a "tremendously well-organized and broad repressive ideological apparatus" that gathered "feminist apparatchiks" while "serious activists" stayed away because "the real work may be elsewhere."[8]

Given these critiques, how can I defend my focus on global rules and global politics, my point of departure from an interstate organization, and my suggestion that there is a place for emancipatory politics at these locales? I would argue that the disregard for global gender rules and the hostility toward activism which centers around interstate organizations among some feminists is based on a confusion of the universal and the global, on a tendency to consider the universal and the global as synonymous. In one of their meanings, both terms denote "worldwide"; but in the context of feminist critiques of theories on women's oppression, the term "universal" meant something quite different. These theories claimed logical universality: they stated (or implied) that the sources of oppression identified were the same for all members of an objective category called women. Whereas universality thus denotes a logical proposition and an epistemological position, the global, as I use the term here, signifies a social space that emerges from the diverse interactions of influentials across state boundaries. It is the locus of social construction and politics, including perhaps a disproportionate number of appeals to universal rights, but nonetheless, like any other social space, creating specific social rules.

If the global and the universal are distinct, what is the meaning of the local? The term interweaves an image of territory with a justificatory strategy. In opposition to the universal, the local signifies the recognition that all knowledge is ultimately situated and that claims to universality are therefore strategies of power. Thus the local yields a location of potential resistance, a site that makes possible emancipatory politics.[9] But in its opposition to the global, the local evokes as well a territorial image that designates geographical communities. It is in this understanding that the study of such communities has achieved primacy against investigations of international organization or processes of global governance. Emancipatory critique emerges from the knowledge of geographically bounded communities against knowledge that is not so rooted. However, many have argued that modernity increasingly has divorced space from territory or place and fostered networks between distant agents. Like territorially bounded communities, these global networks create historically specific rules. From this perspective, the distinction between the global and the local becomes problematic. While they occupy different geographical scales (or levels of analysis), they are both imbued with history and realize processes of both empowerment and disempowerment.

In addition to geographical communities, international organizations are locales where global processes become visible. Clearly, universal claims pervade ILO conventions, and they carry the disempowering implications of such claims. But labor conventions do not simply issue from universal aspirations; they are the focus of intense negotiation and consequently reflect the politics that brought them about. The rules emerging from such politics may differ significantly from those at other geographical scales, but they impact at other levels as activists employ global claims to effect particular outcomes. For example, the right of home-based workers to be considered employees carries different meaning in India, where the self-employed are striving for protection, than in Europe, where workers are fighting to retain employment rights and benefits. In their local practices, social movements use the global understanding that home-based workers should receive the same or similar treatment as other wage-earners while developing distinct meanings of this understanding in specific cultural and historical situations.[10]

Because the ILO, in addition to providing a forum for its institutionalized constituents, also is a site of movement politics, it sometimes becomes a location for emancipatory claims. For example, its focus on the informal sector in the 1970s provided a reorientation of state policies that gained some previously marginalized workers easier access to credit or less police harassment. Similarly, its feminist-inspired technical assistance projects for home-based workers offered a conduit for alternative interpretations of employment relations and helped destabilize the gendered opposition between work and home. These aspects of ILO activity have led some to consider it a counterforce to the disempowering, system-conforming policies of the World Bank and the International Monetary Fund. But, as I have shown, ILO debates also marginalize and exclude, creating, in Foucault's words, subjects in both senses of the word. In this respect global space resembles any other social space.

The force with which processes of capital accumulation assert themselves at a global scale today gives urgency to probing political spaces that provide openings for alternative interpretations. Such spaces exist at different levels of analysis, including the level of international organization. Intergovernmental and NGO meetings, development projects, research financed by international institutions, exchanges of written communications between movement participants, and the many other occasions for global conversation constitute historically specific events that are defined by rules and that provide a terrain for the reconstruction of rules. Exploring such rules illuminates the social dimension of capitalist restructuring and creates emancipatory knowledge that can help subvert power politics coded in class and gender.

Appendix
ILO Convention Concerning
Home Work

The General Conference of the International Labour Organization,

Having been convened at Geneva by the Governing Body of the International Labour Office, and having met in its Eighty-third session on 4 June 1996, and

Recalling that many international labour Conventions and Recommendations laying down standards of general application concerning work conditions are applicable to homeworkers, and

Noting that the particular conditions characterizing home work make it desirable to improve the application of those Conventions and Recommendations to homeworkers, and to supplement them by standards which take into account the special characteristics of home work, and

Having decided upon the adoption of certain proposals with regard to home work, which is the fourth item on the agenda of the session, and

Having determined that these proposals shall take the form of an international Convention;

adopts, this twentieth day of June of the year one thousand nine hundred and ninety-six, the following Convention, which may be cited as the Home Work Convention, 1996:

Article 1

For the purposes of this Convention:

(a) the term "home work" means work carried out by a person, to be referred to as a homeworker,

  (i)   in his or her home or in other premises of his or her choice, other than the workplace of the employer;
  (ii) for remuneration;
  (iii) which results in a product or service as specified by the employer, irrespective of who provides the equipment, materials or other inputs used,

  unless this person has the degree of autonomy and of economic independence necessary to be considered an independent worker under national laws, regulations or court decisions;

(b) persons with employee status do not become homeworkers within the meaning of this Convention simply by occasionally performing their work as employees at home, rather than their usual workplaces;

(c) the term "employer" means a person, natural or legal, who, either directly or through an intermediary, whether or not intermediaries are provided for in national legislation, gives out home work in pursuance of his or her business activity.

Article 2

This Convention applies to all persons carrying out home work within the meaning of Article 1.

Article 3

Each Member which has ratified this Convention shall adopt, implement and periodically review a national policy on home work aimed at improving the situation of homeworkers, in consultation with the most representative organizations of employers and workers and, where they exist, with organizations concerned with homeworkers and those of employers of homeworkers.

Article 4

1. The national policy on home work shall promote, as far as possible, equality of treatment between homeworkers and other wage earners, taking into account the special characteristics of home work and, where appropriate, conditions applicable to the same or a similar type of work carried out in an enterprise.

2. Equality of treatment shall be promoted, in particular, in relation to:

(a) the homeworkers' right to establish or join organizations of their own choosing and to participate in the activities of such organizations;
(b) protection against discrimination in employment and occupation;
(c) protection in the field of occupational safety and health;
(d) remuneration;
(e) statutory social security protection;
(f) access to training;
(g) minimum age for admission to employment or work; and
(h) maternity protection.

Article 5

The national policy on home work shall be implemented by means of laws and regulations, collective agreements, arbitration awards or in any other appropriate manner consistent with national practice.

Article 6

Appropriate measures shall be taken so that labour statistics include, to the extent possible, home work.

Article 7

National laws and regulations on safety and health at work shall apply to home work, taking account of its special characteristics, and shall establish conditions under which certain types of work and the use of certain substances may be prohibited in home work for reasons of safety and health.

Article 8

Where the use of intermediaries in home work is permitted, the respective responsibilities of employers and intermediaries shall be determined by laws and regulations or by court decisions, in accordance with national practice.

Article 9

1. A system of inspection consistent with national law and practice shall ensure compliance with the laws and regulations applicable to home work.
2. Adequate remedies, including penalties where appropriate, in case of violation of these laws and regulations shall be provided for and effectively applied.

Article 10

This Convention does not affect more favourable provisions applicable to homeworkers under other international labour Conventions.

Article 11

The formal ratifications of this Convention shall be communicated to the Director-General of the International Labour Office for registration.

Article 12

1. This Convention shall be binding only upon those Members of the International Labour Organization whose ratifications have been registered with the Director-General of the International Labour Office.

2. It shall come into force 12 months after the date on which the ratifications of two Members have been registered with the Director-General.

3. Thereafter, this Convention shall come into force for any Member 12 months after the date on which its ratification has been registered.

Article 13

1. A Member which has ratified this Convention may denounce it after the expiration of ten years from the date on which the Convention first comes into force, by an act communicated to the Director-General of the International Labour Office for registration. Such denunciation shall not take effect until one year after the date on which it is registered.

2. Each Member which has ratified this Convention and which does not, within the year following the expiration of the period of ten years mentioned in the preceding paragraph, exercise the right of denunciation provided for in this Article, will be bound for another period of ten years and, thereafter, may denounce this Convention at the expiration of each period of ten years under the terms provided for in this Article.

Article 14

1. The Director-General of the International Labour Office shall notify all Members of the International Labour Organization for the registration of all ratifications and denunciation communicated by the Members of the Organization.

2. When notifying the Members of the Organization of the registration of the second ratification, the Director-General shall draw the attention of the Members of the Organization to the date upon which the Convention shall come into force.

Article 15

The Director-General of the International Labour Office shall communicate to the Secretary-General of the United Nations, for registration in accordance with article 102 of the Charter of the United Nations, full particulars of all ratifications and acts of denunciation registered by the Director-General in accordance with the provisions of the preceding Articles.

Article 16

At such times as it may consider necessary, the Governing Body of the International Labour Office shall present to the General Conference a report on the working of this Convention and shall examine the desirability of placing on the agenda of the Conference the question of its revision in whole or in part.

Article 17

1. Should the Conference adopt a new Convention revising this Convention in whole or in part, then, unless the new Convention otherwise provides -

(a) the ratification by a Member of the new revising Convention shall *ipso jure* involve the immediate denunciation of this Convention, notwithstanding the provisions of Article 13 above, if and when the new revising Convention shall have come into force;
(b) as from the date when the new revising Convention comes into force, this Convention shall cease to be open to ratification by the Members.

2. This Convention shall in any case remain in force in its actual form and content for those Members which have ratified it but have not ratified the revising Convention.

Article 18

The English and French versions of the text of this Convention are equally authoritative.

Notes

1. Feminism, Constructivism, and the Global Politics of Home-Based Work

1. *HomeNet* (Leeds, UK), Bulletin No. 4 (July 1996).
2. Karl Marx, *Capital: A Critique of Political Economy, Vol. 1: The Process of Capitalist Production*, ed. Frederick Engels, trans. Samuel Moore and Edward Aveling (New York: International Publishers, 1967), p. 462.
3. In general, I use the term "homeworker" to refer to dependent employees working at home under an industrial division of labor. I use the term "home-based worker" as an inclusive category that encompasses all those who work at home for pay, including industrial homeworkers, the self-employed, crafts producers, and subsistence producers. However, in the debate in the 1990s, the term homeworker became itself a contested category, and the self-employed sometimes included in that category.
4. For a fascinating account of the phenomenology of the home-work distinction in the United States see Christena E. Nippert-Eng, *Home and Work: Negotiating Boundaries through Everyday Life* (Chicago: University of Chicago Press, 1996).
5. V. Spike Peterson, "Security and Sovereign States: What Is at Stake in Taking Feminism Seriously?" in *Gendered States: Feminist (Re)Visions of International Relations Theory*, ed. V. Spike Peterson (Boulder: Lynne Rienner, 1992).
6. V. Spike Peterson, "Seeking World Order Beyond the Gendered Order of Global Hierarchies," in *The New Realism: Perspectives on Multilateralism and World Order*, ed. Robert W. Cox (Tokyo: United Nations University Press, 1997); Maria Mies, *Patriarchy and Accumulation on a World Scale: Women in the International Division of Labour* (London: Zed Books, 1986).
7. Witold Rybczynski, *Home: A Short History of an Idea* (London: Penguin, 1986);

Peter J. Taylor, *The Way the Modern World Works: World Hegemony to World Impasse* (Chichester: John Wiley and Sons, 1996), pp. 202–206. Both of these treatments are strangely silent on the gender implications of these processes. For a fascinating account of the gender and racialist politics of the British imperialist state see Laura Tabili, "Women 'of a Very Low Type': Crossing Racial Boundaries in Imperial Britain," in *Gender and Class in Modern Europe*, ed. Laura L. Frader and Sonya O. Rose (Ithaca: Cornell University Press, 1996), pp. 165–190.

8. For a cross-section of works see Mary K. Meyer and Elisabeth Prügl, ed. *Gender Politics in Global Governance* (Lanham, MD: Rowman and Littlefield, 1999).

9. Sandra Whitworth, *Feminism and International Relations: Towards a Political Economy of Gender in Interstate and Non-Governmental Institutions* (New York: St. Martin's Press, 1994), pp. 41–42.

10. Albert S. Yee, "The Effects of Ideas on Policies," *International Organization* 50 (Winter 1996): 69–108.

11. E.g. Martha Finnemore, *National Interests in International Society* (Ithaca: Cornell University Press, 1996); Peter J. Katzenstein, ed. *The Culture of National Security: Norms and Identity in World Politics* (New York: Columbia University Press, 1996).

12. John Gerard Ruggie, *Constructing the World Polity: Essays on International Institutionalization* (New York: Routledge, 1998), p. 20.

13. Nicholas Onuf, "Constructivism: A User's Manual," in *International Relations in a Constructed World*, ed. Vendulka Kubálková, Nicholas Onuf, and Paul Kowert (Armonk, NY: M.E. Sharpe, 1998), pp. 58–78; Karin M. Fierke, "At the Boundary: Language, Rules, and Social Construction," in *The Aarhus-Norsminde Papers: Constructivism, International Relations and European Studies*, ed. Knud Erik Jørgensen (Aarhus, Denmark: Aarhus University, Department of Political Science), pp. 43–51.

14. For a categorization of constructivists (including some feminists) according to philosophical bases see Ruggie, *Constructing the World Polity*, pp. 35–36. Ruggie does not identify Wittgenstein as providing philosophical roots separate from the sociological classics, and thereby papers over substantial differences. For a forceful argument in favor of a Wittgensteinian constructivism see Fierke, "At the Boundary," p. 45; also Nicholas G. Onuf, *World of Our Making: Rules and Rule in Social Theory and International Relations* (Columbia, SC: University of South Carolina Press, 1989).

15. Audie Klotz and Cecelia Lynch, "Conflicted Constructivism? Positivist Leanings vs. Interpretivist Meanings," presented at the International Studies Association Annual Meeting, Minneapolis, MN, March 1998. For a categorization of constructivists according to methodological disagreements see Emanuel Adler, "Seizing the Middle Ground: Constructivism in World Politics," *European Jour-*

nal of International Relations 3 (3): 335–336. David Dessler and Alexander Wendt ground constructivism in scientific realism in order to legitimize a positivist research program. Alexander E. Wendt, "The Agent-Structure Problem in International Relations Theory," *International Organization* 41 (Summer 1987): 335–370; David Dessler, "What's at Stake in the Agent-Structure Debate?" *International Organization* 43 (Summer 1989): 441–473. Some sociologically grounded constructivists equally argue that constructivism and positivism are in principle compatible. E.g. Nicholas Onuf, "How Things Get Normative," presented at the Conference on "International Norms," Leonard Davis Institute for International Relations, Hebrew University of Jerusalem, May 26–27, 1997; Ronald L. Jepperson, Alexander Wendt, and Peter J. Katzenstein, "Norms, Identity, and Culture in National Security," in *The Culture of National Security*, p. 67. But see Ruggie, *Constructing the World Polity*, chap. 3 for an argument to the contrary. Most feminists in IR are wary of positivist methodologies. E.g. J. Ann Tickner, *Gender in International Relations: Feminist Perspectives on Achieving Global Security* (New York: Columbia University Press, 1992); Christine Sylvester, *Feminist Theory and International Relations in a Postmodern Era* (Cambridge: Cambridge University Press, 1994).

16. The following summary thus excludes the contentions of scholars drawing on French post-structuralist writings as well as the writings of scholars that focus on the causal role of "ideas" in international relations. Writers in neither tradition tend to label themselves constructivists, although some have subsumed them under the category constructivism. E.g. Ruggie, *Constructing the World Polity*, chap. 1.

17. For a succinct analysis of the convoluted arguments around this issue see Harry D. Gould, "What *Is* at Stake in the Agent-Structure Debate?" in *International Relations in a Constructed World*, pp. 79–98.

18. The writings of Anthony Giddens have provided inspiration for many constructivists in IR on this issue. See Anthony Giddens, *The Constitution of Society: Outline of the Theory of Structuration* (Berkeley, Los Angeles: University of California Press, 1984). Giddens is discussed in Onuf, *World of Our Making*, p. 36; Wendt, "The Agent-Structure Problem," p. 356.

19. E.g. Finnemore, *National Interests in International Society*; Alexander Wendt, "Collective Identity Formation and the International State," *American Political Science Review* 88 (June 1994): 384–396; Paul Kowert, "Agent versus Structure in the Construction of National Identity," in *International Relations in a Constructed World*, pp. 101–122.

20. E.g. Ruggie, *Constructing the World Polity*, esp. Part II. Rey Koslovski and Friedrich V. Kratochwil, "Understanding Change in International Politics: The Soviet Empire's Demise and the International System," *International Organization* 48 (Spring 1994): 215–247; Gavan Duffy, Brian K. Frederking, and Seth A. Tucker,

"Language Games: Dialogical Analysis of INF Negotiations," *International Studies Quarterly* 42 (June 1998): 271–294; Klotz and Lynch, "Conflicted Constructivism?"

Note that this ability to explain change is lost in approaches that take norms or culture as explanatory variables. Paul Kowert and Jeffrey Legro, "Norms, Identity, and Their Limits: A Theoretical Reprise," in *The Culture of National Security*, p. 488.

21. However, there is disagreement about which aspects of the world gender encompasses: does it pertain only to the social or does it subsume "sex" and "the material." See Linda Nicholson, "Interpreting Gender," *Signs: Journal of Women in Culture and Society* 20 (Autumn 1994): 79–105.

22. Peterson, "Security and Sovereign States;" Jan Jindy Pettman, *Worlding Women: A Feminist International Politics* (London, New York: Routledge, 1996); Mary Ann Tétreault, ed. *Women and Revolution in Africa, Asia, and the New World* (Columbia, SC: University of South Carolina Press, 1994); Jongwoo Han and L.H.M. Ling, "Authoritarianism in the Hypermasculinized State: Hybridity, Patriarchy, and Capitalism in Korea," *International Studies Quarterly* 42 (March 1998): 53–78.

23. Cynthia Weber, "Performative States," *Millennium: Journal of International Studies* 27 (1): 77–95; Diana Saco, "Gendering Sovereignty: Marriage and International Relations in Elizabethan Times," *European Journal of International Relations* 3 (September 1997): 291–318.

24. Tickner, *Gender in International Relations*.

25. Carol Cohn, "Gays in the Military: Texts and Subtexts," in *The "Man" Question in International Relations*, ed. Marysia Zalewski and Jane Parpart (Boulder: Westview Press, 1998), p. 130; Craig N. Murphy, "Six Masculine Roles in International Relations and Their Interconnection: A Personal Investigation," in *The "Man" Question in International Relations*, pp. 93–108; Steve Niva, "Tough and Tender: New World Order Masculinity and the Gulf War," in *The "Man" Question in International Relations*, pp. 109–128.

26. Jean Bethke Elshtain, *Women and War* (New York: Basic Books, 1987).

27. Cynthia Enloe, *Bananas, Beaches, and Bases: Making Feminist Sense of International Politics* (Berkeley, Los Angeles: University of California Press, 1989); Cynthia Enloe, *The Morning After: Sexual Politics at the End of the Cold War* (Berkeley, Los Angeles, London: University of California Press, 1993).

28. Whitworth, *Feminism and International Relations*; Deborah Stienstra, *Women's Movements and International Organizations* (New York: St. Martin's Press, 1994).

29. The broad literature on Women and Gender in Development has begun to intersect with feminist literature in International Relations. See various articles in Marianne Marchand and Jane L. Parpart, ed. *Feminism/Postmodernism/De-*

velopment (London: Routledge, 1995); Marianne Marchand, "Reconceptualizing 'Gender and Development' in an Era of 'Globalization,'" *Millennium: Journal of International Studies* 25 (Winter 1996): 577–603; also chapters in part 3 of Eleonore Kofman and Gillian Youngs, ed. *Globalization: Theory and Practice* (London: Pinter, 1996).

30. Friedrich Kratochwil and John G. Ruggie, "International Organization: A State of the Art on an Art of the State," *International Organization* 40 (4): 753–775, reprinted in revised form in Ruggie, *Constructing the World Polity*.

31. See Kowert and Legro, "Norms, Identity, and Their Limits: A Theoretical Reprise," pp. 483–497.

32. Richard J. Bernstein, *Beyond Objectivism and Relativism* (Philadelphia: University of Pennsylvania Press, 1983), p. 19.

33. Ruggie, *Constructing the World Polity*, p. 94.

34. Nancy C. M. Hartsock, "The Feminist Standpoint: Developing the Ground for a Specifically Feminist Historical Materialism," in *Discovering Reality: Feminist Perspectives on Epistemology, Metaphysics and Philosophy of Science*, ed. Sandra Harding and Merrill B. Hintikka (Dordrecht: Reidel Publishing Company, 1993), pp. 283–310; reprinted in Nancy C. M. Hartsock, *The Feminist Standpoint Revisited and Other Essays* (Boulder: Westview Press, 1998), pp. 105–132.

35. bell hooks, *Ain't I a Woman: Black Women and Feminism* (Boston: South End Press, 1981); Elizabeth V. Spelman, *Inessential Woman: Problems of Exclusion in Feminist Thought* (Boston: Beacon Press, 1988); Chandra Talpade Mohanty, "Under Western Eyes: Feminist Scholarship and Colonial Discourses," in *Third World Women and the Politics of Feminism*, ed. Chandra Talpade Mohanty, Ann Russo, and Lourdes Torres (Bloomington, Indianapolis: Indiana University Press, 1991), pp. 51–80.

36. Seyla Benhabib, Judith Butler, Drucilla Cornell, and Nancy Fraser, *Feminist Contentions: A Philosophical Exchange* (New York: Routledge, 1995).

37. Marysia Zalewski, "Women, Gender and International Relations Ten Years On. 'To Return as a Woman and Be Heard,'" presented at the 1998 Millennium Conference on "Gender and International Studies: Looking Forward," London School of Economics and Political Science, 13–14 September 1998.

38. Hartsock, *The Feminist Standpoint Revisited*, p. 239.

39. Donna Haraway, "Situated Knowledges: The Science Question in Feminism and the Privilege of Partial Perspective," *Feminist Studies* 14 (Fall 1988): 575–599.

40. Christine Sylvester, "Empathetic Cooperation: A Feminist Method for IR," *Millennium: Journal of International Studies* 23, 2 (1994): 315–334; Sylvester, *Feminist Theory and International Relations*, p. 12. Sylvester builds on Kathy Ferguson's appeal to "mobile subjectivities." Kathy E. Ferguson, *The Man Question: Visions of Subjectivity in Feminist Theory* (Berkeley, Los Angeles, Oxford: Uni-

versity of California Press, 1993). See also Linda Alcoff, "Cultural Feminism Versus Post-Structuralism: The Identity Crisis in Feminist Theory," *Signs: Journal of Women in Culture and Society* 13, 3 (1988): 405–436.

41. Susan Hekman, "Truth and Method: Feminist Standpoint Theory Revisited," *Signs: Journal of Women in Culture and Society* 22 (Winter 1997), p. 356.

42. Donna J. Haraway, *Modest_Witness@Second_Millennium.FemaleMan_Meets_ OncoMouse™: Feminism and Technoscience* (New York: Routledge, 1997), p. 36.

43. Stefano Guzzini, "Machtbegriffe am Ausklang(?): Der Meta-Theoretischen Wende in den internationalen Beziehungen (oder: Gebrauchsanweisung zur Rettung des Konstruktivismus vor seinen neuen Freunden," in *The Aarhus-Norsminde Papers*, pp. 69–79. On the interweaving of rules and rule see Onuf, *World of Our Making*, p. 42.

44. Joan W. Scott, "Gender: A Useful Category of Historical Analysis," *American Historical Review* 91 (December 1986): 1067.

45. Jean L. Cohen and Andrew Arato, *Civil Society and Political Theory* (Cambridge: The MIT Press), p. 542.

46. See various articles in Katzenstein, ed., *The Culture of National Security*.

47. Ruggie, *Constructing the World Polity*, pp. 66–69.

48. For example, Kowert and Legro, "Norms, Identity and Their Limits"; Adler, "Seizing the Middle Ground." For a critique of this inclination see Fierke, "At the Boundary."

49. Nicholson, "Interpreting Gender," p. 86.

50. Haraway, *Modest_Witness*.

51. Judith Butler, *Bodies that Matter: On the Discursive Limits of "Sex"* (New York: Routledge, 1993), p. 9.

52. Carol Cohn, "Sex and Death in the Rational World of Defense Intellectuals," *Signs: Journal of Women in Culture and Society* 12 (4), p. 715.

53. J. K. Gibson-Graham, *The End of Capitalism (As We Knew It): A Feminist Critique of Political Economy* (Cambridge, Mass.: Blackwell Publishers, 1996).

54. E.g. Johanna Meehan, ed., *Feminists Read Habermas: Gendering the Subject of Discourse* (New York: Routledge, 1995).

55. Onuf, *World of Our Making*. Neither Foucault nor Habermas, nor Onuf for that matter, are unproblematic for feminist theorizing. See critiques in Nancy Fraser, *Unruly Practices: Power, Discourse and Gender in Contemporary Social Theory* (Minneapolis: University of Minnesota Press, 1989); also Meehan, ed., *Feminists Read Habermas*. Yet their feminist critics often have eclectically borrowed from these social theorists.

56. Jürgen Habermas, *The Theory of Communicative Action, Volume 1: Reason and the Rationalization of Society*, trans. Thomas McCarthy (Boston: Beacon Press, 1984), pp. 295–305.

57. Onuf, *World of Our Making*, pp. 78–95; Onuf, "Constructivism: A User's Manual," p. 61.
58. Michel Foucault, "Truth and Power," interview by Alessandro Fontana and Pasquale Pasquino, in *Power/Knowledge: Selected Interviews and Other Writings 1972–1977*, ed. and trans. Colin Gordon, Leo Marshall, John Mepham and Kate Soper (New York: Pantheon Books, 1980), p. 117; Michel Foucault, "Powers and Strategies," interview by the editorial collective of Les révoltes logiques, in *Power/Knowledge*, p. 141; Michel Foucault, *Discipline and Punish: The Birth of the Prison*, trans. Alan Sheridan (New York: Random House, Vintage Book Edition, 1975), pp. 135–169; Michel Foucault, "Afterword: The Subject and Power," in *Michel Foucault: Beyond Structuralism and Hermeneutics*, ed. Hubert L. Dreyfus and Paul Rabinow (Chicago: University of Chicago Press, 1982), p. 212; Stephen K. White, "Foucault's Challenge to Critical Theory," *American Political Science Review* 80 (June 1986): 424 and 430; Jana Sawicki, *Disciplining Foucault: Feminism, Power, and the Body* (New York: Routledge, 1991), pp. 20–23.
59. E.g., Lawrence S. Finkelstein, "What Is Global Governance?"*Global Governance: A Review of Multilateralism and International Organizations* 1 (September–December 1995): 367–372.
60. Jan Aart Scholte, "Beyond the Buzzword: Towards a Critical Theory of Globalization," in *Globalization: Theory and Practice*, p. 46. This paragraph draws heavily on Scholte's excellent analysis.
61. Scholte, "Beyond the Buzzword," pp. 46–47.
62. The global is not synonymous with global civil society, a concept that has become popular but that, because of its definition in opposition to states, invites conceptual trouble when extrapolated to the interstate arena. The global designates a social space that cuts across the state/non-state distinction. Works that employ the notion of global civil society include Robert W. Cox, *Approaches to World Order* (Cambridge: Cambridge University Press, 1996); Ronnie D. Lipschutz, "Reconstructing World Politics: The Emergence of Global Civil Society," *Millennium: Journal of International Studies* 21 (Winter 1992): 389–420; Stienstra, *Women's Movements and International Organizations*, p. 30. For a critique see R. B. J. Walker, "Social Movements/World Politics," *Millennium: Journal of International Studies* 23, 3 (1994), esp. pp. 690–699.
63. Cohen and Arato, *Civil Society and Political Theory*, chap. 10.
64. R. B. J. Walker, "Social Movements/World Politics," p. 677.
65. Sidney Tarrow defines social movements as "collective challenges by people with common purposes and solidarity in sustained interaction with elites, opponents and authorities." Sidney Tarrow, *Power in Movement: Social Movements, Collective Action and Politics* (Cambridge: Cambridge University Press,

1994), p. 2. I owe to him the insight that argumentations have to be sustained in order to qualify as social movements.

66. This is clearly illustrated in the criticisms of various women's movements as exclusionary.

67. Compare Warren Magnusson, "Social Movements and the Global City," *Millennium: Journal of International Studies* 23, 3 (1994): 636–637.

68. For an overview of this literature see the special issue of *Social Research* 52 (Winter 1985) .

69. See also Tarrow, *Power in Movement*.

70. Tarrow, *Power in Movement*, Part I.

71. Walker, "Social Movements/World Politics," p. 672; James N. Rosenau, *Along the Domestic-Foreign Frontier: Exploring Governance in a Turbulent World* (Cambridge: Cambridge University Press, 1997).

72. Compare Leila J. Rupp, *Worlds of Women: The Making of an International Women's Movement* (Princeton: Princeton University Press, 1997); and Joan W. Scott, Cora Kaplan, and Debra Keates, ed., *Transitions, Environments, Translations: Feminisms in International Politics* (New York: Routledge, 1997).

73. See for example, Doreen Massey, *Space, Place, and Gender* (Minneapolis: University of Minneapolis Press, 1994); Lourdes Benería and Shelley Feldman, ed., *Unequal Burden: Economic Crises, Persistent Poverty, and Women's Work* (Boulder: Westview Press, 1992); June Nash, ed., *Crafts in the World Market: The Impact of Global Exchange on Middle American Artisans* (Albany: State University of New York Press, 1993); June Nash and María Patricia Fernández-Kelly, ed., *Women, Men and the International Division of Labor* (Albany: State University of New York Press, 1983); Kathryn Ward, ed., *Women Workers and Global Restructuring* (Ithaca: ILR Press, 1990).

74. Pettman, *Worlding Women*, chap. 9.

75. For a review of this literature see Elisabeth Prügl, "Gender in International Organization and Global Governance: A Critical Review of the Literature," *International Studies Notes* 21 (Winter 1996): 15–24.

76. For a comprehensive historical overview see Stienstra, *Women's Movements and International Organizations*; contemporary issues are addressed in Irene Tinker, "Non-Governmental Organizations: An Alternative Power Base for Women?" Mary K. Meyer, "Negotiating International Norms: The Inter-American Commission of Women and The Convention on Violence Against Women," Amy J. Higer, "International Women's Activism and the 1994 Cairo Population Conference," Jutta Joachim, "Shaping the Human Rights Agenda: The Case of Violence Against Women," Alice M. Miller, "Realizing Women's Human Rights: Non-Governmental Organizations and the United Nations Treaty Bodies," Lois A. West, "The United Nations Women's Conferences and Feminist Politics,"

all in *Gender Politics and Global Governance*. On the four UN Women's Conferences and policies toward women in different UN agencies see Anne Winslow, ed., *Women, Politics, and the United Nations* (Westport, CT: Greenwood
Press, 1995). Whitworth, *Feminism and International Relations* explores the interaction of global forces with changes in policy in the International Planned
Parenthood Federation and the International Labor Organization.

77. Anne Sisson Runyan, "Women in the Neoliberal 'Frame'," in *Gender Politics
and Global Governance*, pp. 210–220; Anne Sisson Runyan, "The Places of
Women in Trading Places: Gendered Global/Regional Regimes and Inter-nationalized Feminist Resistance," and Marianne H. Marchand, "Selling NAFTA:
Gendered Metaphors and Silenced Gender Implications," both in *Globalization: Theory and Practice*.

78. Carol Riegelman Lubin and Anne Winslow, *Social Justice for Women: The International Labor Organization and Women*. Durham, NC: Duke University
Press, 1990.

79. Ann Therese Lotherington and Anne Britt Flemmen, "Negotiating Gender: The
Case of the International Labour Organization, ILO," in *Gender and Change
in Developing Countries*, ed. Kristi Anne Stølen and Mariken Vaa (Norwegian
University Press, 1991), pp. 273–307.

80. Lubin and Winslow, *Social Justice for Women*, p. 229.

81. Whitworth, *Feminism and International Relations*, esp. chaps. 3 and 5.

82. Ibid., p. 119.

83. For an elaboration see Elisabeth Prügl and Irene Tinker, "Microentrepreneurs
and Homeworkers: Convergent Categories," *World Development* 25 (September
1997): 1471–1482.

84. Onuf, *World of Our Making*, pp. 78–95; Onuf, "Constructivism: A User's Manual," pp. 67–68.

85. Note that Onuf rejects the common constructivist distinction between regulative
and constitutive rules. He argues that all categories of rules are both regulative
and constitutive. In other words, all elicit action on the part of others while also
establishing social facts.

*2. Motherly Women—Breadwinning Men: Industrial Homework and the
Construction of Western Welfare States*

1. Marx, *Capital*, p. 461.

2. Ibid, p. 470.

3. Eileen Boris, "Sexual Division, Gender Constructions: The Historical Meaning
of Homework in Western Europe and the United States," in *Homeworkers in*

Global Perspective: Invisible No More, ed. Eileen Boris and Elisabeth Prügl (New York and London: Routledge, 1996), p. 23; Vivien Hart, *Bound by Our Constitution: Women, Workers, and the Minimum Wage* (Princeton: Princeton University Press, 1994), pp. 20–21.

4. Marx, *Capital*, p. 503.

5. Marilyn Boxer, "Protective Legislation and Home Industry: The Marginalization of Women Workers in Late Nineteenth- Early Twentieth-Century France," *Journal of Social History* 20 (Fall 1986): 47.

6. Rosmarie Beier, *Frauenarbeit und Frauenalltag im Deutschen Kaiserreich: Heimarbeiterinnen in der Berliner Bekleidungsindustrie 1880–1914* (Frankfurt, New York: Campus Verlag, 1983), p. 36.

7. Käthe Gaebel, *Die Heimarbeit: Das jüngste Problem des Arbeiterschutzes* (Jena: Gustav Fischer, 1913), pp. 92–126; Remark by Mrs. Kjelsberg, Government Delegate from Norway, International Labour Organisation (hereafter ILO), *International Labour Conference, 11th Session: Proceedings, Vol. I* (Geneva, 1928), p. 401; Hans Dockendorf, *Der Entgeltschutz in der deutschen Heimarbeit* (Jena: Gustav Fischer, 1936), pp. 5–17.

8. Eileen Boris, *Home to Work: Motherhood and the Politics of Industrial Homework in the United States* (Cambridge: Cambridge University Press, 1994), pp. 39–44.

9. For an overview of literature see Elizabeth Pleck, "Two Worlds in One: Work and Family," *Journal of Social History* 10 (Winter 1976): 178–195.

10. Sonya O. Rose, *Limited Livelihoods: Gender and Class in Nineteenth-Century England* (Berkeley: University of California Press, 1992), pp. 138–153.

11. Ellen Carol DuBois, "Woman Suffrage and the Left: An International Socialist-Feminist Perspective," *New Left Review* 186 (1991), 24–25.

12. DuBois, "Woman Suffrage and the Left," 20; Rupp, *Worlds of Women*, chap. 3.

13. Lewis L. Lorwin, *The International Labor Movement: History, Policies, Outlook* (New York: Harper & Brothers, 1953; reprint, Westport, CT: Greenwood Press, 1973), p. 35; G.A. Johnston, *The International Labour Organisation: Its Work for Social and Economic Progress* (London: Europa Publications, 1970), p. 10; Sheila Rowbotham, "Strategies Against Sweated Work in Britain, 1820–1920," in *Dignity and Daily Bread: New Forms of Economic Organising Among Poor Women in the Third World and the First*, ed. Sheila Rowbotham and Swasti Mitter (London, New York: Routledge, 1994), pp. 167 and 183; Hugo Karpf, *Heimarbeit und Gewerkschaft: Ein Beitrag zur Sozialgeschichte der Heimarbeit im 19. und 20. Jahrhundert* (Cologne: Bund-Verlag, 1980), pp. 32–41 and 63–72; Boris, "Sexual Division, Gender Construction," p. 30.

14. Robin Miller Jacoby, *The British and American Women's Trade Union Leagues, 1890–1925: A Case Study of Feminism and Class* (Brooklyn: Carlson Publishing

Inc., 1994), pp. 165 and 175; Lorwin, *The International Labor Movement*, p. 63; Julia Varley, "Heimarbeit," presented at the International Congress of Women Workers, Paris, 1927.

15. Stienstra, *Women's Movements and International Organizations*, p. 49; Whitworth, *Feminism and International Relations*, p. 136; Susan D. Becker, *The Origins of the Equal Rights Amendment: American Feminism Between the Wars* (Westport, CT and London: Greenwood Press, 1981), chap. 5; Rupp, *Worlds of Women*, pp. 141–142.

16. See Rupp, *Worlds of Women*, p. 140; for a review of literature on maternalism in the U.S. see Felicia A. Kornbluh, "The New Literature on Gender and the Welfare State: The U.S. Case," *Feminist Studies* 22 (Spring 1996): 171–197.

17. Antony Alcock, *History of the International Labour Organisation* (London: Macmillan, 1971), p. 11. The Association is considered to be the forerunner of the ILO.

18. See *Catalogue of Publications of the International Association for Labour Legislation, International Association on Unemployment, and International Association for Social Progress and their National Sections*, Bibliographical Contributions No. 22 (Geneva: ILO Library, 1962).

19. Ulla Wikander, "Some 'Kept the Flag of Feminist Demands Waving': Debates at International Congresses on Protecting Women Workers," in *Protecting Women: Labor Legislation in Europe, the United States, and Australia, 1880–1920*, ed. Ulla Wikander, Alice Kessler-Harris, and Jane Lewis (Urbana: University of Illinois Press, 1995), p. 51.

20. "Beschlüsse der dritten Delegiertenversammlung der internationalen Vereinigung für gesetzlichen Arbeiterschutz," Kapsel 10405, Mapp "Basel 1904, Protokoll und Resolutionen," Basle Files, ILO Archives, Geneva; Gaebel, *Die Heimarbeit*, p. 206.

21. *International Congress of Home Work (Reports, Resolutions and Papers)* (n.p.: International Association for Labour Legislation [1912?]), Section 4, pp. 61–65.

22. Ernst B. Haas, *Beyond the Nation-State: Functionalism and International Organization* (Stanford: Stanford University Press, 1964), pp. 140–142.

23. *International Congress of Home Work*, p. 61; Gaebel, *Die Heimarbeit* , p. 94; Frieda Wunderlich, *Die Deutsche Heimarbeitausstellung 1925* (Jena: Gustav Fischer, 1927), pp. 1–2; Karpf, *Heimarbeit und Gewerkschaft*, p. 50; *Deuxième Conférence Internationale des Ligues Sociales d'Acheteurs*, Antwerp, 25–28 September 1913 (Lyon: Secretariat General de la L.S.A. de France, n.d.), p. 58. The notion of "repertoire of contention" is from Tarrow, *Power in Movement*, p. 19. He adopts the term from Charles Tilly.

24. *International Congress of Home Work*, Section 1, pp. 60 and 67; Section 2, pp. 12–13; Section 3, p. 6; Section 4, p. 34; my translation.

25. Boris, "Sexual Divisions, Gender Constructions," p. 25; Judith Coffin, *The Politics of Women's Work: The Paris Garment Trades 1750–1915* (Princeton: Princeton University Press, 1996): 203–206.
26. Gaebel, *Die Heimarbeit*, p. 37.
27. Jane Jenson argues that in France a tradition that built on the notion of solidarity created women workers as "citizen-producers." Mothering and income-earning emerged as compatible in this context. In contrast, debates about women and work in the U.S. were framed around individual rights, leading to a construction of mothering and income-earning as mutually exclusive. Jane Jenson, "Representations of Gender: Policies to 'Protect' Women Workers and Infants in France and the United States before 1914," in *Women, the State, and Welfare*, ed. Linda Gordon (Madison: University of Wisconsin Press, 1990).
28. H. J. Tennant, *Parliamentary Debates* (Commons), 5th ser., 4 (1909): col. 344; cited in Hart, *Bound by Our Constitution*, p. 20.
29. Hart, *Bound by Our Constitution*, p. 20; citing "Evidence of Mrs. Ramsey Mac-Donald, *Select Committee 1907*, 213, and Edward Cadbury and George Shann, *Sweating* (London: Headley Brothers, 1907), p. 75.
30. Judith Coffin, "Social Science Meets Sweated Labor: Reinterpreting Women's Work in Late Nineteenth-Century France," *Journal of Modern History* 63 (June 1991): 255–257; quotes are from a pamphlet by E. Rist, *Travail à domicile et salubrité publique* (Paris, 1914), p. 9, and Report of section on hygiene, *Exposition du travail à domicile: Premier congrès international*, vol.1, *Compte rendu des séances* (Brussels, 1910), pp. 38–44, all quoted in Coffin; also Boris, *Home to Work*, p. 89; Robert Wilbrandt, *Arbeiterinnenschutz und Heimarbeit* (Jena: Gustav Fischer, 1906), p. 18, my translation.
31. D. Pesl, "Leitsätze über Massnahmen zur Verbesserung der Lage der Heimarbeiterinnen," in *Zur Erhaltung und Mehrung der Volkskraft: Arbeiten einer vom Ärztlichen Verein München eingesetzten Kommission* (Munich: Verlag von J.F. Lehmann, 1918), p. 169, my translation; see also Alice Kessler-Harris, Jane Lewis, and Ulla Wikander, "Introduction," in *Protecting Women*, pp. 16–17.
32. Rupp, *Worlds of Women*, 83–89.
33. *International Congress of Home Work*, p. xxx; Section 1, pp. 14, 60 and 63; Section 4, Reports.
34. Rowbotham, "Strategies Against Sweated Work in Britain," p. 183; Tuckwell is quoted ibid., p. 184.
35. Wilbrandt, *Arbeiterinnenschutz und Heimarbeit*, p. 136, my translation.
36. Coffin, *The Politics of Women's Work*, p. 174.
37. Hart, *Bound by Our Constitution*, p. 45; Boris, "Sexual Divisions, Gender Constructions," p. 30; Karpf, *Heimarbeit und Gewerkschaft*, p. 48; Beier, *Frauenarbeit und Frauenalltag im Deutschen Kaiserreich*, p.165; quote is from M. Ver-

haegen, Provincial Councilor, Belgium, *International Congress of Home Work*, Section 1, p. 65, my translation.

38. Antony Neuckens, Communal Administrator, Belgium, *International Congress of Home Work*, Section 1, p. 68; my translation.

39. *International Congress of Home Work; Deuxième Conférence Internationale des Ligues Sociales D'Acheteurs*, pp. 55, 63, and 134.

40. Raoul Jay, Professor of Law at the University of Paris, *International Congress on Home Work*, Section 1, pp. 35–36, my translation.

41. A. J. de Maguerie, Director of the journal "Les Idées Contemporaines," *International Congress of Home Work*, Section 1, p. 33, my translation.

42. Coffin, "Social Science Meets Sweated Labor," p. 233, *fn*4; Hart, *Bound by Our Constitution*, pp. 12, 29, and 57.

43. See letters in *11th International Labour Conference, 1928, Reply to questionnaire on minimum wage fixing machinery*, File No. D611/102/25/1, ILO Archives, Geneva.

44. Gaebel, *Die Heimarbeit*, pp. 143ff.

45. ILO, *International Labour Conference, 10th Session: Proceedings, Vol.I* (Geneva, 1927), p. 393.

46. Ibid.; my emphasis.

47. ILO, *International Labour Conference, 10th Session: Proceedings*, p. 391.

48. ILO, *International Labour Conference, 11th Session: Proceedings, Vol. 1* (Geneva, 1928), p. 726.

49. ILO, *International Labour Conference, 11th Session: Minutes of the Committee on Minimum Wage Fixing Machinery*, 13th Sitting (Geneva 1928), p. 5.

50. *The International Labour Code 1951, Vol. 1* (Geneva: ILO, 1952), p. 169; footnotes deleted.

51. ILO, *International Labour Conference, 82nd Session: Report III (Part 5): Lists of Ratifications by Convention and by Country* (Geneva, 1995), pp. 40–41.

52. ILO, *International Labour Conference, 11th Session: Minutes of the Committee on Minimum Wage*, Sixth Sitting, p. 12; Wunderlich, *Die Deutsche Heimarbeitausstellung 1925*, p. 29.

53. The Open Door International for the Economic Emancipation of the Woman Worker, "Manifesto and Charter adopted at Berlin, June 1929," File WN1000/7/1, ILO Archives, Geneva.

54. Ibid.

55. Dr. Alison Hunter, "Open Door Council Dinner—March 5th 1932," File No. WN1000/7/0/2, ILO Archives, Geneva; "Women and the International Labour Organisation," *The Vote: The Organ of the Women's Freedom League* Vol. 32, No. 1,154 (Friday, December 4, 1931).

56. "Minute Sheet" and "Documents envoyés par 'The Open Door International'," File No. WN1000/7/1, ILO Archives, Geneva.

57. "Statement of The Open Door Council, Six Point Group, Women's Freedom League, St. Joan's Social and Political Alliance, National Union of Women Teachers (being five British feminist organisations), and of the International Committee of The Open Door Council," File D611/2010/01,ILO Archives, Geneva, p. 2, emphases in the original.

58. Elizabeth Abbott, Helen Douglas-Irvine, Ethel E. Froud, E. Knight, M.D., Chrystal Macmillan, Rhondda [sic], "Draft Letter to Delegates to the Assembly of the League of Nations," File No. D611/2010/01, ILO Archives, Geneva; see also Whitworth, *Feminism and International Relations*.

59. ILO, *International Labour Conference, 11th Session: Minutes of the Committee on Minimum Wage*, Sixth Sitting, p.14.

60. Ibid., 13th Sitting, pp. 10–11.

61. Ibid., p. 9.

62. Robert W. Cox, "Labor and Hegemony," *International Organization* 31 (Summer 1977): 387.

63. Boris, *Home to Work*, pp. 246–252.

64. Ibid., Part III.

65. Winslow also headed the Inter-American Commission of Women. She had managed to oust in 1933 a U.S. equal rights feminist, Doris Stevens, who had used the platform to gain support for the Equal Rights Treaty in Latin America. Becker, *The Origins of the Equal Rights Amendment*, pp. 183–184.

66. ILO, *Second Labour Conference of the American States Which Are Members of the International Labour Organisation: Record of Proceedings* (Montreal 1941), p. 230.

67. Ibid, p 229.

68. "Industrial Home Work," *International Labour Review* 53 (December 1948): 735 and 751.

69. ILO, "99th Session of the Governing Body," in *International Labour Review* 54 (November–December 1946): 357; ILO, Governing Body, *99th Session: Minutes* (Montreal, 1946), p. 36; ILO, Governing Body, *103rd Session: Minutes* (Geneva, 1947), p. 135.

70. Frieda S. Miller, "Industrial Home Work in the United States," *International Labour Review* 43 (January 1941): 1.

71. Ibid.

72. Alice Zimmermann, "Home Work in Switzerland," *International Labour Review* 62 (September-October 1950): 242–244.

73. Valentine Paulin, "Home Work in France: Its Origin, Evolution, and Future," *International Labour Review* 37 (February 1938): 193–225; quotes appear on pp. 223 and 224.

74. "Industrial Homework," p. 751.

75. Ministry of Labour and National Service to Mildred Fairchild, ILO, April 23, 1947; Marit Aarum to M. Fairchild, March 20, 1947; Kerstin Hesselgren to M. Fairchild, June 20, 1947; Ministère du Travail et de la Sécurité Sociale, République Française to Diréteur Général, BIT, May 15, 1943, pp. 1 and 20; Anne Larrabee to M. Fairchild, p. 1; all in File WN 1001/06, ILO Archives, Geneva.

  Governments also were not worried about unfair international competition resulting from homework, an issue that concerned Miller who had seen standards undermined in the U.S. because of divergent state regulations. In part this was because many governments had imposed rigid import and export controls to help economic recovery. Miller pondered in a letter to Mildred Fairchild, the ILO officer in charge of the survey: "I can't quite understand why there should have been no international competitive aspects in France and Belgium since their lace industries, and in France embroideries as well, were certainly on an international basis before the war." Fairchild conveyed some of the realities of the post-War economy in Europe: "The best explanation I can see lies in the rigid controls exercised over exports and imports not only of materials but of money." The French response to the questionnaire supported Fairchild's analysis. Luxury clothing, including *haute couture*, lingerie, and fur, were the main employers of homeworkers in France; these items had simply become too expensive for most people during the war. After the war, Britain leveled import restrictions on luxury items, the U.S. slapped a tariff of 70 percent on luxury goods, and countries in South America, Sweden, Norway and the Netherlands required export licenses. Frieda Miller to Mildred Fairchild, January 23, 1947; M. Fairchild to F. Miller, January 25, 1947; Ministère du Travail et de la Sécurité Sociale, République Française to Diréteur Général, BIT, May 15, 1943, p. 13; all in File WN 1001/06, ILO Archives, Geneva.

76. Government figures on homework should be treated with caution, however. Homeworker advocates have amply demonstrated that government surveys often miss substantial numbers of home-based workers. Indeed, Boris describes an expansion of clerical homework in the U.S. in the 1940s. Similarly, a union activist in Germany recounts fierce competition for homework after the war when refugee entrepreneurs reopened their former enterprises in the West and drew heavily on homework. Boris, *Home to Work*, p. 308; Karpf, *Heimarbeit und Gewerkschaft*, p. 104.

77. Ministère du Travail et de la Sécurité Sociale, République Française to Diréteur Général, BIT, May 15, 1943, pp. 1 and 20, File WN 1001/06, ILO Archives, Geneva.

78. Miller's close collaboration with Mildred Fairchild of the ILO in drafting the survey questionnaire resembled that between British bureaucrats and ILO offi-

cers in the 1920s. See exchange of letters between Mildred Fairchild and Frieda Miller in "Committee on Women's Work: Industrial Homework," ILO Archives, Geneva, File WN 1001/06.

3. *Supplemental Earners and National Essence: Home-Based Crafts Producers and Nation-Building in Post-Colonial States*

1. Geoffrey Barraclough, *An Introduction to Contemporary History* (London: Penguin Books, 1967, c1964), chap. 6.
2. Haas, *Beyond the Nation-State*, pp. 155–183.
3. Alcock, *History of the International Labour Organisation*, p. 215.
4. Johnston, *The International Labour Organisation*, pp. 251–254; Alcock, *History of the International Labour Organisation*, pp. 217 and 235.
5. Lubin and Winslow, *Social Justice for Women*, pp. 69–70.
6. Ibid., pp. 229–230.
7. Maryse Gaudier, "The Development of the Women's Question at the ILO, 1919–1994: 75 Years of Progress Towards Equality," Prepared for International Forum on Equality for Women in the World of Work: Challenges for the Future, Geneva, June 1–3, 1994, International Institute for Labour Studies; Whitworth, *Feminism and International Relations*, p. 140.
8. Mies, *Patriarchy and Accumulation*; Helen I. Safa, *The Myth of the Male Breadwinner: Women and Industrialization in the Caribbean* (Boulder: Westview Press, 1995). For a critique of Mies's functionalism see Elisabeth Prügl, "Home-Based Workers: A Comparative Exploration of Mies's Theory of Housewifization," *Frontiers: A Journal of Women Studies* 17, 1 (1996): 114–135.
9. Barbara Rogers, *The Domestication of Women: Discrimination in Developing Societies* (London: St. Martin's Press, 1980).
10. E.g. Pettman, *Worlding Women*, p. 48.
11. Andrew Parker, Mary Russo, Doris Sommer, and Patricia Yaeger, "Introduction," in *Nationalisms and Sexualities*, ed. Parker et al. (New York and London: Routledge, 1992); Pettman, *Worlding Women*, chap. 3. For an elaboration of this apparently global rule in the local context of the Confucian patriarchy of South Korea see Han and Ling, "Authoritarianism in the Hypermasculinized State."
12. Barraclough, *An Introduction to Contemporary History*, p. 159.
13. Ibid., pp. 177 and 196.
14. Kumari Jayawardena, *Feminism and Nationalism in the Third World* (London: Zed Books, 1986), pp. 77, 93–94 and 99; Sheila Rowbotham, *Women in Movement: Feminism and Social Action* (New York, London: Routledge, 1992), pp. 199–203 and 210.

15. Jasleen Dhamija, "Handicrafts: A Source of Employment for Women in Developing Rural Economies," *International Labour Review* 112 (December 1975): 460.

16. Consider for example the following statement in Senegal's Second Five-Year Plan (1965–69): "The crafts industry does not afford the same interest as the industrial sector for the country's economic growth, mainly because it does not give rise to capital formation or to the cumulative process that this sets in motion. The development of this pre-industrial sector does, however, present a very definite interest as a desirable preliminary stage towards the industrialisation of the country," quoted in J. Trouvé, "Development of Rural Industries in French-Speaking Africa: A Critical Review." In *Rural Small-Scale Industry and Employment in Africa and Asia: A Review of Programmes and Policies* (Geneva: International Labour Office, 1984), p. 65.

17. M. Allal and E. Chuta, *Cottage Industries and Handicrafts: Some Guidelines for Employment Promotion* (Geneva: International Labour Office, 1982), pp. 38–58; Enyinna Chuta and S. V. Sethuraman, ed., *Rural Small-Scale Industries and Employment in Africa and Asia: A Review of Programmes and Policies* (Geneva: International Labour Office, 1984).

18. On feminist nationalism see Lois A. West, ed. *Feminist Nationalism* (New York: Routledge, 1997); also Pettman, *Worlding Women*, 61. Works documenting the role of women in revolutionary and nationalist movements include Jayawardena, *Feminism and Nationalism*; Christine Obbo, "Sexuality and Economic Domination in Uganda," in Nira Yuval-Davis and Floya Anthias, ed. *Woman—Nation—State* (New York: St. Martin's Press, 1989), pp. 85–89; Tétreault, ed. *Women and Revolution*; Georgina Waylen, *Gender in Third World Politics* (Boulder: Lynne Rienner, 1996), chap. 4.

19. Jayawardena, *Feminism and Nationalism*, p. 259.

20. ILO, *International Labour Conference, 39th Session, Report VIII (1): Living and Working Conditions of Indigenous Populations in Independent Countries* (Geneva, 1955), pp. 7–8.

21. United Nations Economic and Social Council, *22d Session: Official Records, Supplement No. 4: Commission on the Status of Women, Report to the Economic and Social Council on the Tenth Session of the Commission* (New York, 1956) p. 12.

22. United Nations Economic and Social Council, *24th Session: Official Records, Supplement No. 3: Commission on the Status of Women: Report to the Economic and Social Council on the Eleventh Session of the Commission* (New York, 1957), p.19.

23. ILO, *Fourth Asian Regional Conference: Record of Proceedings* (Geneva, 1958), pp. 173–174.

24. United Nations Economic and Social Council, Commission on the Status of

Women, *Ninth Session: Development of Opportunities for Women in Handicrafts and Cottage Industries : Report Prepared by the International Labour Office*, 1955 (E/CN.6/267), p. 3; cited later as United Nations, *Development of Opportunities.*

25. Ibid., p. 22; United Nations Economic and Social Council, *22d Session*, p. 12; and United Nations Economic and Social Council, *24th Session*, p. 19.

26. United Nations Economic and Social Council, *20th Session: Official Records, Supplement No. 2: Commission on the Status of Women, Report to the Economic and Social Council on the Ninth Session of the Commission* (New York, 1955), p. 12.

27. United Nations *Development of Opportunities* ; United Nations Economic and Social Council, Commission on the Status of Women, *Tenth Session: Opportunities for Women in Handicrafts and Cottage Industries: Progress Report Prepared by the International Labour Office*, 1956 (E/CN.6/282); later cited as United Nations, *Progress Report*; United Nations Economic and Social Council, Commission on the Status of Women, *Eleventh Session: Opportunities for Women in Handicrafts and Cottage Industries: Second Progress Report Prepared by the International Labour Office for the Commission on the Status of Women*, 1957 (E/CN.6/303); later cited as United Nations, *Second Progress Report.*

28. United Nations Economic and Social Council, *20th Session*, p. 11.

29. United Nations, *Second Progress Report*, p. 41.

30. United Nations, *Progress Report*, p. 3.

31. United Nations, *Second Progress Report*, p. 33.

32. United Nations, *Progress Report*, p. 5.

33. Organización de los Estados Americanos, Comisión Interamericana de Mujeres, *Reunión de Técnicas y Dirigentes de las Oficinas del Trabajo de la Mujer: Oficina Internacional del Trabajo, Trabajo a Domicilio*, Washington, D.C., 1957 (RT-Doc. 5/57, Abril 1957), pp. 12 and 31–32; later quoted as Organización de los Estados Americanos, *Reunión de Técnicas y Dirigentes.*

34. Catherine Scott, *Gender and Development: Rethinking Modernization and Dependency Theory* (Boulder, London: Lynne Rienner, 1995), p. 29.

35. ILO, *International Labour Conference, 39th Session: Report VIII (1)*, p. 11.

36. United Nations Economic and Social Council, *22nd Session*, p. 12.

37. United Nations Economic and Social Council, *24th Session*, p. 19.

38. ILO, *Fourth Asian Regional Conference*, p. 175.

39. "Handicrafts and Small-Scale Industries in Asian Countries: Possibilities of Cooperative Organisation," *International Labour Review* 62 (July-December 1950): 507; "Women's Employment in Asian Countries," *International Labour Review* 68 (September 1953): 303–304.

40. Eugene Staley and Richard Morse, *Modern Small Industry for Developing Countries* (New York: McGraw-Hill, 1965), p. 1

41. Ibid., pp. 92, 47, and 7.

42. Ibid., p. 23.
43. Ibid., p. 85.
44. Ibid., pp. 86–87. Compare also David C. McClelland: "A crucial way to break with tradition and introduce new norms is via the emancipation of women. . . . The most general explanation lies in the fact that women are the most conservative members of a culture. They are less subject to influences outside the home than the men and yet they are the ones who rear the next generation and give it the traditional values of the culture." Quoted in Scott, *Gender and Development*, p. 26.
45. Staley and Morse, *Modern Small Industry*, p. 87.
46. Ibid.
47. Allal and Chuta, *Cottage Industries and Handicrafts*, p. 56. A typical ILO manual neglecting home-based industries is Philip A. Neck, ed. *Small Enterprise Development: Policies and Programmes* (Geneva: International Labour Office, 1977).
48. E.g. International Labour Office, *Report to the Government of Libya on the Role of Handicrafts in a Rapidly Developing Economy* (Geneva, 1967), pp. 5 and 55; International Labour Office, *Report to the Government of the Yemen Arab Republic on the Development of Handicrafts and Small-Scale Industries* (Geneva, 1967), p. 11; International Labour Office and Swedish International Development Authority, *Report on ILO/ECA/YWCA/SIDA Workshop on Participation of Women in Handicrafts and Small Industries*, Geneva, 1975, pp. 103 and 177.
49. International Labour Office and Swedish International Development Authority, *Report on ILO/ECA/YWCA/SIDA Workshop*, p. 103.
50. Malcolm Harper and Tan Thiam Soon, *Small Enterprises in Developing Countries: Case Studies and Conclusions* (London: Intermediate Technology Publications Ltd., 1979), p. 114.
51. "Handicrafts and Small-Scale Industries in Asian Countries," p. 508.
52. Dhamija, "Handicrafts," p. 463.
53. ILO, *International Labour Conference, 39th Session: Report VIII (1)*, p. 34.
54. ILO, *International Labour Conference, 40th Session: Record of Proceedings* (Geneva, 1958), p. 812. The Convention was revised in 1989 and the two paragraphs on handicrafts totally rewritten. The significance of handicrafts is reduced and appears as one type of economic activity among others, including subsistence production; references to "modern methods" are eliminated as are any suggestions that the cultural heritage and artistic expressions of indigenous peoples needed development. The revised text (Article 23 of Convention 169) reads as follows:
    "1. Handicrafts, rural and community-based industries, and subsistence economy and traditional activities of the peoples concerned, such as hunting, fishing, trapping and gathering, shall be recognised as important factors in the mainte-

nance of their cultures and in their economic self-reliance and development. Governments shall, with the participation of these people and whenever appropriate, ensure that these activities are strengthened and promoted.

"2. Upon the request of the peoples concerned, appropriate technical and financial assistance shall be provided wherever possible, taking into account the traditional technologies and cultural characteristics of these peoples, as well as the importance of sustainable and equitable development."

55. ILO, *International Labor Conference, 39th Session: Report VIII (1)*, pp. 84–85.
56. International Labour Office, *Report to the Government of St. Lucia on the Development of Handicrafts* (Geneva, 1969), pp. 12–13.
57. International Labour Office, *Report to the Government of Libya*, pp. 33 and 13.
58. Ibid., p. 35.
59. Allal and Chuta, *Cottage Industries and Handicrafts*, pp. 101–107.
60. Johnston, *The International Labour Organisation*, pp. 230–231. In the late 1950s older workers were added to the responsibilities of this section. Lubin and Winslow, *Social Justice for Women*, p. 210.
61. International Labour Office, *Report to the Government of the Republic of Cyprus on the Development of Handicrafts* (Geneva, 1967), p. 34; International Labour Office, *Report to the Government of St. Lucia on the Development of Handicrafts* (Geneva, 1969), p. 8.
62. United Nations Economic and Social Council, *22nd Session*, p. 12; and United Nations Economic and Social Council, *24th Session*, p. 19.
63. According to Alcock the Andean Indian Programme was "one of the most far-reaching technical co-operation projects ever mounted. The project was lead by the ILO and involved collaboration of UN, UNESCO, FAO, and WHO. Its purpose was to improve the social and economic conditions of indigenous peoples of the Andes and integrate them into their countries' economies and societies." Alcock, *History of the International Labour Organisation*, p. 251. See also Johnston, *The International Labour Organisation*, p. 259.
64. United Nations, *Progress Report*, p. 8.
65. ILO, *International Labour Conference, 40th Session*, p. 812.
66. ILO, *International Labour Conference, 39th Session: Report VIII (1)*, p. 86.
67. Ibid., pp. 18, 45, and 89.
68. "Vocational Training and the Establishment of Service Workshops in a Poor Rural Area: The Experience of the Andean Indian Programme," *International Labour Review* 85 (January–June 1962): 146–147.
69. ILO, *International Labour Conference, 49th Session: Record of Proceedings* (Geneva, 1965), pp. 663–664.
70. Organización de los Estados Americanos, *Reunión de Técnicas y Dirigentes*, p. 26; International Labour Office, *Report to the Government of the Republic of Cyprus*, p. 33.

71. Jayawardena, *Feminism and Nationalism*, pp. 22 and 259.
72. International Labour Office, *Report to the Government of Botswana on the Co-operative Marketing of Handicraft Products* (Geneva, 1967), p. 37.
73. United Nations, *Second Progress Report*, pp. 48–49.
74. International Labour Office and Swedish International Development Authority, *Report on ILO/ECA/YWCA/SIDA Workshop*, pp. 128, 133, 138, 160, and 166.
75. ILO, Asian Regional Skill Development Programme, *Report of the Regional Workshop on Income Generating Skills for Women in Asia* (Bangkok, 1979).
76. United Nations, *Development of Opportunities*, pp. 36–39.
77. Ibid., pp. 24–33.
78. International Labour Office, *Report to the Government of the Republic of Cyprus*, p. 20.
79. At the same time they acknowledged that "handicrafts were in many cases unprofitable because of poor marketing organization." United Nations, *Progress Report*, p. 3.
80. International Labour Office, *Report to the Government of the Yemen Arab Republic on the Development of Handicrafts and Small-Scale Industries* (Geneva, 1967), p. 7.
81. International Labour Office, *Report to the Government of Botswana*, p. 28.
82. United Nations Economic and Social Council, *20th Session*, p. 12; my emphasis.
83. United Nations, *Development of Opportunities*, pp. 14–16.
84. "Women's Employment in Asian Countries," *International Labour Review* 68 (September 1953): 309–310.
85. United Nations, *Development of Opportunities*, p.22.
86. Trouvé, "Development of Rural Industries in French-Speaking Africa,"p. 65.
87. International Labour Office and Swedish International Development Authority, *Report on ILO/ECA/YWCA/SIDA Workshop*, pp. 132, 160, and 185.
88. Ibid., p. 185, my emphasis.
89. International Labour Office, *Report to the Government of the Republic of Cyprus*, pp. 31–32.
90. Ibid., p. 43.

4. Marginal Survivors or Nurturant Entrepreneurs: Home-Based Work in the Informal Sector

1. David A. Morse, Director-General of the ILO, "The World Employment Programme," *International Labour Review* 97 (June 1968): 517.
2. ILO, *International Labour Conference, 53rd session: The World Employment Programme: Report of the Director-General/Part 1* (Geneva, 1969), p. 7.

3. *Employment, Incomes, and Equality: A Strategy for Increasing Productive Employment in Kenya*, Report of an inter-agency team financed by the United Nations Development Programme and organised by the International Labour Office (Geneva: International Labour Office, 1972), p. 5. For a detailed overview of ILO studies see Harold Lubell, *The Informal Sector in the 1980s and 1990s* (Paris: OECD, 1991).

4. The following were points of controversy: Did the informal sector describe enterprises or workers? How could it be distinguished clearly from the formal sector? What was the relationship between the formal sector and the informal sector? What was the relationship between the informal sector and the state, between informality and illegality? Was the informal sector a transitional phenomenon or a permanent feature of "Third World" economies? For overviews of the early debate see Harry W. Richardson, "The Role of the Urban Informal Sector: An Overview," *Regional Development Dialogue* 5, 2 (1984): 3–40; Ray Bromley, "Introduction—The Urban Informal Sector: Why Is It Worth Discussing?" *World Development* 6 (September–October 1978): 1033–1039; Caroline O.N. Moser, "Informal Sector or Petty Commodity Production: Dualism or Dependence in Urban Development?" *World Development* 6 (September–October 1978): 1041–1064. For recent overviews see Cathy A. Rakowski, "The Informal Sector Debate, Part 2: 1984–1993," in *Contrapunto: The Informal Sector Debate in Latin America*, ed. Cathy A. Rakowski (Albany: State University of New York Press, 1994) pp. 31–50; Alejandro Portes and Richard Schauffler, "The Informal Economy in Latin America: Definition, Measurement, and Policies," in *Work Without Protections: Case Studies of the Informal Sector in Developing Countries* (Washington, D.C.: U.S. Department of Labor, Bureau of International Labor Affairs, 1993), pp. 3–39; Alejandro Portes, Manuel Castells, Lauren A. Benton, ed. *The Informal Economy: Studies in Advanced and Less Developed Countries* (Baltimore: The Johns Hopkins University Press, 1989).

5. Gustavo Márquez, "Inside Informal Sector Policies in Latin America: An Economist's View," in *Contrapunto*, p. 165.

6. Irene Tinker, *Street Foods: Testing Assumptions about Informal Sector Activity by Women and Men.* Special Issue of *Current Sociology* 35 (Winter 1987): 28–30; Bromley, "Introduction," p. 1036.

7. Carl Liedholm and Donald Mead, "Small Scale Industries in Developing Countries: Empirical Evidence and Policy Implications," MSU International Development Paper No. 9 (East Lansing: Michigan State University, 1987), pp. 35–36.

8. Michael Lipton, "Family, Fungibility and Formality: Rural Advantages of Informal Non-farm Enterprise versus the Urban-formal State," in *Human Resources, Employment and Development, Vol. 5: Developing Countries. Proceedings of the Sixth World Congress of the International Economic Association*, ed. Samir Amin (London: Macmillan, 1980).

9. E.g. Jeffrey Ashe, "Synthesis and Overall Findings," in *The Pisces Studies: Assisting the Smallest Economic Activities of the Urban Poor* ed. Michael Farbman (Washington, D.C.: U.S. Agency for International Development, 1981), p. 43.

10. Stienstra, *Women's Movements and International Organizations*, p. 91.

11. See Virginia R. Allen, Margaret E. Galey, and Mildred E. Persinger, "World Conference of International Women's Year," in *Women, Politics, and the United Nations*, pp. 29–44; Jane S. Jaquette, "Losing the Battle/Winning the War: International Politics, Women's Issues, and the 1980 Mid-Decade Conference," in *Women, Politics, and the United Nations*, pp. 45–59; Irene Tinker and Jane Jaquette, "UN Decade for Women: Its Impact and Legacy," *World Development* 15, 3: 419–424; Charlotte G. Patton, "Women and Power: The Nairobi Conference, 1985," in *Women, Politics, and the United Nations*, pp. 61–76; Hilary Charlesworth, "Women as Sherpas: Are Global Summits Useful for Women?" *Feminist Studies* 22 (Fall 1996): 537–547.

12. "Beijing Marks New Era of NGOs Holding Governments Accountable," *Mobilizing Beyond Beijing: A Quarterly Newsletter of InterAction's Commission on the Advancement of Women* No. 7 (Summer 1996), p. 1.

13. Márquez, "Inside Informal Sector Policies," p. 163.

14. María Otero, "Solidarity Group Programs: A Working Methodology for Enhancing the Economic Activities of Women in the Informal Sector," in *Women's Ventures: Assistance to the Informal Sector in Latin America*, ed. Marguerite Berger and Mayra Buvinic (West Hartford, CT: Kumarian Press, 1989), pp. 83–101; Elisabeth Rhyne and María Otero, "Financial Services for Microenterprises: Principles and Institutions," *World Development* 20, 11 (1992): 1561–1571; María Otero and Elisabeth Rhyne, ed., *The New World of Microenterprise Finance: Building Healthy Financial Institutions for the Poor* (West Hartford, CT: Kumarian Press, 1994).

15. James J. Boomgard, Dennis De Santis, Mohini Mahotra, and Anastasia Tzavaras, "Taking Stock of A.I.D.'s Microenterprise Portfolio: Background and Conceptual Overview," A.I.D. Evaluation Special Study No. 66 (Washington, D.C.: U.S. Agency for International Development, December 1989), p. 10.

16. Farbman, ed., *The Pisces Studies*. Crucial, more recent AID publications on microenterprise development include James J. Boomgard, "A.I.D. Microenterprise Stocktaking: Synthesis Report," A.I.D. Evaluation Special Study No. 65 (Washington, D.C.: U.S. Agency for International Development, 1989); Otero and Rhyne, ed., *The New World of Microenterprise Finance*.

17. Barbara Crosette, "U.N. Report Raises Questions About Small Loans to the Poor," *The New York Times* (September 3, 1998), p. A8.

18. Hernando de Soto, *The Other Path: The Invisible Revolution in the Third World* (New York: Harper and Row, 1989); for a critical discussion see Ray Bromley, "Informality, de Soto Style: From Concept to Policy," in *Contrapunto*, pp. 131–151.

19. *The Microcredit Summit Report* [Washington, D.C.: RESULTS Educational Fund, 1997], p. iii.
20. See interview with James Gustave Speth, the Administrator of the UNDP in *Countdown 2005: The Newsletter of the Microcredit Summit Campaign* 1 (September 1997). Also interview with Brian Atwood, the Administrator at USAID in *Countdown 2005: The Newsletter of the Microcredit Summit Campaign* 1 (December 1997). But also Crossette, "U.N. Report Raises Questions."
21. Margaret Lycette and Karen White, "Improving Women's Access to Credit in Latin America and the Caribbean," in *Women's Ventures*, pp. 19–44.
22. See *Bibliography of Published Research of the World Employment Programme*, 8th edition (Geneva: International Labour Office, 1990).
23. *Employment, Incomes and Equality*, p. 5; Caroline O.N. Moser, "The Informal Sector Debate, Part 1: 1970–1983," in *Contrapunto*, p. 15.
24. Allal and Chuta, *Cottage Industries and Handicrafts*, p. 14.
25. Staley and Morse, *Modern Small Industry*, p. 15.
26. Allal and Chuta, *Cottage Industries and Handicrafts*, p. 11; 27. S. V. Sethuraman, ed., *The Urban Informal Sector in Developing Countries: Employment, Poverty and Environment* (Geneva: International Labour Office, 1981), p. 214.
27. *Employment, Incomes and Equality*, p. 6. Similar ideas pertained to rural crafts. See Allal and Chuta, *Cottage Industries and Handicrafts*, p. 14.
28. Victor E. Tokman, "An Exploration into the Nature of Informal-Formal Sector Relationships," *World Development* 5, 9/10 (1978): 1067, summarizing the position put forward in R. Webb, "Income and Employment in the Urban Traditional Sector: The Case of Peru" (Princeton University, 1974, unpublished).
29. Tokman, "An Exploration," p. 1067; Moser, "Informal Sector or Petty Commodity Production," p. 1060; Chris Gerry, "Small-scale Manufacturing and Repairs in Dakar: A Survey of Market Relations within the Urban Economy," in *Casual Work and Poverty in Third World Cities*, ed. Ray Bromley and Chris Gerry (Chichester: John Wiley and Sons, 1979), pp. 229–250; Chris Gerry, "Petty Production and Capitalist Production in Dakar: The Crisis of the Self-Employed," *World Development* 6, 9 (1978): 1147–1160.
30. Alejandro Portes and Saskia Sassen-Koob, "Making It Underground: Comparative Material on the Informal Sector in Western Market Economies," *American Journal of Sociology* 93 (July 1987): 31; see also Victor E. Tokman, "Policies for a Heterogeneous Informal Sector in Latin America," *World Development* 17 (July 1989): 1067–1076.
31. William J. House, "Nairobi's Informal Sector: Dynamic Entrepreneurs or Surplus Labor?" *Economic Development and Cultural Change* 32, 2 (1984): 280.
32. Victor E. Tokman, "Policies for a Heterogeneous Informal Sector in Latin America," p. 1069.
33. *Gender and Poverty in India: A World Bank Country Study* (Washington, D.C.: The World Bank, 1991), p. 337.

34. United Nations Office at Vienna, Centre for Social Development and Human-itarian Affairs, *1989 World Survey on the Role of Women in Development* (New York, 1989).

35. Marguerite Berger, "Giving Women Credit: The Strengths and Limitations of Credit as a Tool for Alleviating Poverty," *World Development* 17 (July 1989): 1021.

36. Namely in Congo, Zambia, Venezuela, Indonesia, and Malaysia; but not in Gambia. *The World's Women 1970–1990: Trends and Statistics*, Social Statistics and Indicators, Series K, No. 8 (New York: United Nations, 1991), p. 93.

37. Ibid., p. 93; The World Bank, *World Development Report 1995: Workers in an Integrating World* (New York: Oxford University Press, 1995), p. 73; Helen I. Safa and Peggy Antrobus, "Women and the Economic Crisis in the Caribbean," in *Unequal Burden: Economic Crises, Persistent Poverty, and Women's Work*, ed. Lourdes Benería and Shelley Feldman (Boulder: Westview Press, 1992), p. 61; Lourdes Benería, "The Mexican Debt Crisis: Restructuring in the Economy and the Household," in *Unequal Burden*, p. 92; Aili Mari Tripp, "The Impact of Crisis and Economic Reform on Women in Urban Tanzania," in *Unequal Burden*; Victoria Daines and David Seddon, "Confronting Austerity: Women's Responses to Economic Reform," in *Women's Lives and Public Policy: The International Experience*, ed. Meredeth Turshen and Briavel Holcomb (Westport, CT: Praeger, 1993): 3–32; June Nash, "Maya Household Production in the World Market: The Potters of Amatenango del Valle, Chiapas, Mexico," in *Crafts in the World Market: The Impact of Global Exchange on Middle American Artisans*, ed. J. Nash (Albany: State University of New York Press, 1993), p. 129. For evidence on the prevalence of women in informal activities under conditions of flexible specialization see Vittorio Capecchi, "The Informal Economy and the Development of Flexible Specialization in Emilia-Romagna," in *The Informal Economy*, p. 212.

38. Ashe, "Synthesis and Overall Findings," p. 19.

39. Berger, "Giving Women Credit," p. 1021.

40. United Nations Office at Vienna, *1989 World Survey*, p. 219.

41. Alejandro Portes, Silvia Blitzer, and John Curtis, "The Urban Informal Sector in Uruguay: Its Internal Structure, Characteristics, and Effects," *World Development* 14, 6 (1986): 729, 734–735, and 739; see also Portes and Sassen-Koob, "Making It Underground," p. 40.

42. For a summary see United Nations Office in Vienna, *1989 World Survey*, pp. 221–223.

43. W. Paul Strassmann, "Home-based Enterprises in Cities of Developing Countries," *Economic Development and Cultural Change* 36, 1 (1987): 135 and 131.

44. Boomgard, "A.I.D. Microenterprise Stocktaking," p. xiii.

45. Irene Tinker, *Street Foods: Urban Food and Employment in Developing Countries* (New York, Oxford: Oxford University Press, 1997), p. 197; Caren A. Grown

and Jennefer Sebstad, "Introduction: Toward a Wider Perspective on Women's Employment," *World Development* 17 (July 1989): 940.

46. Ashe, "Synthesis and Overall Findings," p. 19.

47. "Proceedings of the Senior Management Seminar: Micro and Small Enterprise, January 12, 1989" prepared for the U.S. Agency for International Development (Washington, D.C.: Development Alternatives, Inc.), p. 6.

48. Lourdes Benería, "Accounting for Women's Work," in *Women and Development: The Sexual Division of Labor in Rural Societies*, ed. L. Benería (New York: Praeger, 1982): 119–147.

49. Irene Tinker, "The Adverse Impact of Development on Women," in *Women and World Development* ed. I. Tinker and Michelle Bo Bramsen (New York: Praeger, 1976); Irene Tinker, "The Making of a Field: Advocates, Practitioners, and Scholars," in *Persistent Inequalities: Women and World Development*, I. Tinker ed. (New York: Oxford University Press, 1990), pp. 27–53. Representative works include essays in *Persistent Inequalities*; Roslyn Dauber and Melinda L. Cain, ed., *Women and Technological Change in Developing Countries* (Boulder: Westview, 1981); Ester Boserup, *Women's Role in Economic Development* (New York: St. Martin's Press, 1970); Rogers, *The Domestication of Women*. For a comprehensive treatment of the WID movement, its arguments, and its critics, see Naila Kabeer, *Reversed Realities: Gender Hierarchies in Development Thought* (London: Verso, 1994), esp. chapters 1–3. On cooperatives and handicrafts see Devaki Jain, *Women's Quest For Power: Five Indian Case Studies* (Ghaziabad, India: Vikas Publishing House Pvt Ltd, 1980); Manoshi Mitra, "Women's Work: Gains Analysis of Women's Labour in Dairy Production," in *Invisible Hands: Women in Home-based Production* ed. Andrea Menefee Singh and Anita Kelles-Viitanen (New Delhi: Sage Publications, 1987).

50. Boserup, *Women's Role in Economic Development*; Sue Ellen M. Charlton, *Women in Third World Development* (Boulder: Westview Press, 1984); Irene Tinker, "Feminizing Development—For Growth with Equity," *Care Briefs on Development Issues*, No. 6 (n.d.), pp. 3–4; Lynne Brydon and Sylvia Chant, *Women in the Third World: Gender Issues in Rural and Urban Areas* (New Brunswick, NJ: Rutgers University Press, 1993). In a study in the early 1990s, the UN Development Program systematically applied this approach to thirty-one countries, finding that "women work longer hours than men in nearly every country" and that "of the total burden of work, women carry on average 53% in developing countries and 51% in industrial countries." Furthermore, "of men's total work time in industrial countries, roughly two-thirds is spent in paid SNA [i.e. System of National Accounts] activities and one-third in unpaid non-SNA activities. For women, these shares are reversed." United Nations Development Program, *Human Development Report 1995* (New York: Oxford University Press, 1995), p. 88.

51. This is also true for family firms in the informal sector which employ many women—often as unpaid family labor. Liedholm and Mead, "Small Scale Industries in Developing Countries," p. 36; Strassmann, "Home-based Enterprises," p. 125.

52. Rebecca Reichmann, "Women's Participation in Two PVO Credit Programs for Microenterprise: Cases from the Dominican Republic and Peru," in *Women's Ventures*, p. 142; Strassmann, "Home-based Enterprises"; Irene Tinker, *Street Foods: Testing Assumptions*.

53. Lourdes Benería and Gita Sen, "Accumulation, Reproduction, and Women's Role in Economic Development: Boserup Revisited," *Signs: A Journal of Women in Culture and Society* 7 (Winter 1981): 279–298; Gita Sen and Caren Grown, *Development, Crises, and Alternative Visions: Third World Women's Perspectives* (New York: Monthly Review Press, 1987); Kabeer, *Reversed Realities*, chap. 3.

54. Maria Mies, *The Lace Makers of Narsapur: Indian Housewives Produce for the World Market* (London: Zed Press, 1982).

55. Ibid.; Singh and Kelles-Viitanen, *Invisible Hands*; Zarina Bhatty, *The Economic Role and Status of Women in the Beedi Industry in Allahabad, India* (Saarbrücken: Verlag Breitenbach, 1981); Günseli Berik, *Women Carpet Weavers in Rural Turkey: Patterns of Employment, Earnings and Status* (Geneva: International Labour Office, 1987).

56. Richard Longhurst, "Resource Allocation and the Sexual Division of Labor: A Case Study of a Moslem Hausa Village in Northern Nigeria," in *Women and Development*, p. 110.

57. Anita M. Weiss, *Walls Within Walls: Life Histories of Working Women in the Old City of Lahore* (Boulder, San Francisco, Oxford: Westview Press, 1992); Anita M. Weiss, "Within the Walls: Home-based Work in Lahore," in *Homeworkers in Global Perspective*, pp. 81–92.

58. Zohreh Ghavamshahidi, " 'Bibi Khanum': Carpet Weavers and Gender Ideology in Iran," in *Homeworkers in Global Perspective*, pp. 111–128; Dewi Haryani Susilastuti, "Home-Based Work as a Rural Survival Strategy," in *Homeworkers in Global Perspective*, pp. 129–141. For a review of evidence on Thailand see Prügl, "Home-Based Workers: A Comparative Exploration ," pp. 124–126.

59. Lourdes Benería and Martha Roldán, *The Crossroads of Class and Gender: Industrial Homework, Subcontracting, and Household Dynamics in Mexico City* (Chicago: The University of Chicago Press, 1987); Bryan R. Roberts, "Employment Structure, Life Cycles, and Life Chances: Formal and Informal Sectors in Guadalajara," in *The Informal Economy*, pp. 41–59; Alice Rangel de Paiva Abreu and Bila Sorj, " 'Good Housewives': Seamstresses in the Brazilian Garment Industry," in *Homeworkers in Global Perspective*, pp. 93–110; Alice Rangel de Paiva Abreu and Bila Sorj, ed., *O Trabalho Invisível: Estudos Sobre Trabalhadores A Domicílio No Brasil* (Rio de Janeiro, RJ: Rio Fundo Editora Ltda.,

1993); Faranak Miraftab, "Space, Gender, and Work: Home-Based Workers in Mexico," in *Homeworkers in Global Perspective*, pp. 63–80; José Antonio Alonso, "The Domestic Clothing Workers in the Mexican Metropolis and Their Relation to Dependent Capitalism," in *Women, Men and the International Division of Labor*; José Antonio Alonso, *Mujeres Maquiladoras Y Microindustria Domestica* (Mexico, D.F.: Distribuciones Fontamara, S.A., 1991); Nash, ed., *Crafts in the World Market*.

60. Parimal Das, "Women under India's Community Development Programme," *International Labour Review* 80 (July–December 1959): 41.

61. *Selected Standards and Policy Statements of Special Interest to Women Workers Adopted Under the Auspices of the International Labour Office* (Geneva: International Labour Office, 1980), pp. 11–12. One resolution concerned the Economic and Social Advancement of Women in Developing Countries and the other Women Workers in a Changing World.

62. ILO, *International Labour Conference, 45th Session: Record of Proceedings* (Geneva, 1962), p. 567, my emphasis; Lubin and Winslow, *Social Justice for Women*, p. 100.

63. ILO, *International Labour Conference, 48th Session: Record of Proceedings* (Geneva, 1965), p. 469.

64. International Labour Office and Swedish International Development Authority, *Report on ILO/ECA/YWCA/SIDA Workshop*, p. 189.

65. Dhamija, "Handicrafts," p. 464.

66. United Nations Economic Commission for Africa, *Report of the Workshop on Handicrafts and Small-Scale Industries Development for Women in Francophone Countries* (Addis Ababa, 1980), p. 31; later cited as United Nations, *Report of the Workshop on Handicrafts*.

67. United Nations Economic Commission for Africa, *Report of the Workshop on the Participation of Women in Development* (Addis Ababa, 1979), p. 9.

68. Mayra Buvinic, "Investing in Poor Women: The Psychology of Donor Support," *World Development* 17 (July 1989): 1052.

69. Jasleen Dhamija, "Women and Handicrafts: Myth and Reality," in *Seeds: Supporting Women's Work in the Third World*, ed. Ann Leonard (New York: The Feminist Press, 1989), p. 195; Sue Ellen M. Charlton, *Women in Third World Development* (Boulder: Westview, 1984), p. 129.

70. Dhamija, "Women and Handicrafts," p. 195.

71. International Labour Office and Swedish International Development Agency, *Report on ILO/ECA/YWCA/SIDA Workshop*, p. 70.

72. See Caroline O. N. Moser, *Gender Planning and Development: Theory, Practice and Training* (London, New York: Routledge, 1993), chap. 4.

73. United Nations, *Report of the Workshop on Handicrafts*, pp. 25–26.

74. ILO, *Tripartite Asian Regional Seminar on Rural Development and Women in Asia: Proceedings and Conclusions* (Geneva, 1982), p. 31.
75. United Nations, *Report of the Workshop on Handicrafts*, pp. 30 and 35; International Labour Office and Swedish International Development Authority, *Report on ILO/ECA/YWCA/SIDA Workshop*, p. 21.
76. Ibid., p. 14.
77. See e.g. Sethuraman, ed., *The Urban Informal Sector*, p. 189.
78. Allal and Chuta, *Cottage Industries and Handicrafts*, p. 3.
79. Ibid.
80. Irene Tinker, "Credit for Poor Women: Necessary, But Not Always Sufficient for Change," *Change* 10 (Spring 1989), p. 41; Judith Bruce, "Homes Divided," *World Development* 17 (July 1989): 987–988; Benería and Roldán, *The Crossroads of Class and Gender*, chapter 7.
81. Bruce, "Homes Divided," p. 985; see also Benjamin Senauer, "The Impact of the Value of Women's Time on Food and Nutrition," in *Persistent Inequalities*, p. 158.
82. Irene Tinker, "The Human Economy of Microentrepreneurs," in *Women in Micro- and Small-Scale Enterprise Development*, ed. Louise Dignard and José Havet (Boulder, San Francisco: Westview Press, 1995), pp. 25, and 39; Tinker, "The Making of a Field," p. 47.
83. Berger, "Giving Women Credit," p. 1018.
84. *Women at Work* No. 1 (Geneva: International Labour Office, 1987), pp. 12–13.
85. Muhammad Yunus, "Does the Capitalist System Have to be the Handmaiden of the Rich," Keynote Address delivered at 85th Rotary International Convention held at Taipei, Taiwan, June 12–15, 1994, p. 2.
86. David Bornstein, *The Price of a Dream: The Story of the Grameen Bank and the Idea That Is Helping the Poor to Change Their Lives* (New York: Simon and Schuster, 1996), p. 19.
87. Yunus, "Does the Capitalist System Have to be the Handmaiden of the Rich," p. 2.
88. *The Microcredit Summit Report*, p. 26.
89. Tinker, "The Making of a Field," p. 47.

5. Fordist Gender Rules at Issue: The Debate Over the ILO Home Work Convention

1. Robert W. Cox, *Production, Power, and World Order: Social Forces in the Making of History* (New York: Columbia University Press, 1987), pp. 274–279.

2. Folker Fröbel, Otto Kreye, and Jürgen Heinrichs, *The New International Division of Labour: Structural Unemployment in Industrialised Countries and Industrialisation in Developing Countries*, trans. Pete Burgess (Cambridge: Cambridge University Press, 1980), p. 61 and Table 2 in the appendix; Nash and Fernandez-Kelly, ed. *Women, Men, and the International Division of Labor*.
3. For an overview of these processes see Michael Storper and Allen J. Scott, "Work Organisation and Local Labour Markets in an Era of Flexible Production," World Employment Programme Research Working Paper No. 30 (Geneva: ILO, 1989) p. 15. For related issues see Guy Standing, "Labour Flexibility: Towards a Research Agenda," World Employment Programme Research Working Paper (Geneva: ILO, 1986); Richard S. Belous, "Flexibility and American Labour Markets: The evidence and implications," World Employment Programme Research Working Paper No. 14 (Geneva: ILO, 1987); Bennett Harrison and Barry Bluestone, "The dark side of labour market 'flexibility': Falling wages and growing income inequality in America," World Employment Programme Research Working Paper No. 17 (Geneva: ILO, 1987); Guy Standing, "European Unemployment, Insecurity and Flexibility: A Social Dividend Solution," World Employment Programme Research Working Paper No. 23 (Geneva: ILO, 1988).

For feminist interpretations see Swasti Mitter, *Common Fate, Common Bond: Women in the Global Economy* (London: Pluto Press, 1986); Swasti Mitter, "Computer-Aided Manufacturing and Women's Employment: A Global Critique of Post-Fordism," in *Women, Work and Computerization: Understanding and Overcoming Bias in Work and Education*, ed. Inger V. Eriksson, Barbara A. Kitchenham, and Kea G. Tijdens (Amsterdam: North-Holland, 1991); Swasti Mitter, "On Organising Women in Casualised Work: A Global Overview," in *Dignity and Daily Bread*; Rosalinda Pineda-Ofreneo, "Women and Work: Focus on Homework in the Philippines," *Review of Women's Studies* 1, 1 (1990): 42–55; Kathryn Ward, ed. *Women Workers and Global Restructuring*; Jamie Faricellia Dangler, *Hidden in the Home: The Role of Waged Homework in the Modern World-Economy* (Albany: State University of New York Press, 1994).
4. Robert W. Cox, "The Global Political Economy and Social Choice," in *Approaches to World Order*, by Robert W. Cox and Timothy J. Sinclair (Cambridge: Cambridge University Press, 1996), p. 193.
5. Cox, *Production, Power, and World Order*, pp. 274–279.
6. For example, the government of Indonesia promoted linkages between large-scale modern industries and small-scale home-based firms as "father and son" relationships. The government of the Republic of Cyprus encouraged subcontracting linkages as a new model of development. Swasti Mitter, "Homeworking: An Evaluation in a Global Context," March 1990, unpublished, p. 33, ILO-CONDI/T Files on Homework, Geneva. The government of Sri Lanka set up "export production villages" enlisting private firms to export the products of rural

producers whose villages are organized into companies. Vidyamali Samara-singhe, "The Last Frontier or a New Beginning? Women's Microenterprises in Sri Lanka," in *Women at the Center: Development Issues and Practices for the 1990s*, ed. Gay Young, Vidyamali Samarasinghe, and Ken Kusterer (West Hart-ford, CT: Kumarian Press, 1993), pp. 38–39; Lakshmi Perera, "Women in Mi-cro- and Small-Scale Enterprise Development in Sri Lanka," in *Women in Mi-cro- and Small-Scale Enterprise Development*, p. 103. The government of the Philippines encouraged homework as part of its export-oriented, labor-intensive development strategy. Pineda-Ofreneo, "Women and Work," p. 51. Even before globalization pushed other countries towards encouraging home-based subcon-tracting, the government of Taiwan had built its export-oriented industrialization on the work of home-based producers. Ping-Chun Hsiung, *Living Rooms as Factories: Class, Gender, and the Satellite Factory System in Taiwan* (Philadel-phia: Temple University Press, 1996), chap. 2.

7. Catherine Hakim, "Homework and Outwork: National Estimates From Two Surveys," *Employment Gazette* 92 (January 1984): 9 and 11; Government of Germany, Ministry of Labor and Social Affairs, *Bundesarbeitsblatt* (Bonn) 3/ 1985, p.133, and 10/1988, p. 70; Assefa Bequele, "Homework: Why Should We Care?" in ILO, *Asian Subregional Tripartite Seminar on the Protection of Ho-meworkers: Proceedings* (Geneva, 1988), pp. 37f; Council of Europe, *The Pro-tection of Persons Working at Home* (Strasbourg, 1989), p. 16; Portes and Sassen-Koob. "Making It Underground," p. 46; Ruth Rose and Michel Grant, "Le Travail à Domicile Dans L'Industrie Du Vêtement Au Quebec" (Montréal: Université du Québec à Montréal, 1983), p. 78.

8. ILO, *Meeting of Experts on the Social Protection of Homeworkers: Documents* (Geneva, 1991), p. 78; Safa and Antrobus, "Women and the Economic Crisis in the Caribbean," p. 61; Benería, "The Mexican Debt Crisis, p. 92; Aili Mari Tripp, "The Impact of Crisis and Economic Reform"; Daines and Seddon, "Confronting Austerity ; Nash, "Maya Household Production in the World Mar-ket," p. 129.

9. Hsiung, *Living Rooms as Factories*; Tai-Lok Lui, *Wage Work at Home: The Social Organization of Industrial Outwork in Hong Kong* (Aldershot: Avebury, 1994).

10. It is not at all clear that the ILO will have a role to play in the new global regime of accumulation. Much will depend on its ability to carve out a role in the new mode of regulation. Proposals to the World Trade Organization to make free trade privileges contingent on good labor practices are troubling in this respect because they constitute an infringement on ILO competencies. While some member states have rejected such proposals, rescuing the ILO may be to the detriment of workers who would benefit from such a powerful tool.

11. Michel Aglietta, *A Theory of Capitalist Regulation: The U.S. Experience*, trans. David Fernbach (London: New Left Books, 1985); Alain Lipietz, *Mirages and*

Miracles: The Crisis of Global Fordism, trans. David Macey (London: Verso, 1987); Robert Boyer, *The Regulation School: A Critical Introduction*, trans. Craig Charney (New York: Columbia University Press, 1990); David Harvey, *The Condition of Postmodernity: An Enquiry into the Origins of Cultural Change* (Oxford: Basil Blackwell, 1989); John Grahl and Paul Teague, "The Cost of Neo-Liberal Europe," *New Left Review* 174 (March–April 1989): 37.

12. Noël has argued that it is useful to combine the insights from the regulation school with theories of international regimes. He also provides a useful review of major works of the regulation school. Alain Noël, "Accumulation, regulation, and social change: an essay on French political economy," *International Organization* 41, 2 (Spring 1987): 303–333.

13. Robert W. Cox, "Labor and Hegemony," in *Approaches to World Order*, p. 444.

14. The notion of the "unprotected worker" is from Jeffrey Harrod, *Power, Production, and the Unprotected Worker* (New York: Columbia University Press, 1987). See also Cox, *Power, Production, and World Order*, p. 297.

15. *International Labour Conventions and Recommendations, 1919–1991* (Geneva: International Labour Office, 1992), pp. 225, 560, and 693.

16. ILO, *International Labour Conference, 82nd Session: Report V (1): Home Work* (Geneva, 1994), p. 77.

17. Diane Elson and Ruth Pearson, " 'Nimble Fingers Make Cheap Workers': An Analysis of Women's Employment in Third World Export Manufacturing," *Feminist Review* 8 (Spring 1981), esp. pp. 92–99.

18. Susan Tiano, *Patriarchy on the Line: Labor, Gender, and Ideology in the Mexican Maquila Industry* (Philadelphia: Temple University Press, 1994), pp. 92–96. In Puerto Rico and the Dominican Republic married women always played an important role in export-processing attesting to the divergent outcomes that global rules effect in local interactions. Safa, *The Myth of the Male Breadwinners*.

19. Warren Magnusson, *The Search for Political Space: Globalization, Social Movements, and the Urban Political Experience* (Toronto: University of Toronto Press, 1996), pp. 86–87.

20. Cox, *Production, Power, and World Order*, p. 282; Cox, "The Global Political Economy and Social Choice," p. 198; Stephen Gill, *American Hegemony and the Trilateral Commission* (New York, Port Chester, Melbourne, Sydney: Cambridge University Press, 1990).

    Capital is pervasively organized at the global level. John Boli and George M. Thomas found that between 1875 and 1973 industry, trade, and industrial groups accounted for 17.6 percent of all international nongovernmental organizations listed in the Yearbook of International Organizations, constituting the largest category of such organizations. See John Boli and George M. Thomas, "World Culture in the World Polity: A Century of International Non-Governmental Organizations," *American Sociological Review* 62 (April 1997): 183.

21. Runyan, "Women in the Neoliberal 'Frame';" Runyan, "The Places of Women in Trading Places," and Marchand, "Selling NAFTA." On private and public patriarchy see Safa, *The Myth of the Male Breadwinner*. For critiques of structural adjustment see Pamela Sparr, ed. *Mortgaging Women's Lives: Feminist Critiques of Structural Adjustment* (London, New Jersey: Zed Press, 1994); Daines and Seddon, "Confronting Austerity," pp. 3–32. On women organizing see Ann Bookman and Sandra Morgen, *Women and the Politics of Empowerment* (Philadelphia: Temple University Press, 1988); Rowbotham and Mitter, *Dignity and Daily Bread*; Margaret Hosmer Martens and Swasti Mitter, ed. *Women in Trade Unions: Organizing the Unorganized* (Geneva: International Labour Office, 1994); Boris and Prügl, ed. *Homeworkers in Global Perspective*.

22. Jane Tate, "Making Links: The Growth of Homeworker Networks," in *Homeworkers in Global Perspective*, pp. 273–289.

23. ILO, *International Labour Conference, 83rd Session: Provisional Record 10* (Geneva, 1996), p. 17.

24. See chapter 4, note 55.

25. Kalima Rose, *Where Women Are Leaders: The SEWA Movement in India* (London: Zed Press, 1992), p. 124.

26. Lucita Lazo, "Women's Empowerment in the Making: The Philippine Bid for Social Protection," in *Homeworkers in Global Perspective..*

27. Lucita Lazo and Phanomwan Yoodee, "Networking for Economic Empowerment: The Chiangmai Homenet," in *From the Shadows to the Fore: Practical Actions for the Social Protection of Homeworkers in Thailand*, ed. Lucita Lazo (Bangkok: ILO Regional Office for Asia and the Pacific, 1993), pp. 31–70.

28. Yayasan Pengembangan Pedesaan, "Grassroots Organizing of Homeworkers: The Gondang Experiment," in *From the Shadows to the Fore: Practical Actions for the Social Protection of Homeworkers in Indonesia*, ed. Lucita Lazo (Bangkok: ILO Regional Office for Asia and the Pacific, 1993), pp. 59–74.

29. See for example, ILO, Governing Body, Industrial Activities Committee, *214th Session, Seventh Item on the Agenda: Periodic Report on the Effect Given to the Requests of Industrial Committees and Similar Bodies*, Geneva, 1980; ILO, Textiles Committee, *Eleventh Session: General Report* (Geneva, 1984), p. 94; ILO, *Tripartite Technical Meeting for the Leather and Footwear Industry: General Report* (Geneva, 1985), p. 61.

30. Results are published as an issue entitled *Home Work* of the *Conditions of Work Digest* 8, 2 (1989). Luz Vega Ruiz provides a summary of the results in "Home Work: Towards a New Regulatory Framework?" *International Labour Review* 131, 2 (1992): 197–216.

31. Gisela Schneider de Villegas, "Home Work: A Case for Social Protection," *International Labour Review* 129, 4 (1990): 423–439; *Telework*, Issue of *Conditions of Work Digest* 9, 1 (1990). None of the monographs were published by

the ILO although some authors published findings from their research through other venues. The monographs included Julio César Neffa, "Condiciones Y Medio Ambiente De Trabajo De Los Trabajadores A Domicilio En Argentina"; Anuradha Prasad and K. V. Eswara Prasad, "Home-Working in India: A Review"; Rosalinda Pineda-Ofreneo, "Industrial Homework in the Philippines"; S.E.G. Perera, "National Monograph on Home Work in Sri Lanka"; Chulalongkorn Social Research Institute, "Thailand Rural Women Homeworkers"; and Miguel Angel Lacabana, "Trabajo A Domicilio En Paises En Desarrollo: El Caso De Venezuela." Swasti Mitter, "Homeworking: An Evaluation in a Global Context," provided an overview of the major findings from the monographs. All can be found in ILO-CONDI/T files on Homework, Geneva.

32. Results are published in ILO, *International Labour Conference, 82nd Session: Report V (2): Home Work* (Geneva, 1995).

33. Published in ILO, *International Labour Conference, 83rd Session: Report IV (2A): Home Work* (Geneva, 1996).

34. "Employment Rights for Homeworkers," *HomeNet Newsletter* No. 9 (Summer 1998): 3.

35. Speech by Ela Bhatt at ILO Meeting of Experts on the Social Protection of Homeworkers, Geneva, October 1–5, 1990, author's notes.

36. Elia Ramirez, "HomeNet International: Launch of the International Network for Home-based Workers," *News from IRENE: International Restructuring Education Network Europe* (Tilburg, Netherlands) No. 22 (March 1995): 29–30; *Working Together: Recognition for Homebased Workers at the International Labour Organisation* (n.p.: Self-Employed Women's Association and HomeNet, March 1996); also various articles in Boris and Prügl, ed. *Homeworkers in Global Perspective.*

37. See for example, Swasti Mitter, "On Organising Workers in the Informal Sector."

38. ILO, *International Labour Conference, 82nd Session, Provisional Record 27* (Geneva, 1995), p. 34. There are still a number of national unions that favor a total ban on homework. ILO *Meeting of Experts*, p. 27.

39. See *Need for an ILO Convention for Homebased Workers* (Ahmedabad: Self-Employed Women's Association, n.d.).

40. ILO, *International Labour Conference, 82nd Session: Provisional Record 27*, pp. 30 and 41.

41. ILO Meeting of Experts, author's notes.

42. Jhabvala, "Self-Employed Women's Association," pp. 117–118.

43. ILO, *International Labour Conference, 82nd Session: Report V (1)*, p. 59.

44. ILO Meeting of Experts, author's notes.

45. ILO, *International Labour Conference, 83rd Session, Provisional Record 10* (Geneva, 1996), p. 4.

46. ILO, *International Labour Conference, 82nd Session, Provisional Record 27*, p. 43.
47. ILO, *International Labour Conference, 83rd Session, Report IV (2A)*, pp. 17–18.
48. ILO, *International Labour Conference, 82nd Session: Provisional Record 27*, p. 23.
49. Ibid., p. 26.
50. ILO, *International Labour Conference, 83rd Session: Report IV (2A)*, pp. 224–225.
51. ILO, *International Labour Conference, 82nd Session: Provisional Record 27*, p. 41.
52. Ibid., pp. 37–38.

6. Fordist Class Categories at Issue: Are Homeworkers Employees or Self-Employed?

1. ILO, *International Labour Conference, 77th Session: Report VII: The Promotion of Self-Employment* (Geneva, 1990), pp. 63–68.
2. Ibid., pp. 14–21.
3. Cox, "Labor and Hegemony," pp. 440–442.
4. For a theoretical elaboration of heteronomy as a form of rule see Onuf, *World of Our Making*, pp. 212–219.
5. John W. Cairns, "Blackstone, Kahn-Freund and the Contract of Employment," *The Law Quarterly Review* 105 (April 1989): 300–314.
6. Christopher L. Tomlins, "Law and Power in the Employment Relationship," in *Labor Law in America: Historical and Critical Essays*, ed. Christopher L. Tomlins and Andrew J. King (Baltimore: The Johns Hopkins University Press, 1992), pp. 74–76; Marc Linder, *Farewell to the Self-Employed: Deconstructing a Socioeconomic and Legal Solipsism* (New York: Greenwood Press, 1992), p. 37.
7. For an incisive interpretation of state and movement interventions fostering this understanding in the United States see Linder, *Farewell to the Self-Employed*, especially chap. 5.
8. ILO, *Ninth International Conference of Labour Statisticians, Committee on the International Classification According to Status* (Geneva, 1957), p. 32; ILO, *Ninth International Conference of Labour Statisticians, Report III: International Classification According to Status* (Geneva, 1957), p. 22; ILO, *Sixth International Conference of Labor Statisticians: International Standards for Statistics of Employment, Unemployment and the Labour Force, Cost of Living and Industrial Injuries* (Montreal, 1947), p. 9; International Labour Office, *Yearbook of Labour Statistics*, 14th Issue (Geneva, 1954), p. 2.

9. ILO Meeting of Experts, author's notes.
10. Ibid.
11. For an elaboration see Prügl and Tinker, "Microentrepreneurs and Homeworkers."
12. Rose, *Where Women Are Leaders*, p. 195. SEWA's interpretation gained some popularity in international development circles. See A. Graham Tipple, "Shelter as Workplace: A Review of Home-Based Enterprise in Developing Countries," *International Labour Review* 132, 4 (1993): 521–539.
13. Carole Pateman, *The Sexual Contract* (Stanford, CA: Stanford University Press, 1988), esp. chap. 5.
14. In the ILO, flexible employment practices often were subsumed under the term "atypical employment," reflecting their status outside the regulatory structures of the institution. E.g. Efrén Córdova, "From Full-Time Wage Employment to Atypical Employment: A Major Shift in the Evolution of Labour Relations?" *International Labour Review* 129, 4 (1990): 641–657.
15. Cynthia B. Costello, "The Clerical Homework Program at the Wisconsin Physicians Services Insurance Corporation," in *Homework: Historical and Contemporary Perspectives on Paid Labor at Home*, ed. Eileen Boris and Cynthia Daniels (Urbana: University of Illinois Press, 1989), p. 205.
16. Mirai Chatterjee, "Occupational Health Issues of Home-Based Piece-Rate Workers," in *Report of a National Workshop on Home-Based Piece-Rate Workers* (Ahmedabad: Mahila Sewa Trust, 1987), pp. 28–29.
17. Soumyajit Ghoshal and Debkumar Chakraborti, "Man, Machine, Environment: An Ergonomic Study on the Readymade Garment Workers at Ahmedabad for Improvement of Health, Safety, Efficiency at Work and Productivity," in *Report of a National Workshop*, p. 34 (emphasis deleted).
18. For a discussion of these various problems see Ruiz, "Home Work,"pp. 205–214.
19. Kathleen E. Christensen, "Independent Contracting," in *The New Era of Home-Based Work: Directions and Policies*, ed. Kathleen E. Christensen (Boulder: Westview Press, 1988), p. 81; Sheila Allen and Carol Wolkowitz, *Homeworking: Myth and Realities* (London: Macmillan, 1987), p. 110.
20. Hisham R. Hashem, *Arab Contract of Employment: Conflict and Concord, A Comparative Study* (The Hague: Martinus Nijhoff, 1964), p. ix.
21. The continental law tradition has its origins in Roman law, became the basis of the Napoleonic Code, and today underlies the French and German legal systems. These systems rely on written legal codes that cover all major areas of civil affairs. In contrast, British common law draws on precedent rather than preformulated rules in judicial decisionmaking. The French introduced the continental law tradition to their colonies in sub-Saharan Africa. Latin American law also is strongly influenced by the Napoleonic Code. The German system influ-

enced the development of law in Hungary and Greece as well as in China, Japan, and Thailand. The British exported common law to their colonies; nearly one-third of all people today live in regions influenced by the common law tradition. Konrad Zweigert and Hein Kötz, *Introduction to Comparative Law. Volume I—The Framework*, trans. Tony Weir (Oxford: Clarendon Press, 1987), pp. 116–118, 159–160, and 227.

22. E. Herz, "The Contract of Employment: I," *International Labour Review* 31 (May 1935): 845.

23. The case of homeworkers who are connected to their companies' mainframe computer forms an important, albeit rare, exception.

24. Herz, "The Contract of Employment: I," p. 847. A judge in a U.S. court combined these understandings when, in 1939, he denied a seasonally employed woman unemployment benefits because he considered her to be "self-employed as a housewife." Marc Linder, *Farewell to the Self-Employed*, p. 102.

25. E.g. in Britain: *Gookey v. Expert Clothing Services & Sales Ltd.*, case number Q22/76/E, Industrial Tribunal, reprinted in *Homeworking: A TUC Statement* (London: Trades Union Congress, 1978), pp. 22–26.

26. Marc Linder, "The Joint Employment Doctrine: Clarifying Joint Legislative-Judicial Confusion," *Hamline Journal of Public Law and Policy* 10 (Fall 1989): 323. See also Patricia Davidson, "Comment: The Definition of 'Employee' under Title VII: Distinguishing Between Employees and Independent Contractors," *University of Cincinnati Law Review* 53 (1984): 208; Jeanne M. Glader, "Harvest of Shame: The Imposition of Independent Contractor Status on Migrant Farmworkers and Its Ramifications for Migrant Children," *Hastings Law Journal* 42 (July 1992): 1475–1476; Marc Linder, "Employees, Not-So-Independent Contractors, and the Case of Migrant Farmworkers: A Challenge to the 'Law and Economics' Agency Doctrine," *New York University Review of Law and Social Change* 15, 3 (1986–1987): 449–450; Donald Elisburg, "Legalities,"*Telematics and Informatics* 2 (1985): 182.

27. Simon Brown, Untitled Paper reviewing legislation on employment status in the European Union, presented at the International Conference on Homeworking, 7th–10th May 1990, Helvoirt, The Netherlands; H. Barbagelata, "Different Categories of Workers and Labour Contracts," in *Comparative Labour Law and Industrial Relations*, ed. R. Blanpain (Deventer: Kluwer Law and Taxation Publishers, 1987), p. 428.

28. Marc Linder, "What Is an Employee? Why It Does, But Should Not, Matter," *Law and Inequality: A Journal of Theory and Practice* 7 (March 1989): 175.

29. Linder, *Farewell to the Self-Employed*, p. 38; also pp. 149–150.

30. ILO, *International Labour Conference, 83rd Session: Record of Proceedings*, p. 221.

31. International Labour Conference, *Convention 177: Convention Concerning Home Work* (ILO pamphlet), Article 1 (a). See Appendix.

32. ILO, *International Labor Conference, 83rd Session: Provisional Record 10* (Geneva, 1996), p. 5.

33. ILO, *International Labour Conference, 83rd Session, Report IV (2A)*, p. 35.

34. ILO, *International Labour Conference, 82nd Session: Provisional Record 27*, p. 34.

35. Ibid., p. 24.

36. ILO, *International Labour Conference, 83rd Session: Provisional Record 10*, p. 5.

37. ILO, *International Labour Conference, 82nd Session: Provisional Record 27*, p. 25.

38. Zubeida M. Ahmad and Martha F. Loutfi, *Women Workers in Rural Development: A Programme of the ILO* (Geneva: ILO, 1982), p. 1.

39. Martha F. Loutfi, "Development with Women: Action, Not Alibis," *International Labour Review* 126 (January-February 1987): 121.

40. Ahmad and Loutfi, *Women Workers in Rural Development*, p. 23.

41. Jhabvala, "Self-Employed Women's Association," esp. pp. 127–137. For an extensive history of SEWA see Rose, *Where Women Are Leaders*.

42. The project was part of a multi-bilateral program financed by the government of Finland from 1986 to 1990. "Empowering Women: Self-Employment Schemes for Female-Headed Households," Terminal Evaluation Report, Project ILO/RAS/81/10/FIN (Geneva: International Labour Office, 1989).

43. ILO, Multi-Bilateral Programme of Technical Co-operation, *Participatory Action-Research Project on the Development of Effective Monitoring Systems and Application of Legislation on Home-Based Piece-Rate Producers*, [photocopy], ILO-CONDI/T files on homework, International Labor Office, Geneva, p. 3.

44. "Empowering Women: Self-Employment Schemes for Female-headed Households." Terminal Evaluation Report, Project ILO/RAS/81/10/FIN (Geneva: International Labour Office, 1989), pp. 30–32 and Annex B1.

45. ILO, Multi-Bilateral Programme of Technical Co-operation, *Employment promotion and social and legal protection of home-based workers in Asia*, Summary Project Outline, [photocopy], ILO-CONDI/T files on homework, International Labor Office, Geneva.

46. W. B. Greigton, "Social and Legal Protection of Home-Based Workers in Asia," Minute transmitted to A. Kelles-Viitanen, May 17, 1989 [photocopy], ILO-CONDI/T files on homework, International Labor Office, Geneva, p.2.

47. ILO, Multibilateral Programme of Technical Cooperation, "Rural Women Workers in the New Putting Out System," Project Document, ILO-CONDI/T files on homework, International Labor Office, Geneva, p. 6.

48. Azita Berar, "Report on the mission to Bangkok and to Nepal from 31/5/89 to 11/6/89," [photocopy] ILO-CONDI/T files on homework, International Labor Office, Geneva, p. 3.

49. ILO, *Subregional Meetings I and II of the ILO-DANIDA Subregional Project on Rural Women Workers in the Putting Out System: Proceedings* (Bangkok, 1993), RAS/91/M14/DAN, pp. 6–7.

50. Ibid., p. 33.

51. Ibid., pp. 64–65, 89, 94, and 96. Replicating some of the concerns of SEWA to break through the work-home dichotomy, participants also took up the question whether unpaid reproductive work should enter the definition, some arguing that isolating reproductive from productive work may result in ignoring important needs of homeworkers. Again, the ILO definition was cited to preempt inclusion of this issue.

52. ILO, Multibilateral Programme of Technical Cooperation, "Rural Women Workers," p. 6.

53. Hesti Wijaya and Heru Santoso, "Village-Based Action Research in East Java: Rural Women Homeworkers in the Garments Industry," in *From the Shadows to the Fore: Practical Actions for the Social Protection of Homeworkers in Indonesia*, p. 21.

54. Moedjiman, "Breaking through Statistical and Policy Invisibility: Pilot Monitoring Scheme for Homebased Workers of Indonesia," in *From the Shadows to the Fore: Practical Actions for the Social Protection of Homeworkers in Indonesia*, p. 13.

55. Yayasan Pengembangan Pedesaan, "Grassroots Organizing of Homeworkers: The Gondang Experiment," p. 61.

56. Ibid., p. 19.

57. Antonina Tiña and Rosalinda Ofreneo, "PATAMABA Speaks: More Successes, Many More Challenges," in *From the Shadows to the Fore: Practical Actions for the Social Protection of Homeworkers in the Philippines* (Bangkok: ILO Regional Office for Asia and the Pacific, 1993), pp. 38–39.

7. *Studying Global Politics*

1. Whitworth, *Feminism and International Relations*, chap. 5; Lubin and Winslow, *Social Justice for Women*.

2. I am grateful to Nick Onuf for pointing out this connection.

3. Verena Stolcke, "Women's Labours: The Naturalisation of Social Inequality and Women's Subordination," in *Of Marriage and the Market*, ed. Kate Young, Carol Wolkowitz, and Roslyn McCullagh (London, New York: Routledge,

1981), p. 163; Heidi Hartmann, "The Unhappy Marriage of Marxism and Feminism: Towards a More Progressive Union," in *Women and Revolution: A Discussion of the Unhappy Marriage of Marxism and Feminism*, ed. Lydia Sargent (Boston, MA: South End Press, 1981), p. 15; Mies, *Patriarchy and Accumulation*, p. 71; Susan Brownmiller, *Against Our Will: Men, Women and Rape* (New York: Simon and Schuster, Bantam edition 1976), p. 4; Michelle Zimbalist Rosaldo, "Women, Culture, and Society: A Theoretical Overview," in *Women, Culture, and Society* ed. Michelle Zimbalist Rosaldo and Louise Lamphere (Stanford: Stanford University Press, 1974), p. 35.

4. hooks, *Ain't I a Woman*; Spelman, *Inessential Woman*; Mohanty, "Under Western Eyes"; Nancy Fraser and Linda J. Nicholson, "Social Criticism without Philosophy: An Encounter between Feminism and Postmodernism," in *Feminism/Postmodernism*, ed. Linda J. Nicholson (New York, London: Routledge, 1990), pp. 19–38.

5. Donna Haraway, "Situated Knowledges: The Science Question in Feminism and the Privilege of Partial Perspective," *Feminist Studies* 14, 3 (Fall 1988): 575–599; Fraser and Nicholson, "Social Criticism without Philosophy," p. 34

6. Amrita Basu, ed., *The Challenge of Local Feminisms: Women's Movements in Global Perspective* (Boulder: Westview Press, 1995).

7. Joan W. Scott, Cora Kaplan, and Debra Keates, ed., *Transitions, Environments, Translations: Feminisms in International Politics* (New York: Routledge, 1997), p. 2.

8. Gayatri Chakravorty Spivak, " 'Woman' as Theatre: United Nations Conference on Women, Beijing 1995," *Radical Philosophy* 75 (January–February 1996): 2 and 4.

9. Compare Elspeth Probyn, "Travels in the Postmodern: Making Sense of the Local," in *Feminism/Postmodernism*, ed. Linda J. Nicholson (New York, London: Routledge, 1990), pp. 176–189. Also Arif Dirlik, *The Postcolonial Aura: Third World Criticsm in the Age of Global Capitalism* (Boulder: Westview, 1997), esp. chap. 4.

10. For an interesting discussion of the changing meanings of universal human rights in local contexts see Jean Bethke Elshtain, "Exporting Feminism," *Journal of International Affairs* 48 (Winter 1995): 541–558.

Appendix: ILO Convention Concerning Home Work

1. Reprinted from an ILO Pamphlet entitled *International Labour Conference, Convention 177, Convention Concerning Home Work*.

Bibliography

Abreu, Alice Rangel de Paiva and Bila Sorj, ed. *O Trabalho Invisível: Estudos Sobre Trabalhadores A Domicílio No Brasil.* Rio de Janeiro: Rio Fundo Editora Ltda., 1993.

————. " 'Good Housewives': Seamstresses in the Brazilian Garment Industry." In *Homeworkers in Global Perspective: Invisible No More*, ed. Eileen Boris and Elisabeth Prügl, 93–110. New York, London: Routledge, 1996.

Adler, Emanuel. "Seizing the Middle Ground: Constructivism in World Politics." *European Journal of International Relations* 3, 3 (1997): 319–363.

Aglietta, Michel. *A Theory of Capitalist Regulation: The U.S. Experience.* Trans. David Fernbach. London: New Left Books, 1985.

Ahmad, Zubeida M., and Martha F. Loutfi. *Women Workers in Rural Development: A Programme of the ILO.* Geneva: International Labour Office, 1982.

Alcock, Antony. *History of the International Labour Organisation.* London, Basingstoke: The Macmillan Press Ltd., 1971.

Alcoff, Linda. "Cultural Feminism Versus Post-Structuralism: The Identity Crisis in Feminist Theory." *Signs: Journal of Women in Culture and Society* 13, no. 3 (1988): 405–436.

Allal, M. and E. Chuta. *Cottage Industries and Handicrafts: Some Guidelines for Employment Promotion.* Geneva: International Labour Office, 1982.

Allen, Sheila and Carol Wolkowitz. *Homeworking: Myth and Realities.* London: Macmillan, 1987.

Allen, Virginia R., Margaret E. Galey, and Mildred E. Persinger. "World Conference of International Women's Year." In *Women, Politics, and the United Nations*, ed. Anne Winslow, 29–44. Westport: Greenwood Press, 1995.

Alonso, José Antonio. "The Domestic Clothing Workers in the Mexican Metropolis and Their Relation to Dependent Capitalism." In *Women, Men and the International Division of Labor,* ed. June Nash and María Patricia Fernández-Kelly, 160–172. Albany: State University of New York Press, 1983.

———. *Mujeres Maquiladoras Y Microindustria Domestica.* Mexico, D.F.: Distribuciones Fontamara, S.A., 1991.

Ashe, Jeffrey. "Synthesis and Overall Findings." In *The Pisces Studies: Assisting the Smallest Economic Activities of the Urban Poor,* ed. Michael Farbman, 1–55. Washington, D.C.: U.S. Agency for International Development, 1981.

Barbagelata, H. "Different Categories of Workers and Labour Contracts." In *Comparative Labour Law and Industrial Relations,* ed. R. Blanpain, 427–452. Deventer: Kluwer Law and Taxation Publishers, 1987.

Barraclough, Geoffrey. *An Introduction to Contemporary History.* London: Penguin Books, 1967, c1964.

Basu, Amrita, ed. *The Challenge of Local Feminisms: Women's Movements in Global Perspective.* Boulder: Westview Press, 1995.

Becker, Susan D. *The Origins of the Equal Rights Amendment: American Feminism Between the Wars.* Westport, London: Greenwood Press, 1981.

Beier, Rosmarie. *Frauenarbeit und Frauenalltag im Deutschen Kaiserreich: Heimarbeiterinnen in der Berliner Bekleidungsindustrie 1880–1914.* Frankfurt, New York: Campus Verlag, 1983.

"Beijing Marks New Era of NGOs Holding Governments Accountable." *Mobilizing Beyond Beijing: A Quarterly Newsletter of InterAction's Commission on the Advancement of Women.* No.7 (Summer 1996).

Belous, Richard S. "Flexibility and American Labour Markets: The Evidence and Implications." World Employment Programme Research Paper No. 14. Geneva: ILO, 1987.

Benería, Lourdes. "Accounting for Women's Work." In *Women and Development: The Sexual Division of Labor in Rural Societies,* ed. Lourdes Benería, 119–147. New York: Praeger Publishers, 1982.

———. "The Mexican Debt Crisis: Restructuring in the Economy and the Household." In *Unequal Burden: Economic Crises, Persistent Poverty, and Women's Work,* ed. Lourdes Benería and Shelley Feldman, 83–104. Boulder: Westview Press,1992.

Benería, Lourdes and Shelley Feldman, ed. *Unequal Burden: Economic Crises, Persistent Poverty, and Women's Work.* Boulder: Westview Press, 1992.

Benería, Lourdes and Gita Sen. "Accumulation, Reproduction, and Women's Role in Economic Development: Boserup Revisited." *Signs: A Journal of Women in Culture and Society* 7 (Winter 1981): 279–298.

Benería, Lourdes and Martha Roldán. *The Crossroads of Class and Gender: Industrial Homework, Subcontracting, and Household Dynamics in Mexico City.* Chicago: The University of Chicago Press, 1987.

Benhabib, Seyla, Judith Butler, Drucilla Cornell, and Nancy Fraser, ed. *Feminist Contentions: A Philosophical Exchange*. New York: Routledge, 1995.

Bequele, Assefa. "Homework: Why Should We Care?" In ILO, *Asian Subregional Tripartite Seminar on the Protection of Homeworkers: Proceedings*, 35–45. Geneva: International Labour Office, 1988.

Berger, Marguerite. "Giving Women Credit: The Strengths and Limitations of Credit as a Tool for Alleviating Poverty." *World Development* 17 (July 1989): 1017–1032.

Berik, Günseli. *Women Carpet Weavers in Rural Turkey: Patterns of Employment, Earnings and Status*. Geneva: International Labour Office, 1987.

Bernstein, Richard J. *Beyond Objectivism and Relativism*. Philadelphia: University of Pennsylvania Press, 1983.

Bhatty, Zarina. *The Economic Role and Status of Women in the Beedi Industry in Allahabad, India*. Saarbrücken: Verlag Breitenbach, 1981.

Bibliography of Published Research of the World Employment Programme. 8th Edition. Geneva: International Labour Office, 1990.

Biersteker, Thomas J. and Cynthia Weber, ed. *State Sovereignty as Social Construct*. Cambridge: Cambridge University Press, 1996.

Boli, John and George M. Thomas. "World Culture in the World Polity: A Century of International Non-Governmental Organizations." *American Sociological Review* 62 (April 1997): 171–191.

Bookman, Ann and Sandra Morgen, ed. *Women and the Politics of Empowerment*. Philadelphia: Temple University Press, 1988.

Boomgard, James J. *A.I.D. Microenterprise Stocktaking: Synthesis Report*. A.I.D. Evaluation Special Study No. 65. Washington DC: U.S. Agency for International Development, 1989.

Boomgard, James J., Dennis De Santis, Mohini Mahotra, and Anastasia Tzavaras, ed. *Taking Stock of A.I.D.'s Microenterprise Portfolio: Background and Conceptual Overview*. A.I.D. Evaluation Special Study No. 66. Washington DC: U.S. Agency for International Development, December 1989.

Boris, Eileen. *Home to Work: Motherhood and the Politics of Industrial Homework in the United States*. Cambridge: Cambridge University Press, 1994.

———. "Sexual Divisions, Gender Constructions: The Historical Meaning of Homework in Western Europe and the United States." In *Homeworkers in Global Perspective: Invisible No More*, ed. Eileen Boris and Elisabeth Prügl, 19–37. New York, London: Routledge, 1996.

Boris, Eileen and Elisabeth Prügl, ed. *Homeworkers in Global Perspective: Invisible No More*. New York, London: Routledge, 1996.

Bornstein, David. *The Price of a Dream: The Story of the Grameen Bank and the Idea That Is Helping the Poor to Change Their Lives*. New York: Simon and Schuster, 1996.

Boserup, Ester. *Women's Role in Economic Development*. New York: St. Martin's Press, 1970.

Boxer, Marilyn. "Protective Legislation and Home Industry: The Marginalization of Women Workers in Late Nineteenth- Early Twentieth-Century France." *Journal of Social History* 20 (Fall 1986): 45–65.

Boyer, Robert. *The Regulation School: A Critical Introduction*. Trans. Craig Charney. New York: Columbia University Press, 1990.

Bromley, Ray. "Introduction—The Informal Sector: Why Is It Worth Discussing?" *World Development* 6 (September/October 1978): 1033–1039.

———. "Informality, de Soto Style: From Concept to Policy." In *Contrapunto: The Informal Sector Debate in Latin America*, ed. Cathy A. Rakowski, 131–151. Albany: State University of New York Press, 1994.

Brownmiller, Susan. *Against Our Will: Men, Women and Rape*. New York: Simon and Schuster, Bantam Edition 1976.

Bruce, Judith. "Homes Divided." *World Development* 17 (July 1989): 979–991.

Brydon, Lynne and Sylvia Chant. *Women in the Third World: Gender Issues in Rural and Urban Areas*. New Brunswick: Rutgers University Press, 1993.

Butler, Judith. *Gender Trouble: Feminism and the Subversions of Identity*. New York, London: Routledge, 1990.

———. *Bodies that Matter: On the Discursive Limits of "Sex."* New York: Routledge, 1993.

Buvinic, Mayra. "Investing in Poor Women: The Psychology of Donor Support." *World Development* 17 (July 1989): 1045–1057.

Cadbury, Edward and George Shann. *Sweating*. London: Headley Brothers, 1907.

Cairns, John W. "Blackstone, Kahn-Freund and the Contract of Employment." *The Law Quarterly Review* 105 (April 1989): 300–314.

Capecchi, Vittorio. "The Informal Economy and the Development of Flexible Specialization in Emilia-Romagna." In *The Informal Economy: Studies in Advanced and Less Developed Countries*, ed. Alejandro Portes, Manuel Castells, and Lauren Benton, 189–215. Baltimore: The John Hopkins University Press, 1989.

Catalogue of Publications of the International Association for Labour Legislation, International Association on Unemployment, and International Association for Social Progress and their National Sections. Bibliographical Contributions No. 22. Geneva: International Labour Office, Library, 1962.

Charlesworth, Hilary. "Women as Sherpas: Are Global Summits Useful for Women?" *Feminist Studies* 22 (Fall 1996): 537–547.

Charlton, Sue Ellen M. *Women in Third World Development*. Boulder, London: Westview Press, 1984.

Chatterjee, Mirai. "Occupational Health Issues of Home-based Piece-rate Workers." In *Report of a National Workshop on Home-based Piece-rate Workers*, 27–30. Ahmedabad: Mahila Sewa Trust, 1987.

Chowdhry, Geeta. "Engendering Development? Women in Development (WID) in International Development Regimes." In *Feminism/Postmodernism/Development*, ed. Marianne H. Marchand and Jane L. Parpart, 26–41. London, New York: Routledge, 1995.

Christensen, Kathleen E. "Independent Contracting." In *The New Era of Home-Based Work: Directions and Policies*, ed. Kathleen E. Christensen, 79–91. Boulder: Westview Press, 1988.

Chuta, Enyinna and S.V. Sethuraman, ed. *Rural Small-Scale Industries and Employment in Africa and Asia: A Review of Programmes and Policies*. Geneva: International Labour Office, 1984.

Coffin, Judith. "Social Science Meets Sweated Labor: Reinterpreting Women's Work in Late Nineteenth-Century France." *Journal of Modern History* 63 (June 1991): 230–270.

――――. *The Politics of Women's Work: The Paris Garment Trades, 1750–1915*. Princeton: Princeton University Press, 1996.

Cohen, Jean and Andrew Arato. *Civil Society and Political Theory*. Cambridge, London: The MIT Press, 1992.

Cohn, Carol. "Sex and Death in the Rational World of Defense Intellectuals." *Signs: Journal of Women in Culture and Society* 12 ,4 (1987): 687–718.

――――. "Gays in the Military: Texts and Subtexts." In *The "Man" Question in International Relations*, ed. Marysia Zalewski and Jane Parpart, 129–149. Boulder: Westview Press, 1998.

Connell, R.W. *Gender and Power: Society, the Person and Sexual Politics*. Stanford: Stanford University Press, 1987.

Córdova, Efrén. "From Full-Time Wage Employment to Atypical Employment: A Major Shift in the Evolution of Labour Relations." *International Labour Review* 29,4 (1990): 640–657.

Costello, Cynthia B. "The Clerical Homework Program at the Wisconsin Physicians Services Insurance Corporation." In *Homework: Historical and Contemporary Perspectives on Paid Labor at Home*, ed. Eileen Boris and Cynthia Daniels, 198–214. Urbana: University of Illinois Press, 1989.

Council of Europe. *The Protection of Persons Working at Home*. Strasbourg, 1989.

Cox, Robert W. "Labor and Hegemony." *International Organization* 31 (Summer 1977): 385–424.

――――. *Production, Power, and World Order: Social Forces in the Making of History*. New York: Columbia University Press, 1987.

――――. "The Global Political Economy and Social Choice." In *Approaches to World Order*, by Robert W. Cox with Timothy Sinclair, 191–208 . Cambridge: Cambridge University Press, 1996.

――――. "Towards a Posthegemonic Conceptualization of World Order: Reflections on the Relevancy of Ibn Khaldun." In *Approaches to World Order*, by Robert

W. Cox with Timothy Sinclair, 144–173. Cambridge: Cambridge University Press, 1996.

———. *Approaches to World Order.* Cambridge: Cambridge University Press, 1996.

Crosette, Barbara. "U.N Report Raises Questions About Small Loans to the Poor." *The New York Times* (3 September 1998): A8.

Daines, Victoria and David Seddon. "Confronting Austerity: Women's Responses to Economic Reform." In *Women's Lives and Public Policy: The International Experience,* ed. Meredeth Turshen and Briavel Holcomb, 3–32. Westport: Praeger, 1993.

Dangler, Jamie Faricellia. *Hidden in the Home: The Role of Waged Homework in the Modern World-Economy.* Albany: State University of New York Press, 1994.

Das, Parimal. "Women under India's Community Development Programme." *International Labour Review* 80 (July-December 1959): 26–43.

Dauber, Roslyn and Melinda L. Cain, ed. *Women and Technological Change in Developing Countries.* Boulder: Westview Press, 1981.

Davidson, Patricia. "Comment: The Definition of 'Employee' under Title VII: Distinguishing Between Employees and Independent Contractors." *University of Cincinnati Law Review* 53(1984): 203–229.

de Soto, Hernando. *The Other Path: The Invisible Revolution in the Third World.* New York: Harper and Row, 1989.

Dessler, David. "What's at Stake in the Agent-Structure Debate?" *International Organization* 43 (Summer 1989): 441–473.

Deuxième Conférence Internationale des Ligues Sociales d'Acheteurs, Antwerp, 25–28 September 1913. Lyon: Secretariat General de la L.S.A. de France, n.d.

Dhamija, Jasleen. "Handicrafts: A Source of Employment for Women in Developing Rural Economies." *International Labour Review* 112 (December 1975): 459–465.

———. "Women and Handicrafts: Myth and Reality." In *Seeds: Supporting Women's Work in the Third World,* ed. Ann Leonard, 195–212. New York: The Feminist Press, 1989.

Dirlik, Arif. *The Postcolonial Aura: Third World Criticism in the Age of Global Capitalism.* Boulder: Westview Press, 1997.

Dockendorf, Hans. *Der Entgeltschutz in der deutschen Heimarbeit.* Jena: Gustav Fischer, 1936.

DuBois, Ellen Carol. "Woman Suffrage and the Left: An International Socialist-Feminist Perspective." *New Left Review* 186 (1991): 20–45.

Duffy, Gavan, Brian K. Frederking, and Seth A. Tucker. "Language Games: Dialogical Analysis of INF Negotiations. *International Studies Quarterly* 42 (June 1998): 271–294.

Elisburg, Donald. "Legalities." *Telematics and Informatics* 2 (1985): 181–185.

Elshtain, Jean Bethke. *Women and War*. New York: Basic Books, 1987.

———. "Exporting Feminism." *Journal of International Affairs* 48 (Winter 1995): 541–558.

Elson, Diane and Ruth Pearson. "Nimble Fingers Make Cheap Workers: An Analysis of Women's Employment in Third World Manufacturing." *Feminist Review* 8 (Spring 1981): 87–107.

Employment, Incomes, and Equality: A Strategy for Increasing Productive Employment in Kenya. Report of an Inter-Agency Team Financed by the United Nations Development Programme and Organised by the International Labour Office. Geneva: International Labour Office, 1972.

Enloe, Cynthia. *Bananas, Beaches, and Bases: Making Feminist Sense of International Politics*. Berkeley, Los Angeles: University of California Press, 1989.

———. *The Morning After: Sexual Politics at the End of the Cold War*. Berkeley, Los Angeles, London: University of California Press, 1993.

Farbman, Michael, ed. *The Pisces Studies: Assisting the Smallest Economic Activities of the Urban Poor*. Washington, D.C.: U.S. Agency for International Development, 1981.

Ferguson, Kathy E. *The Man Question: Visions of Subjectivity in Feminist Theory*. Berkeley, Los Angeles, Oxford: University of California Press, 1993.

Fierke, Karin M. " At the Boundary: Language, Rules and Social Construction." In *The Aarhus-Norsminde Papers: Constructivism, International Relations and European Studies*, ed. Knud Erik Jørgensen, 43–51. Aarhus, Denmark: Aarhus University, 1997.

Finkelstein, Lawrence S. "What Is Global Governance?" *Global Governance: A Review of Multilateralism and International Organizations* 1 (September-December 1995): 367–372.

Finnemore, Martha. *National Interests in International Society*. Ithaca: Cornell University Press, 1996.

Foucault, Michel. *Discipline and Punish: The Birth of the Prison*. Trans. Alan Sheridan. New York: Random House, Vintage Book Edition, 1975.

———. "Powers and Strategies." Interview by the editorial collective of Les révoltes logiques, In *Power/Knowledge: Selected Interviews and Other Writings 1972–1977*, ed. and trans. Colin Gordon, Leo Marshall, John Mepham, and Kate Soper, 134–145. New York: Pantheon Books, 1980.

———. "Truth and Power." Interview by Alessandro Fontana and Pasquale Pasquino, In *Power/Knowledge: Selected Interviews and Other Writings 1972–1977*, ed. and trans. Colin Gordon, Leo Marshall, John Mepham, and Kate Soper. New York: Pantheon Books, 1980.

———. "Afterword: The Subject and Power." In *Michel Foucault: Beyond Structuralism and Hermeneutics*, ed. Hubert L. Dreyfus and Paul Rabinow, 208–226. Chicago: University of Chicago Press, 1982.

Fraser, Nancy. *Unruly Practices: Power, Discourse and Gender in Contemporary Social Theory*. Minneapolis: University of Minnesota Press, 1989.

Fraser, Nancy and Linda J. Nicholson. "Social Criticism without Philosophy: An Encounter between Feminism and Postmodernism." In *Feminism/ Postmodernism*, ed. Linda J. Nicholson, 19–38. New York, London: Routledge, 1990.

Fröbel, Folker, Otto Kreye, and Jürgen Heinrichs. *The New International Division of Labour: Structural Unemployment in Industrialised Countries and Industrialisation in Developing Countries*. Trans. Pete Burgess. Cambridge: Cambridge University Press, 1980.

Gaebel, Käthe. *Die Heimarbeit: Das jüngste Problem des Arbeiterschutzes*. Jena: Gustav Fischer, 1913.

Gaudier, Maryse. "The Development of the Women's Question at the ILO, 1919–1994: 75 Years of Progress Towards Equality." Prepared for International Forum on Equality for Women in the World of Work: Challenges for the Future, Geneva, June 1–3, 1994, International Institute for Labour Studies.

Gender and Poverty in India: A World Bank Country Study. Washington, D.C.: The World Bank, 1991.

Gerry, Chris. "Petty Production and Capitalist Production in Dakar: The Crisis of the Self-Employed." *World Development* 6, no. 9 (1978): 1147–1160.

———. "Small-scale Manufacturing and Repairs in Dakar: A Survey of Market Relations within the Urban Economy." In *Casual Work and Poverty in Third World Cities*, ed. Ray Bromley and Chris Gerry, 229–250. Chichester, New York, Brisbane, Toronto: John Wiley and Sons, 1979.

Ghavamshahidi, Zohreh. " 'Bibi Khanum': Carpet Weavers and Gender Ideology in Iran." In *Homeworkers in Global Perspective: Invisible No More*, ed. Eileen Boris and Elisabeth Prügl, 111–128. New York, London: Routledge, 1996.

Ghoshal, Soumyajit and Debkumar Chakraborti. "Man, Machine, Environment: An Ergonomic Study on the Readymade Garment Workers At Ahmedabad for Improvement of Health, Safety, Efficiency at Work and Productivity." In *Report of a National Workshop on Home-based Piece-rate Workers*, 31–34. Ahmadabad: Mahila SEWA Trust, 1987.

Gibson-Graham, J.K. *The End of Capitalism (As We Knew It): A Feminist Critique of Political Economy*. Cambridge: Blackwell Publishers, 1996.

Giddens, Anthony. *The Constitution of Society: Outline of the Theory of Structuration*. Berkeley, Los Angeles: University of California Press, 1984.

Gill, Stephen. *American Hegemony and the Trilateral Commission*. New York, Port Chester, Melbourne, Sydney: Cambridge University Press, 1990.

Glader, Jeanne M. "Harvest of Shame: The Imposition of Independent Contractor Status on Migrant Farmworkers and Its Ramifications for Migrant Children." *Hastings Law Journal* 42 (July 1992): 1455–1490.

Goetz, Anne Marie. "Feminism and the Claim to Know: Contradictions in Feminist Approaches to Women in Development." In *Gender and International Relations*, ed. Rebecca Grant and Kathleen Newland, 133–157. Bloomington, Indianapolis: Indiana University Press, 1991.

Gould, Harry D. "What *Is* at Stake in the Agent-Structure Debate?" In *International Relations in a Constructed World*, ed. Vendulka Kubálková, Nicholas Onuf, and Paul Kowert, 79–98. Armonk, NY: M.E. Sharpe, 1998.

Grahl, John and Paul Teague. "The Cost of Neo-Liberal Europe." *New Left Review* 174 (March/April 1989): 33–50.

Grown, Caren A. and Jennefer Sebstad. "Introduction: Toward a Wider Perspective on Women's Employment." *World Development* 17 (July 1989): 937–952.

Guzzini, Stefano. "Machtbegriffe am Ausklang (?): Der Meta-Theoretischen Wende in den internationalen Beziehungen (oder: Gebrauchsanweisung zur Rettung des Konstruktivismus vor seinen neuen Freunden)." In *The Aarhus-Norsminde Papers: Constructivism, International Relations and European Studies*, ed. Knud Erik Jørgensen, 69–79. Aarhus, Denmark: Aarhus University, 1997.

Haas, Ernst B. *Beyond the Nation-State: Functionalism and International Organization*. Stanford: Stanford University Press, 1964.

Habermas, Jürgen. *The Theory of Communicative Action. Volume 1: Reason and the Rationalization of Society*. Trans. Thomas McCarthy. Boston: Beacon Press, 1984.

Hakim, Catherine. "Homework and Outwork: National Estimates From Two Surveys." *Employment Gazette* 92 (January 1984): 7–12.

Hale, Sylvia M. "Using the Oppressor's Language in the Study of Women and Development." *Women and Language* 11, no. 2 (1989): 38–43.

Han, Jongwoo and L.H.M. Ling. "Authoritarianism in the Hypermasculinized State: Hybridity, Patriarchy, and Capitalism in Korea." *International Studies Quarterly* 42 (March 1998): 53–78.

"Handicrafts and Small Industries in Asian Countries: Possibilities of Co-operative Organizations." *International Labour Review* 62 (July-December 1950): 500–524.

Haraway, Donna. "Situated Knowledges: The Science Question in Feminism and the Privilege of Partial Perspective." *Feminist Studies* 14, no. 3 (Fall 1988): 575–599.

———. *Modest_Witness@Second_Millenium. FemaleMan©_Meets_OncoMouse™: Feminism and Technoscience*. New York: Routledge, 1997.

Harding, Sandra. *The Science Question in Feminism*. Ithaca, London: Cornell University Press, 1986.

———. "Introduction: Is there a Feminist Methodology." In *Feminism and Methodology*, ed. Sandra Harding, 1–14. Bloomington: Indiana University Press, 1987.

Harper, Malcolm and Tan Thiam Soon. *Small Enterprises in Developing Countries: Case Studies and Conclusions*. London: Intermediate Technology Publications Ltd., 1979.

Harrison, Bennett and Barry Bluestone. "The Dark Side of Labour Market 'Flexibility': Falling Wages and Growing Income Inequality in America." World Employment Programme Research Paper No. 17. Geneva: ILO, 1987.

Hart, Vivien. *Bound by Our Constitution: Women, Workers, and the Minimum Wage*. Princeton: Princeton University Press, 1994.

Hartmann, Heidi. "The Unhappy Marriage of Marxism and Feminism: Towards a More Progressive Union." In *Women and Revolution: A Discussion of the Unhappy Marriage of Marxism and Feminism*, ed. Lydia Sargent, 1–41. Boston: South End Press, 1981.

Hartsock, Nancy C.M. "The Feminist Standpoint: Developing the Ground for a Specifically Feminist Historical Materialism." In *Discovering Reality: Feminist Perspectives on Epistemology, Metaphysics and Philosophy of Science*, ed. Sandra Harding and Merrill B. Hintikka, 283–310. Dordrecht: Reidel Publishing Company, 1993. Reprinted in Nancy C.M. Hartsock, *The Feminist Standpoint Revisited and Other Essays*, 105–132. Boulder: Westview Press, 1998.

Hashem, Hisham R. *Arab Contract of Employment: Conflict and Concord, A Comparative Study*. The Hague: Martinus Nijhoff, 1964.

Hekman, Susan. "Truth and Method: Feminist Standpoint Theory Revisited." *Signs: Journal of Women in Culture and Society* 22 (Winter 1997): 341–365.

Herz, E. "The Contract of Employment: I." *International Labour Review* 31 (May 1935): 837–858.

Higer, Amy J. "International Women's Activism and the 1994 Cairo Population Conference." In *Gender Politics and Global Governance*, ed. Mary K. Meyer and Elisabeth Prügl, 122–141. Lanham, MD: Rowman and Littlefield, 1999.

hooks, bell. *Ain't I a Woman: Black Women and Feminism*. Boston: South End Press, 1981.

Hosmer Martens, Margaret and Swasti Mitter, ed., *Women in Trade Unions: Organizing the Unorganized*. Geneva: International Labour Office, 1994.

Hossain, Mahabub. "Employment Generation Through Cottage Industries — Potentials and Constraints: The Case of Bangladesh." Asian Employment Programme Working Papers. Bangkok: ILO/ARTEP, June 1984.

House, William J. "Nairobi's Informal Sector: Dynamic Entrepreneurs or Surplus Labor?" *Economic Development and Cultural Change* 32, no. 2 (1984): 277–302.

Hsiung, Ping-Chun. *Living Rooms as Factories: Class, Gender, and the Satellite Factory System in Taiwan*. Philadelphia: Temple University Press, 1996.

"Industrial Home Work." *International Labour Review* 58 (December 1948): 735–751.

International Congress of Home Work (Reports, Resolutions and Papers). N.p.: International Association for Labour Legislation [1912?].

*International Labour Conventions and Recommendations, 1919–1991.*Geneva: International Labour Office, 1992.

International Labour Office. *International Labour Code 1951, Vol 1*. Geneva: International Labour Office, 1952.

———. *Report to the Government of Botswana on Co-operative Marketing of Handicraft Products*. Geneva, 1967.

———. *Report to the Government of Libya on the Role of Handicrafts in a Rapidly Developing Economy*. Geneva, 1967.

———. *Report to the Government of St. Lucia on the Development of Handicrafts*. Geneva, 1969.

———. *Report to the Government of the Yemen Arab Republic on the Development of Handicrafts and Small-Scale Industries*. Geneva, 1967.

———. *Report to the Republic of Cyprus on the Development of Handicrafts*. Geneva, 1967.

———. *Yearbook of Labor Statistics*, 14th Issue. Geneva, 1954.

International Labor Office and Swedish International Development Authority. *Report on ILO/ECA/YWCA/SIDA Workshop on Participation of Women in Handicrafts and Small Industries*. Geneva, 1975.

International Labour Organization. *Fourth Asian Regional Conference: Record of Proceedings*. Geneva, 1958.

———. *International Labour Conference, 10th Session: Proceedings Vol.I*. Geneva, 1927.

———. *International Labour Conference, 11th Session: Minutes of the Committee on Minimum Wage Fixing Machinery*. Geneva, 1928.

———. *International Labour Conference, 11th Session: Proceedings. Vol. I*. Geneva, 1928.

———. *International Labour Conference, 39th Session: Living and Working Conditions of Indigenous Populations in Independent Countries. Report VIII (1)*. Geneva, 1955.

———. *International Labour Conference, 40th Session: Record of Proceedings*. Geneva, 1958.

———. *International Labour Conference, 45th Session: Record of Proceedings*. Geneva, 1962.

———. *International Labour Conference, 48th Session: Record of Proceedings*. Geneva, 1965.

———. *International Labour Conference, 53rd Session: Report of the Director-General Part 1: The World Employment Programme*. Geneva, 1969.

———. *International Labour Conference, 77th Session: The Promotion of Self-Employment. Report VII*. Geneva, 1990.

———. *International Labour Conference, 82nd Session: Provisional Record 27.* Geneva, 1995.

———. *International Labour Conference, 82nd Session: Lists of Ratifications by Convention and by Country. Report III (Part 5).* Geneva, 1995.

———. *International Labour Conference, 82nd Session: Home Work. Report V (1).* Geneva, 1994.

———. *International Labour Conference, 83rd Session: Provisional Record 10.* Geneva, 1996.

———. *International Labour Conference, 83rd Session: Home Work. Report IV (2A).* Geneva, 1996.

———. *International Labour Conference, 83rd Session: Record of Proceedings.* Geneva, 1996.

———. *Meeting of Experts on the Social Protection of Homeworkers: Documents.* Geneva, 1991.

———. *Ninth International Conference of Labour Statisticians, Committee on the International Classification According to Status.* Geneva, 1957.

———. *Ninth International Conference of Labour Statisticians: International Classification According to Status. Report III.* Geneva, 1957.

———. "99th Session of the Governing Body." *International Labour Review* 54 (November-December 1946): 353–358.

———. *Report of the Regional Workshop on Income Generating Skills for Women in Asia.* Geneva, 1979.

———. *Second Labour Conference of the American States Which Are Members of the International Labour Organisation: Record of Proceedings.* Montreal, 1941.

———. *Selected Standards and Policy Statements of Special Interest to Women Workers Adopted Under the Auspices of the International Labour Office.* Geneva, 1980.

———. *Sixth International Conference of Labour Statisticians: International Standards for Statistics of Employment, Unemployment and the Labor Force, Cost of Living and Industrial Injuries.* Montreal, 1947.

———. *Social Protection of Homeworkers: Documents of the Meeting of Experts on the Social Protection of Homeworkers.* Geneva, 1990.

———. *Subregional Meetings I and II of the ILO-DANIDA Subregional Project on Rural Women Workers in the Putting Out System: Proceedings.* Bangkok, 1993, RAS/91/M14/DAN.

———. *Tripartite Asian Regional Seminar on Rural Development and Women in Asia: Proceedings and Conclusions.* Geneva, 1982.

———. *Tripartite Technical Meeting for the Leather and Footwear Industry: Report.* Geneva, 1985.

ILO Asian Regional Skill Development Programme. *Report of the Regional Workshop on Income Generating Skills for Women in Asia.* Bangkok, 1979.

ILO Governing Body. *99th Session: Minutes.* Montreal, 1946.

————. *103rd Session: Minutes*. Geneva, 1947.

ILO Governing Body, Industrial Activities Committee, *214th Session, Seventh Item on the Agenda: Periodic Reports on the Effect Given to the Requests of Industrial Committees and Similar Bodies*. Geneva, 1980.

ILO Textiles Committee. *Eleventh Session: General Report*. Geneva, 1984.

Jacoby, Robin Miller. *The British and American Women's Trade Union Leagues, 1890–1925: A Case Study of Feminism and Class*. Brooklyn: Carlson Publishing Inc., 1994.

Jain, Devaki. *Women's Quest For Power: Five Indian Case Studies*. Ghaziabad, India: Vikas Publishing House Pvt Ltd, 1980.

Jaquette, Jane S. "Losing the Battle/Winning the War: International Politics, Women's Issues, and the 1980 Mid-Decade Conference." In *Women, Politics, and the United Nations*, ed. Anne Winslow, 45–59. Westport: Greenwood Press, 1995.

Jayawardena, Kumari. *Feminism and Nationalism in the Third World*. London, New Jersey: Zed Books, 1986.

Jenson, Jane. "Representations of Gender: Policies to 'Protect' Women Workers and Infants in France and the United States Before 1914." In *Women, the State, and Welfare*, ed. Linda Gordon, 152–177. Madison: University of Wisconsin Press, 1990.

Jepperson, Ronald L., Alexander Wendt and Peter J. Katzenstein. "Norms, Identity, and Culture in National Security." In *The Culture of National Security: Norms and Identity in World Politics*, ed. Peter J. Katzenstein, 33–75. New York: Columbia University Press, 1996.

Jhabvala, Renana. "Self-Employed Women's Association: Organising Women by Struggle and Development." In *Dignity and Daily Bread: New Forms of Economic Organising Among Poor Women in the Third World and the First*, ed. Sheila Rowbotham and Swasti Mitter, 114–138. London: Routledge, 1994.

Joachim, Jutta. " Shaping the Human Rights Agenda: The Case of Violence Against Women." In *Gender Politics and Global Governance*, ed. Mary K. Meyer and Elisabeth Prügl, 142–160. Lanham, MD: Rowman and Littlefield, 1999.

Johnston, G.A. *The International Labour Organisation: Its Work for Social and Economic Progress*. London: Europa Publications, 1970.

Kabeer, Naila. *Reversed Realities: Gender Hierarchies in Development Thought*. London: Verso, 1994.

Karpf, Hugo. *Heimarbeit und Gewerkschaft: Ein Beitrag zur Sozialgeschichte der Heimarbeit im 19. und 20. Jahrhundert*. Cologne: Bund-Verlag, 1980.

Katzenstein, Peter J., ed. *The Culture of National Security: Norms and Identity in World Politics*. New York: Columbia University Press, 1996.

Kessler, Suzanne J. and Wendy McKenna. *Gender: An Ethnomethodological Approach*. New York: John Wiley and Sons, 1978.

Kessler-Harris, Alice, Jane Lewis, and Ulla Wikander. "Introduction." In *Protecting*

Women: Labor Legislation in Europe, the United States, and Australia, 1880–1920, ed. U. Wikander, A. Kessler-Harris, and J. Lewis, 1–27. Urbana, Chicago: University of Illinois Press, 1995.

Klotz, Audie and Cecilia Lynch. "Conflicted Constructivism? Positivist Leanings vs. Interpretivist Meanings." Presented at the International Studies Association Annual Meeting. Minneapolis, MN, March 1998.

Kofman, Eleonore and Gillian Youngs, ed. *Globalization: Theory and Practice*. London: Pinter, 1996.

Kornbluh, Felicia A. "The New Literature on Gender and the Welfare State: The U.S. Case." *Feminist Studies* 22 (Spring 1996): 171–197.

Koslovski, Rey and Friedrich V. Kratochwil. "Understanding Change in International Politics: The Soviet Empire's Demise and the International System." *International Organization* 48 (Spring 1994): 215–247.

Kowert, Paul. "Agency versus Structure in the Construction of National Identity." In *International Relations in a Constructed World*, ed. Vendulka Kubálková, Nicholas Onuf, and P. Kowert, 101–122. Armonk, NY: M. E. Sharpe, 1998.

Kowert, Paul and Jeffrey Legro. "Norms, Identity, and Their Limits: A Theoretical Reprise." In *The Culture of National Security: Norms and Identity in World Politics*, ed. Peter J. Katzenstein, 451–497. New York: Columbia University Press, 1996.

Kratochwil, Friedrich and John G. Ruggie. "International Organization: A State of the Art on an Art of the State." *International Organization* 40 (Autumn 1986): 753–775, reprinted in revised form in John Gerard Ruggie, *Constructing the World Polity: Essays on International Institutionalization*. New York: Routledge, 1998.

Lazo, Lucita. "Women's Empowerment in the Making: The Philippine Bid for Social Protection." In *Homeworkers in Global Perspective: Invisible No More*, ed. Eileen Boris and Elisabeth Prügl, 259–271. New York: Routledge, 1996.

Lazo, Lucita and Phanomwan Yoodee. "Networking for Economic Empowerment: The Chiangmai Homenet." In *From the Shadows to the Fore: Practical Actions for the Social Protection of Homeworkers in Thailand*, ed. Lucita Lazo, 31–70. Bangkok: ILO Regional Office for Asia and the Pacific, 1993.

Liedholm, Carl and Donald Mead. "Small Scale Industries in Developing Countries: Empirical Evidence and Policy Implications." MSU International Development Paper No. 9. East Lansing: Michigan State University, 1987.

Linder, Marc. "Employees, Not-So-Independent Contractors, and the Case of Migrant Farmworkers: A Challenge to the 'Law and Economics' Agency Doctrine." *New York University Review of Law and Social Change* 15, no. 3 (1986–1987): 435–475.

———. "What Is an Employee? Why It Does, But Should Not, Matter." *Law and Inequality: A Journal of Theory and Practice* 7 (March 1989): 155–187.

———. "The Joint Employment Doctrine: Clarifying Joint Legislative-Judicial Con-

fusion." *Hamline Journal of Public Law and Policy* 10 (Fall 1989): 321–345.
———. *Farewell to the Self-Employed: Deconstructing a Socioeconomic and Legal Solipsism*. New York, Westport, London: Greenwood Press, 1992.
Lipietz, Alain. *Mirages and Miracles: The Crisis of Global Fordism*. Trans. David Macey. London: Verso, 1987.
Lipschutz, Ronnie D. "Reconstructing World Politics: The Emergence of Global Civil Society." *Millennium: Journal of International Studies* 21 (Winter 1992): 389–420.
Lipton, Michael. "Family, Fungibility and Formality: Rural Advantages of Informal Non-farm Enterprise versus the Urban-formal State." In *Human Resources, Employment and Development, Vol. 5: Developing Countries. Proceedings of the Sixth World Congress of the International Economic Association*, ed. Samir Amin, 189–242. London: Macmillan, 1980.
Longhurst, Richard. "Resource Allocation and the Sexual Division of Labor: A Case Study of a Moslem Hausa Village in Northern Nigeria." In *Women and Development: The Sexual Division of Labor in Rural Societies*, ed. Lourdes Benería, 95–117. New York: Praeger Publishers, 1982.
Lorber, Judith. *Paradoxes of Gender*. New Haven: Yale University Press, 1994.
Lorwin, Lewis L. *The International Labor Movement: History, Policies, Outlook*. New York: Harper & Brothers, 1953. Reprint, Westport: Greenwood Press, 1973.
Lotherington, Ann Therese and Anne Britt Flemmen. "Negotiating Gender: The Case of the International Labour Organization, ILO." In *Gender and Change in Developing Countries*, eds. Kristi Anne Stølen and Mariken Vaa, 273–307. Norwegian University Press, 1991.
Loutfi, Martha F. "Development with Women: Action, Not Alibis." *International Labour Review* 126 (January-February 1987): 111–124.
Lubell, Harold. *The Informal Sector in the 1980s and 1990s*. Paris: OECD, 1991.
Lubin, Carol Riegelman and Anne Winslow. *Social Justice for Women: The International Labor Organization and Women*. Durham, London: Duke University Press, 1990.
Lycette, Margaret and Karen White. "Improving Women's Access to Credit in Latin America and the Caribbean." In *Women's Ventures: Assistance to the Informal Sector in Latin America*, ed. Marguerite Berger and Mayra Buvinic, 19–44. West Hartford: Kumarian Press, 1989.
Magnusson, Warren. "Social Movements and the Global City." *Millennium: Journal of International Studies* 23, no. 3 (1994): 621–645.
———. *The Search for Political Space: Globalization, Social Movements, and the Urban Political Experience*. Toronto: University of Toronto Press, 1996.
Marchand, Marianne. "Reconceptualizing 'Gender and Development' in an Era of 'Globalization.'" *Millennium: Journal of International Studies* 25 (Winter 1996): 577–603.
———. " Selling NAFTA: Gendered Metaphors and Silenced Gender Implica-

tions." In *Globalization: Theory and Practice*, ed. Eleonore Kofman and Gillian Youngs, 253–270. London: Pinter, 1996.

Marchand, Marianne and Jane L. Parpart, ed. *Feminism/Postmodernism/Development*. London: Routledge, 1995.

Márquez, Gustavo. "Inside Informal Sector Policies in Latin America: An Economist's View." In *Contrapunto: The Informal Sector Debate in Latin America*, ed. Cathy A. Rakowski, 153–173. Albany: State University of New York Press, 1994.

Marx, Karl. *Capital: A Critique of Political Economy. Vol. 1: The Process of Capitalist Production*, ed. Frederick Engels, trans. Samuel Moore and Edward Aveling. New York: International Publishers, 1967.

Massey, Doreen. *Space, Place, and Gender*. Minneapolis: University of Minnesota Press, 1994.

Meehan, Johanna, ed. *Feminists Read Habermas: Gendering the Subject of Discourse*. New York: Routledge, 1995.

Meyer, Mary K. "Negotiating International Norms: The Inter-American Commission of Women and the Convention on Violence Against Women." In *Gender Politics in Global Governance*, ed. Mary K. Meyer and Elisabeth Prügl, 58–71. Lanham, MD: Rowman and Littlefield, 1999.

Meyer, Mary K. and Elisabeth Prügl, ed. *Gender Politics in Global Governance*. Lanham, MD: Rowman and Littlefield, 1999.

Mies, Maria. *The Lace Makers of Narsapur: Indian Housewives Produce for the World Market*. London: Zed Press, 1982.

———. *Patriarchy and Accumulation on a World Scale: Women in the International Division of Labour*. London: Zed Books, 1986.

Miller, Alice M. " Realizing Women's Human Rights: Non-Governmental Organizations and the United Nations Treaty Bodies." In *Gender Politics and Global Governance*, ed. Mary K. Meyer and Elisabeth Prügl, 161–176. Lanham, MD: Rowman and Littlefield, 1999.

Miller, Frieda S. "Industrial Home Work in the United States." *International Labour Review* 43 (January 1941): 1–50.

Miraftab, Faranak. "Space, Gender, and Work: Home-Based Workers in Mexico." In *Homeworkers in Global Perspective: Invisible No More*, ed. Eileen Boris and Elisabeth Prügl, 63–80. New York, London: Routledge, 1996.

Mitra, Manoshi. "Women's Work: Gains Analysis of Women's Labor in Dairy Production." In *Invisible Hands: Women in Home-Based Production*, ed. Andrea Menefee Singh and Anita Kelles-Viitanen, 109–143. New Delhi: Sage Publications, 1987.

Mitter, Swasti. *Common Fate, Common Bond: Women in the Global Economy*. London: Pluto Press, 1986.

———. "On Organizing Workers in the Informal Sector." A Report Prepared for the International Confederation of Free Trade Unions. Brussels: ICFTU, 1989.

———. "Computer-Aided Manufacturing and Women's Employment: A Global Critique of Post-Fordism." In *Women, Work and Computerization: Understanding and Overcoming Bias in Work and Education*, ed. Inger V. Eriksson, Barbara A. Kitchenham, and Kea G. Tijdens, 53–65. Amsterdam: North-Holland, 1991.

———. "On Organising Women in Casualised Work: A Global Overview." In *Dignity and Daily Bread: New Forms of Economic Organising Among Poor Women in the Third World and the First*, ed. Sheila Rowbotham and Swasti Mitter, 14–52. London: Routledge, 1994.

Moedjiman. "Breaking through Statistical and Policy Invisibility: Pilot Monitoring Scheme for Homebased Workers of Indonesia." In *From the Shadows to the Fore: Practical Actions for the Social Protection of Homeworkers in Indonesia*, ed. Lucita Lazo, 7–19. Bangkok: ILO Regional Office for Asia and the Pacific, 1993.

Mohanty, Chandra Talpade. "Under Western Eyes: Feminist Scholarship and Colonial Discourses." In *Third World Women and the Politics of Feminism*, ed. Chandra Talpade Mohanty, Ann Russo, and Lourdes Torres, 51–80. Bloomington: Indiana University Press, 1991.

Morse, David A. "The World Employment Programme." *International Labour Review* 97 (June 1968): 517–524.

Moser, Caroline O.N. "Informal Sector or Petty Commodity Production: Dualism or Dependence in Urban Development?" *World Development* 6, no. 9/10 (1978): 1041–1064.

———. *Gender Planning and Development: Theory, Practice and Training*. London, New York: Routledge, 1993.

———. "The Informal Sector Debate, Part 1: 1970–1983." In *Contrapunto: The Informal Sector Debate in Latin America*, ed. Cathy A. Rakowski, 11–29. Albany: State University of New York Press, 1994.

Mueller, Adele. " 'In and Against Development': Feminists Confront Development on Its Own Ground." *Women and Language* 11, no. 2 (1989): 35–37.

Murphy, Craig N. "Six Masculine Roles in International Relations and Their Interconnection: A Personal Investigation." In *The "Man" Question in International Relations*, ed. Marysia Zalewski and Jane Parpart, 93–108. Boulder: Westview Press, 1998.

Nash, June, ed. *Crafts in the World Market: The Impact of Global Exchange on Middle American Artisans*. Albany: State University of New York Press, 1993.

———. "Maya Household Production in the World Market: The Potters of Amatenango del Valle, Chiapas, Mexico." In *Crafts in the World Market: The Impact of Global Exchange on Middle American Artisans*, ed. J. Nash, 127–153. Albany: State University of New York Press, 1993.

Nash, June and María Patricia Fernández-Kelly, ed. *Women, Men, and the Inter-*

national Division of Labor. Albany: State University of New York Press, 1983.

Neck, Philip A. ed. Small Enterprise Development: Policies and Programmes. Geneva: International Labour Office, 1977.

Nicholson, Linda. "Interpreting Gender." Signs: Journal of Women in Culture and Society 20 (Autumn 1994): 79–105.

Nippert-Eng, Christena E. Home and Work: Negotiating Boundaries through Everyday Life. Chicago: University of Chicago Press, 1996.

Niva, Steve. "Tough and Tender: New World Order Masculinity and the Gulf War." In The "Man" Question in International Relations, ed. Marysia Zalewski and Jane Parpart, 109–128. Boulder: Westview Press, 1998.

Noël, Alain. "Accumulation, Regulation, and Social Change: An Essay on French Political Economy." International Organization 41, no. 2 (Spring 1987): 303–333.

Obbo, Christine. "Sexuality and Economic Domination in Uganda." In Woman-Nation-State, ed. Nira Yuval-Davis and Floya Anthias, 79–91. New York: St. Martin's Press, 1989.

Onuf, Nicholas G. World of Our Making: Rules and Rule in Social Theory and International Relations. Columbia: University of South Carolina Press, 1989.

———. "Constructivism: A User's Manual." In International Relations in a Constructed World, ed. Vendulka Kubálková, N. Onuf, and Paul Kowert, 58–78. Armonk, NY: M.E. Sharpe, 1998.

———. "How Things Get Normative." Unpublished manuscript, 1997.

Organización de los Estados Americanos, Comisión Interamericana de Mujeres. Reunión de Técnicas y de Dirigentes de las Oficinas del Trabajo de la Mujer. Washington, D.C., 1957. RT-Doc. 5/7, Abril 1957.

Otero, María. "Solidarity Group Programs: A Working Methodology for Enhancing the Economic Activities of Women in the Informal Sector." In Women's Ventures: Assistance to the Informal Sector in Latin America, ed. Marguerite Berger and Mayra Buvinic, 83–101. West Hartford: Kumarian Press, 1989.

Otero, Maria and Elisabeth Rhyne, ed., The New World of Microenterprise Finance: Building Healthy Financial Institutions for the Poor. West Hartford: Kumarian Press, 1994.

Parker, Andrew, Mary Russo, Doris Sommer, and Patricia Yaeger. "Introduction." In Nationalisms and Sexualities, ed. A. Parker, M. Russo, D. Sommer, and P. Yaeger, 1–18. New York, London: Routledge, 1992.

Parpart, Jane L. "Who is the 'Other'?: A Postmodern Feminist Critique of Women and Development Theory and Practice." Development and Change 24 (1993): 439–464.

Pateman, Carole. The Sexual Contract. Stanford: Stanford University Press, 1988.

Patton, Charlotte G. "Women and Power: The Nairobi Conference, 1985." In Women, Politics, and the United Nations, ed. Anne Winslow, 61–76. Westport: Greenwood Press, 1995.

Paulin, Valentine. "Home Work in France: Its Origin, Evolution, and Future." *International Labour Review* 37 (February 1938): 193–225.

Perera, Lakshmi. "Women in Micro- and Small-Scale Enterprise Development in Sri Lanka." In *Women in Micro- and Small-Scale Enterprise Development*, ed. Louise Dignard and José Havet, 101–116. Boulder: Westview Press, 1995.

Pesl, D. "Leitsätze über Massnahmen zur Verbesserung der Lage der Heimarbeiterinnen." In *Zur Erhaltung und Mehrung der Volkskraft: Arbeiten einer vom Ärztlichen Verein München eingesetzten Kommission*, 169–178. Munich: Verlag von J.F. Lehmann, 1918.

Peterson, V. Spike. "Security and Sovereign States: What Is at Stake in Taking Feminism Seriously?" In *Gendered States: Feminist (Re)Visions of International Relations Theory*, ed. V. Spike Peterson, 31–64 . Boulder: Lynne Rienner, 1992.

———. "Seeking World Order Beyond the Gendered Order of Global Hierarchies." In *The New Realism: Perspectives on Multilateralism and World Order*, ed. Robert W. Cox, 38–56. Tokyo: United Nations University Press, 1997.

Peterson, V. Spike and Anne Sisson Runyan. *Global Gender Issues*. Boulder, San Francisco, Oxford: Westview Press, 1993.

Pettman, Jan Jindy. *Worlding Women: A Feminist International Politics*. London, New York: Routledge, 1996.

Pineda-Ofreno, Rosalinda. "Women and Work: Focus on Homework in the Philippines." *Review of Women's Studies* 1,1 (1990): 42–55.

Pleck, Elizabeth. "Two Worlds in One: Work and Family." *Journal of Social History* 10 (Winter 1976): 178–195.

Portes, Alejandro, Silvia Blitzer, and John Curtis. "The Urban Informal Sector in Uruguay: Its Internal Structure, Characteristics, and Effects." *World Development* 14, no. 6 (1986): 727–741.

Portes, Alejandro, Manuel Castells, and Lauren A. Benton, ed. *The Informal Economy: Studies in Advanced and Less Developed Countries*. Baltimore: The John Hopkins University Press, 1989.

Portes, Alejandro and Saskia Sassen-Koob. "Making It Underground: Comparative Material on the Informal Sector in Western Market Economies." *American Journal of Sociology* 93 (July 1987): 30–60.

Portes, Alejandro and Richard Schauffler. "The Informal Economy in Latin America: Definition, Measurement, and Policies." In *Work without Protections: Case Studies of the Informal Sector in Developing Countries*, 3–39. Washington, D.C.: U.S Department of Labor, Bureau of International Labor Affairs, 1993.

Price, Patricia. "Bodies, Faith, and Inner Landscapes: Rethinking Change from the Very Local." *Latin American Perspectives*. 26,3 (1999): 37–59.

Probyn, Elspeth. "Travels in the Postmodern: Making Sense of the Local." In *Feminism/Postmodernism*, ed. Linda J. Nicholson, 176–189. New York, London: Routledge, 1990.

"Proceedings of the Senior Management Seminar: Micro and Small Enterprise,

January 12, 1989." Prepared for the U.S. Agency for International Development. Washington, D.C.: Development Alternatives, Inc.

Prügl, Elisabeth. "Gender in International Organization and Global Governance: A Critical Review of the Literature." *International Studies Notes* 21 (Winter 1996): 15–24.

———."Home-Based Workers: A Comparative Exploration of Mies's Theory of Housewifization." *Frontiers: A Journal of Women Studies* 17, no. 1 (1996): 114–135.

Prügl, Elisabeth and Irene Tinker. "Microentrepreneurs and Homeworkers: Convergent Categories." *World Development* 25 (September 1997): 1471–1482.

Rakowski, Cathy A. "The Informal Sector Debate, Part 2: 1984–1993." In *Contrapunto: The Informal Sector Debate in Latin America*, ed. C. A. Rakowski, 31–50. Albany: State University of New York Press, 1994.

Ramirez, Elia. "HomeNet International: Launch of the International Network for Home-Based Workers." *News from IRENE: International Restructuring Education Network Europe* (Tilburg, Netherlands) No. 22 (March 1995): 29–30.

Reichmann, Rebecca. "Women's Participation in Two PVO Credit Programs for Microenterprise: Cases from the Dominican Republic and Peru." In *Women's Ventures: Assistance to the Informal Sector in Latin America*, ed. Marguerite Berger and Mayra Buvinic, 132–160. West Hartford: Kumarian Press, 1989.

Rhyne, Elisabeth and Maria Otero. "Financial Services for Microenterprises: Principles and Institutions." *World Development* 20, no. 11 (1992): 1561–1571.

Richardson, Harry W. "The Role of the Urban Informal Sector: An Overview." *Regional Development Dialogue* 5,2 (1984): 3–40.

Roberts, Bryan R. "Employment Structure, Life Cycles, and Life Chances: Formal and Informal Sectors in Guadalajara." In *The Informal Economy: Studies in Advanced and Less Developed Countries*, ed. Alejandro Portes, Manuel Castells, and Lauren A. Benton, 41–59. Baltimore: The Johns Hopkins University Press, 1989.

Rogers, Barbara. *The Domestication of Women: Discrimination in Developing Societies*. London: St. Martin's Press, 1980.

Rosaldo, Michelle Zimbalist. "Women, Culture, and Society: A Theoretical Overview." In *Women, Culture, and Society*, ed. Michelle Zimbalist Rosaldo and Louise Lamphere, 17–42. Stanford: Stanford University Press, 1974.

Rose, Kalima. *Where Women Are Leaders*. London: Zed Books, 1992.

Rose, Ruth and Michel Grant. "Le Travail à Domicile Dans L'Industrie Du Vêtement Au Quebec." Montréal: Université du Québec à Montréal, 1983.

Rose, Sonya O. *Limited Livelihoods: Gender and Class in Nineteenth-Century England*. Berkeley: University of California Press, 1992.

Rosenau, James N. *Along the Domestic-Foreign Frontier: Exploring Governance in a Turbulent World*. Cambridge: Cambridge University Press, 1997.

Rowbotham, Sheila. *Women in Movement: Feminism and Social Action*. New York, London: Routledge, 1992.

———. "Strategies Against Sweated Work in Britain, 1820–1920." In *Dignity and Daily Bread: New Forms of Economic Organising Among Poor Women in the Third World and the First*, ed. Sheila Rowbotham and Swasti Mitter, 158–192. London, New York: Routledge, 1994.

Ruggie, John Gerard. *Constructing the World Polity: Essays on International Institutionalization*. New York: Routledge, 1998.

Ruiz, Luz Vega. "Home Work: Towards a New Regulatory Framework?" *International Labour Review* 131, 2 (1992): 197–216.

Runyan, Anne Sisson. "The Places of Women in Trading Places: Gendered Global/ Regional Regimes and Inter-nationalized Feminist Resistance." In *Globalization: Theory and Practice*, ed. Eleonore Kofman and Gillian Youngs, 238–252. London: Pinter, 1996.

———. "Women in the Neoliberal 'Frame.'" In *Gender Politics and Global Governance*, ed. Mary K. Meyer and Elisabeth Prügl, 210–220. Lanham, MD: Rowman and Littlefield, 1999.

Rupp, Leila J. *Worlds of Women: The Making of an International Women's Movement*. Princeton: Princeton University Press, 1997.

Rybczynski, Witold. *Home: A Short History of an Idea*. London: Penguin, 1986.

Saco, Diana. "Gendering Sovereignty: Marriage and International Relations in Elizabethan Times." *European Journal of International Relations* 3 (September 1997): 291–318.

Safa, Helen I. *The Myth of the Male Breadwinner: Women and Industrialization in the Caribbean*. Boulder: Westview Press, 1995.

Safa, Helen I. and Peggy Antrobus. "Women and the Economic Crisis in the Caribbean." In *Unequal Burden: Economic Crises, Persistent Poverty, and Women's Work*, ed. Lourdes Benería and Shelley Feldman, 49–82. Boulder: Westview Press, 1992.

Samarasinghe, Vidyamali. "The Last Frontier or a New Beginning? Women's Microenterprises in Sri Lanka." In *Women at the Center: Development Issues and Practices for the 1990s*, ed. Gay Young, Vidyamali Samarasinghe and Ken Kusterer, 30–44. West Hartford: Kumarian Press, 1993.

Sawicki, Jana. *Disciplining Foucault: Feminism, Power, and the Body*. New York: Routledge, 1991.

Scholte, Jan Aart. "Beyond the Buzzword: Towards a Critical Theory of Globalization." In *Globalization: Theory and Practice*, ed. Eleonore Kofman and Gillian Youngs, 43–57. London: Pinter, 1996.

Scott, Catherine V. *Gender and Development: Rethinking Modernization and Dependency Theory*. Boulder, London: Lynne Rienner Publishers, 1995.

Scott, Joan W. "Gender: A Useful Category of Historical Analysis." *American Historical Review* 91 (December 1986): 1053–1075.

Scott, Joan W., Cora Kaplan, and Debra Keates, ed. *Transitions, Environments, Translations: Feminisms in International Politics.* New York: Routledge, 1997.

Sen, Gita and Caren Grown. *Development, Crises, and Alternative Visions: Third World Women's Perspectives.* New York: Monthly Review Press, 1987.

Senauer, Benjamin. "The Impact of the Value of Women's Time on Food and Nutrition." In *Persistent Inequalities: Women and World Development,* ed. Irene Tinker, 150–161. New York, Oxford: Oxford University Press, 1990.

Sethuraman, S.V., ed. *The Urban Informal Sector in Developing Countries: Employment, Poverty and Environment.* Geneva: International Labour Office, 1981.

Sheldon, Kathleen. "Women and Revolution in Mozambique: A Luta Continua." In *Women and Revolution in Africa, Asia, and the New World,* ed. Mary Ann Tétreault, 33–61. Columbia: University of South Carolina Press, 1994.

Singh, Andrea Menefee and Anita Kelles-Viitanen, ed. *Invisible Hands: Women in Home-Based Production.* New Delhi: Sage Publications, 1987.

Sparr, Pamela, ed. *Mortgaging Women's Lives: Feminist Critiques of Structural Adjustment.* London: Zed Press, 1994.

Spelman, Elizabeth V. *Inessential Woman: Problems of Exclusion in Feminist Thought.* Boston: Beacon Press, 1988.

Spivak, Gayatri Chakravorty. " 'Woman' as Theatre: United Nations Conference on Women, Beijing 1995." *Radical Philosophy* 75 (January/February 1996): 2–4.

Staley, Eugene and Richard Morse. *Modern Small Industry for Developing Countries.* New York, London, Sydney, Toronto: McGraw-Hill Book Company, 1965.

Standing, Guy. "Labour Flexibility: Towards a Research Agenda." World Employment Programme Research Working Paper. Geneva: ILO, 1986.

———. "European Unemployment, Insecurity and Flexibility: A Social Dividend Solution." World Employment Programme Research Working Paper No. 23. Geneva: ILO, 1988.

Stienstra, Deborah. *Women's Movements and International Organizations.* New York: St. Martin's Press, 1994.

Stolcke, Verena. "Women's Labours: The Naturalisation of Social Inequality and Women's Subordination." In *Of Marriage and the Market,* ed. Kate Young, Carol Wolkowitz, and Roslyn McCullagh, 159–177. London, New York: Routledge, 1981.

Storper, Michael and Allen J. Scott. "Work Organisation and Local Labour Markets in an Era of Flexible Production." World Employment Programme Research Working Paper No. 30. Geneva: ILO, 1989.

Strassmann, Paul W. "Home-Based Enterprises in Cities of Developing Countries." *Economic Development and Cultural Change* 36, no. 1 (1987): 121–144.

Susilastuti, Dewi Haryani. "Home-Based Work as a Rural Survival Strategy." In

Homeworkers in Global Perspective: Invisible No More, ed. Eileen Boris and Elisabeth Prügl, 129–141. New York, London: Routledge, 1996.

Sylvester, Christine. "Empathetic Cooperation: A Feminist Method for IR." *Millennium: Journal of International Studies* 23,2 (1994): 315–334.

———. *Feminist Theory and International Relations in a Postmodern Era*. Cambridge: Cambridge University Press, 1994.

Tabili, Laura. "Women 'of a Very Low Type': Crossing Racial Boundaries in Imperial Britain." In *Gender and Class in Modern Europe*, ed. Laura L. Frader and Sonya O. Rose, 165–190. Ithaca: Cornell University Press, 1996.

Tarrow, Sidney. *Power in Movement: Social Movements, Collective Action and Politics*. Cambridge: Cambridge University Press, 1994.

Taylor, Peter J. *The Way the Modern World Works: World Hegemony to World Impasse*. Chichester: John Wiley and Sons, 1996.

Tétreault, Mary Ann. "Women and Revolution in Vietnam." In *Women and Revolution in Africa, Asia, and the New World*, ed. M. A. Tétreault, 111–136. Columbia: University of South Carolina Press, 1994.

———, ed. *Women and Revolution in Africa, Asia, and the New World*. Columbia: University of South Carolina Press, 1994.

Tickner, J. Ann. *Gender in International Relations: Feminist Perspectives on Achieving Global Security*. New York: Columbia University Press, 1992.

Tiña, Antonina and Rosalinda Ofreneo. "PATAMABA Speaks: More Successes, Many More Challenges." In *From the Shadows to the Fore: Practical Actions for the Social Protection of Homeworkers in the Philippines*, ed. Lucita Lazo, 33–59. Bangkok: ILO Regional Office for Asia and the Pacific, 1993.

Tinker, Irene. "Feminizing Development—For Growth with Equity." *Care Briefs on Development Issues* No. 6 (n.d.).

———. "The Adverse Impact of Development on Women." In *Women and World Development*, ed. I. Tinker and Michelle Bo Bramsen, 22–34. New York: Praeger, 1976.

———. *Street Foods: Testing Assumptions about Informal Sector Activity by Women and Men*. Special Issue of *Current Sociology* 35 (Winter 1987).

———. "Credit for Poor Women: Necessary, But Not Always Sufficient for Change." *Change* 10 (Spring 1989): 31–48.

———. "The Making of a Field: Advocates, Practitioners, and Scholars." In *Persistent Inequalities: Women and World Development*, ed. I. Tinker, 27–53. New York: Oxford University Press, 1990.

———. "The Human Economy of Microentrepreneurs." In *Women in Micro- and Small-Scale Enterprise Development*, ed. Louise Dignard and José Havet, 25–39. Boulder, San Francisco: Westview Press, 1995.

———. *Street Foods: Urban Food and Employment in Developing Countries*. New York, Oxford: Oxford University Press, 1997.

——. "Non-Governmental Organizations: An Alternative Power Base for Women?" In *Gender Politics and Global Governance*, ed. Mary K. Meyer and Elisabeth Prügl, 88–104. Lanham, MD: Rowman and Littlefield, 1999.

Tinker, Irene and Jane Jaquette. "UN Decade for Women: Its Impact and Legacy." *World Development* 15, 3 (1987): 419–424.

Tipple, A. Graham. "Shelter as Workplace: A Review of Home-Based Enterprise in Developing Countries" *International Labour Review* 132, no. 4 (1993): 521–539.

Tokman, Victor E. "An Exploration into the Nature of Informal-Formal Sector Relationships." *World Development* 5 (September/October 1978): 1065–1075.

——. "Policies for a Heterogeneous Informal Sector in Latin America." *World Development* 17 (July 1989): 1067–1076.

Tomlins, Christopher L. "Law and Power in the Employment Relationship." In *Labor Law in America: Historical and Critical Essays*, ed. Christopher L. Tomlins and Andrew J. King, 71–97. Baltimore: The Johns Hopkins University Press, 1992.

Tripp, Aili Mari. "The Impact of Crisis and Economic Reform on Women in Urban Tanzania." In *Unequal Burden: Economic Crises, Persistent Poverty, and Women's Work*, ed. Lourdes Benería and Shelley Feldman, 159–180. Boulder: Westview Press, 1992.

Trouvé, J. "Development of Rural Industries in French-Speaking Africa: A Critical Review." In *Rural Small-Scale Industry and Employment in Africa and Asia: A Review of Programmes and Policies*, 59–75. Geneva: International Labour Office, 1984.

United Nations. *The World's Women 1970–1990: Trends and Statistics*. Social Statistics and Indicators, Series K, No. 8. New York, 1991.

United Nations Development Program. *Human Development Report 1995*. New York: Oxford University Press, 1995.

United Nations Economic and Social Council. *20th Session: Official Records, Supplement No. 2: Report of the Commission on the Status of Women*. New York, 1955.

——. *22d Session: Official Records, Supplement No. 4: Report of the Commission on the Status of Women*. New York, 1956.

——. *24th Session: Official Records, Supplement No. 3: Report of the Commission on the Status of Women*. New York, 1957.

United Nations Economic and Social Council, Commission on the Status of Women. *Ninth Session: Development of Opportunities for Women in Handicrafts and Cottage Industries: Report Prepared by the International Labor Office*. New York, 1955.

——. *Tenth Session: Opportunities for Women in Handicrafts and Cottage Industries: Progress Report Prepared by the International Labor Office*. New York, 1956.

———. *Eleventh Session: Opportunities for Women in Handicrafts and Cottage Industries: Second Progress Report Prepared by the International Labor Office for the Commission on the Status of Women.* New York, 1957.

United Nations Economic Commission for Africa. *Report of the Workshop on the Participation of Women in Development.* Addis Ababa, 1979.

———. *Report of the Workshop on Handicrafts and Small-Scale Industries Development for Women in Francophone Countries.* Addis Ababa, 1980.

United Nations Office at Vienna, Center for Social Development and Humanitarian Affairs. *1989 World Survey on the Role of Women in Development.* New York, 1989.

"Vocational Training and the Establishment of Service Workshops in a Poor Rural Area: The Experience of the Andean Indian Programme." *International Labour Review* 85 (January–June 1962): 129–147.

Walker, R.B.J. *One World, Many Worlds: Struggles for a Just World Peace.* Boulder: Lynne Rienner Publishers, 1988.

———. *Inside/Outside: International Relations as Political Theory.* Cambridge: Cambridge University Press, 1993.

———. "Social Movements/World Politics," *Millennium: Journal of International Studies* 23, no. 3 (1994): 669–700.

Walker, R.B.J. and Saul H. Mendlovitz, ed. *Contending Sovereignties: Redefining Political Community.* Boulder, London: Lynne Rienner Publishers, 1990.

Ward, Kathryn, ed. *Women Workers and Global Restructuring.* Ithaca: ILR Press, 1990.

Waylen, Georgina. *Gender in Third World Politics.* Boulder: Lynne Rienner, 1996.

Weber, Cynthia. *Simulating Sovereignty: Intervention, the State and Symbolic Exchange.* Cambridge: Cambridge University Press, 1995.

———. "Performative States." *Millennium: Journal of International Studies* 27, 1 (1998): 77–95.

Weiss, Anita M. *Walls Within Walls: Life Histories of Working Women in the Old City of Lahore.* Boulder, San Francisco, Oxford: Westview Press, 1992.

———. "Within the Walls: Home-Based Work in Lahore." In *Homeworkers in Global Perspective: Invisible No More,* ed. Eileen Boris and Elisabeth Prügl, 81–92. New York, London: Routledge, 1996.

Wendt, Alexander. "The Agent-Structure Problem in International Relations Theory." *International Organization* 41 (Summer 1987): 335–370.

———. "Collective Identity Formation and the International State." *American Political Science Review* 88 (June 1994): 384–396.

West, Lois A., ed. *Feminist Nationalism.* New York: Routledge, 1997.

———. " The United Nations Women's Conference and Feminist Politics." In *Gender Politics and Global Governance,* ed. Mary K. Meyer and Elisabeth Prügl, 177–193. Lanham, MD: Rowman and Littlefield, 1999.

White, Stephen K. "Foucault's Challenge to Critical Theory." *American Political Science Review* 80 (June 1986): 419–431.

Whitworth, Sandra. *Feminism and International Relations: Towards a Political Economy of Gender in Interstate and Non-Governmental Institutions.* New York: St. Martin's Press, 1994.

Wijaya, Hesti and Heru Santoso. "Village-Based Action Research in East Java: Rural Women Homeworkers in the Garments Industry." In *From the Shadows to the Fore: Practical Actions for the Social Protection of Homeworkers in Indonesia,* ed. Lucita Lazo, 20–58. Bangkok: ILO Regional Office for Asia and the Pacific, 1993.

Wikander, Ulla. "Some 'Kept the Flag of Feminist Demands Waving:' Debates at International Congresses on Protecting Women Workers." In *Protecting Women: Labor Legislation in Europe, the United States, and Australia, 1880–1920,* ed. U. Wikander, Alice Kessler-Harris, and Jane Lewis, 29–62. Urbana, Chicago: University of Illinois Press, 1995.

Wilbrandt, Robert. *Arbeiterinnenschutz und Heimarbeit.* Jena: Gustav Fischer, 1906.

Winslow, Anne, ed. *Women, Politics, and the United Nations.* Westport: Greenwood Press, 1995.

"Women's Employment in Asian Countries." *International Labour Review* 68 (September 1953): 303–318.

The World Bank. *World Development Report 1995: Workers in an Integrating World.* New York: Oxford University Press, 1995.

Wunderlich, Frieda. *Die Deutsche Heimarbeitausstellung 1925.* Jena: Gustav Fischer, 1927.

Yayasan Pengembangan Pedesaan. "Grassroots Organizing of Homeworkers: The Gondang Experiment." In *From the Shadows to the Fore: Practical Actions for the Social Protection of Homeworkers in Indonesia,* ed. Lucita Lazo, 59–74. Bangkok: ILO Regional Office for Asia and the Pacific, 1993.

Yee, Albert S. "The Effects of Ideas on Policies." *International Organization* 50 (Winter 1996): 69–108.

Yunus, Muhammad, "Does the Capitalist System Have to be the Handmaiden of the Rich." Keynote Address delivered at 85th Rotary International Convention held at Taipei, Taiwan, 12–15 June 1994.

Zalewski, Marysia. "Women, Gender and International Relations Ten Years On: To Return as a Woman and Be Heard." Presented at the 1998 Millennium Conference on "Gender and International Studies: Looking Forward," London School of Economics and Political Science, 13–14 September 1998.

Zimmermann, Alice, "Home Work in Switzerland." *International Labour Review* 62 (September-October 1950): 242–263.

Zweigert, Konrad and Hein Kötz. *Introduction to Comparative Law. Volume I — The Framework.* Trans. Tony Weir. Oxford: Clarendon Press, 1987.

Index